362.767
PRE

Prendergast, William
E.

Sexual abuse of
children and
adolescents.

$29.95

DATE			

17 × 06

BAKER & TAYLOR

SEXUAL ABUSE
OF
CHILDREN
AND
ADOLESCENTS

SEXUAL ABUSE

—— OF ——

CHILDREN

—— AND ——

ADOLESCENTS

A Preventive Guide for
Parents, Teachers, and Counselors

WILLIAM E. PRENDERGAST

CONTINUUM · NEW YORK

1996

The Continuum Publishing Company
370 Lexington Avenue, New York, NY 10017

Copyright © 1996 by William E. Prendergast

Printed in the United States of America

Library of Congress Cataloging-in-Publication Data

Prendergast, William E.
  Sexual abuse of children and adolescents : a preventive guide for parents, teachers, and counselors / William E. Prendergast.
      p.   cm.
  Includes bibliographical references and index.
  ISBN 0-8264-0892-3 (alk. paper)
    1. Child sexual abuse—Prevention.   2. Sexually abused children—Psychology.   3. Sexually abused teenagers—Psychology.   I. Title.
  HV6570.P74   1996
  362.7'67—dc20
                                                                    95–44573
                                                                        CIP

*To all the victims of sexual abuse everywhere
and to the families, friends, therapists,
and others who support them*

CONTENTS

Part 3
RECOGNITION AND TREATMENT

LIST OF FIGURES

ACKNOWLEDGMENTS

My special thanks and heartfelt gratitude go out to the following individuals without whose help this book would not have been possible.

THE READERS: my wife, Mildred, who was my "mother-reader," and Mr. Robert Bolmer, who was my professional reader and critic. Both contributed greatly to this work with their suggestions, criticism, and comments.

THE COMPUTER SPECIALIST: my son, Shawn, without whose technical expertise, encouragement, and prodding I may never have finished the book.

PATIENTS AND FRIENDS: all my patients, past and present, who allowed me to use their stories,* and especially "KATHERINE," who offered her poetry.

MY MENTOR: Dr. Nathaniel Pallone, who got me started on this journey, who edited my first two books, and who remains a treasured friend, colleague, and confidant.

---

*Throughout this book, the names and identities of all these persons have been changed to protect their anonymity.

PREFACE

For the last thirty-three years I have been immersed in cases involving sexual offense and sexual abuse. Throughout this time, I have seen countless children who were abused over and over again and also countless abuse cases that could have been prevented. Consequently, I developed an intense desire to write a prevention manual for parents that would cover three main areas: (1) how, as much as possible, to prevent children and adolescents from being abused; (2) how to recognize the indicators that a child may be in the process of being sexually abused; and (3) how parents can best aid therapists who are treating children who have been abused.

A heavy work schedule, training and lecturing, my private practice for survivors of sexual abuse and for sex offenders, and family commitments prevented me from working on this most important book until I retired. Then, the publication of my first two books — *Treating Sex Offenders in Correctional Institutions and Outpatient Clinics*[1] and *The Merry-Go-Round of Sexual Abuse*[2] — was given priority. Now that both of them are complete and in print, I can finally pay attention to the vital topic at hand.

As discussed in my first two books, sex offenders are predators and choose specific types of victims under specific sets of circumstances that, in their perception, offer the best guarantees of satisfying their deviant needs, of assuring success, and of providing safety. If parents were aware of the potential-victim profiles and, even more importantly, of the specific circumstances that sex offenders look for in their search for new victims, many instances of abuse could be avoided.

---

1. William E. Prendergast, *Treating Sex Offenders in Correctional Institutions and Outpatient Clinics* (New York: Haworth Press, 1991).
2. William E. Prendergast, *The Merry-Go-Round of Sexual Abuse: Identifying and Treating Survivors* (New York: Haworth Press, 1993).

Two factors that will be emphasized and repeated throughout this work are *communication* and *believing* your child. Case after case of survivors whom I have treated involved the absence or mishandling of one or both of these factors. In many cases there was virtually no communication between parents and the children at the time of the offense. In cases where the children did report the abuse to their parents, one of two scenarios occurred. In the first scenario, no action was taken (see the story of **KYLE**, in chapter 2). This leaves the children or adolescents with one of two options to believe: (*a*) they were believed, but the parents either don't care or are giving the offender permission to abuse them; or (*b*) they were not believed, and adults and authority figures are all-powerful and protect each other. In the second scenario, the children may be severely rebuked, punished, and even severely beaten for telling lies about Mr. or Mrs. X, "who is so wonderful and who has done so much for you." The second scenario occurs most frequently with authority figures who are involved with the children, including scoutmasters, priests or ministers, teachers, Big Brothers, foster parents, and so on. This leaves the children or adolescents with the impression, again, that they will not be believed and that adults always side with adults. It also confirms the abuser's prediction to the children that they will not be believed. In the first scenario, the molester's task is made easier and safer; in the second scenario, the molester's power and control are confirmed, and the abuse continues unimpeded. In both cases, helplessness and despair occur, and either submission or flight results. In cases like these, it is no wonder that we see suicidal depression, alcohol and drug abuse, and runaway behaviors. I have treated more than one hundred cases where one or both of these scenarios did occur and were confirmed.

The second scenario involves parental denial and explains the original title of this work: "Not My Child!" When parents deny that their children could ever be victims of sexual abuse, they aid the molester to the highest degree. Individuals with pedophilic or hebophilic desires and needs become bolder in their seductions when they know, and tell their victims, that no one will believe them, including and especially their parents. Further, an almost insane trust results in parents from this denial where individuals in authority or with titles are concerned, especially those with the titles mentioned above. As one homosexual, hebophilic sixth-grade teacher said: "Parents literally give us their children. Permission slips for field trips, camping stay-overs, after school tutoring, and so on, are automatically signed without ever having met me or knowing anything about me. They give permission simply because I'm his teacher. I've even called their homes and asked to keep their son overnight for tutoring and convenience, and they always agreed. They sure made it easy for me."

I have met innumerable offenders with similar stories to tell about how easy it was for them to obtain children and adolescents without worrying about parental or other interference. Ignorance, lack of concern and responsibility, naïveté, a too trusting attitude, abdication of parental rights, and an overly materialistic interpretation of parental love all account for the consistent rise in sexual abuse. The merry-go-round continues unabated and results not only in new victims but also, years later, in compulsive, uncontrolled, and ritual repeat offending against still more children.

Considering the fact that each male pedophile or hebophile will, on average, molest over one hundred children or adolescents before being stopped, the pyramidal numbers become astronomical. If each undiscovered and therefore untreated male survivor some ten or more years later begins ritually offending other male children or adolescents and also follows the pattern of accumulating up to one hundred victims, and then each of those undiscovered and untreated survivors molests another one hundred victims, and so on and so on, the mathematics is simple but horrifying.

One of the only solutions is prevention, which parents must begin to work on almost literally from the birth of their children. This work is an attempt to aid all parents in preventing the merry-go-round from continuing.

❖

It may be helpful here to make two points regarding the language used in this book. First, while this work is intended primarily for parents, teenagers and more mature preteenagers, teachers, and counselors, it could also prove to be a valuable resource to other individuals without professional training who are interested in the subject. I have, therefore, deliberately avoided using too many psychological terms that would be unfamiliar to a large percentage of the population. The work is written in the simplest language possible, and where it is necessary to utilize a psychological or sexological term or phrase, a concise and clear definition or explanation will be found in the glossary of terms at the end of the book.

Second, in several of the cases presented as illustrations of a particular point or concept, the words of the survivor or offender are quoted. These quotes often include graphic sexual descriptions and terms, some openly vulgar and potentially offensive. These terms will appear only in case studies, which are set in a different type face and indented and can therefore be avoided.

Following this preface, I have included a parents' checklist, a type of pretest for all readers to utilize. The checklist should aid the reader in forming a mind-set for what follows.

PARENTS' CHECKLIST

The following list of questions is the result of several hundred interviews with child and adolescent survivors of sexual abuse about their parents and their home life. Parents should answer the questions honestly. Hopefully, the result will be that parents will then take appropriate corrective action in order to prevent any possible sexual or other molestation of their children.

The questions are not meant to be accusatory, although they may sound that way. They not only should be applied to past parental behaviors but can act as a guide to future child-raising behaviors.[1]

- How many of your child's or teenager's friends do you know personally? That is, how many of them have you met, spoken to at some length, and been in social contact with? How many of their parents do you know?

- How often do you permit your child or teen to go out bike riding, or to the park to play ball, or to the mall to meet friends, and so on, unsupervised?

- How often does your child or teen go out to play and is not checked on for at least an hour or more because "I was too busy?"

- What do you know personally about the people who live within a one-block radius of your home? If you live in an apartment, how many people do you know in the other apartments on your floor and the ones above and below your floor?

---

1. For clarity, the singular will be used for child and teenager. However, all questions certainly apply to multioffspring families and apply to both male and female children unless otherwise specified in the question.

- When shopping, do you allow your opposite-sex child to use the public rest room alone? If so, has the child or teen been adequately trained how to behave in public rest rooms and what to be attentive to?

- How often do you spend at least thirty minutes of quality-time with your child or teen and discuss personal and family matters?

- How often are you available when your child needs or asks to talk? How often do you say you are too busy or tired to talk? How often do you just say, "We'll talk later"?

- How many of your child's or teenager's teachers, tutors, coaches, and after-school activity leaders (drama club leader, science club leader, sport's activity leader, and so on) have you met personally, and how much do you know about them? Have they been discussed at home?

- How often do you check on your child's or teen's homework? If he or she says, "I don't have any," do you verify that with the teacher?

- How often have you signed permission slips for class trips, especially hikes, nature walks, overnight trips, and so on, when the entire class is not going and only special students have been chosen to go? In such circumstances do you always check the criteria for the choice of your child or teen and also how many adults will be supervising (if only one, think twice)? If it turned out that only one teacher, scoutmaster, or Big Brother was supervising, what did you know personally about that individual?

- If you use a baby-sitter, nursery school, or day-care setting, how much do you know about the staff and how they are hired, screened, and tested?

- If your child or teen is a "latchkey kid" (a child or teen whose parents work and who comes home from school to an empty apartment or house), isn't there a better solution? Have you asked a trusted and personally known neighbor to keep an eye on your child? Did you provide training and instruction to the child or teen about opening the door to any other adult?

- Is "modesty" so severe or puritanical in your home that it could prevent your child or teen from asking questions regarding bodily functions or regarding sexuality?

- Are religious or social beliefs and attitudes restricting open communication with your child or teen regarding physical or sexual topics?

- Did you adequately prepare your child for entering adolescence, including all of the physical, emotional, and sexual changes accompanying it? For a girl this includes preparation for menses and the knowledge that she may be fertile, and for a boy it includes knowledge of "wet dreams" and the corresponding fact that he may be on the verge of his own fertility.[2]

Where the last three questions are concerned, it has been my experience over the last thirty-three years that boys are more neglected or forgotten in those areas than are girls. Mothers necessarily must discuss menses with their daughters either in preparation for or often when the first shocking "accident" takes place. This often occurs in school or at play and may be horribly traumatic for the young, emerging adolescent female.

Since boys have no counterpart to menses, a discussion about the "facts of life" is often postponed or delayed for one of two reasons: (1) the parents (or parent) do not want to admit or believe that their son is becoming a man; or (2) the parents are too uncomfortable and embarrassed about sexuality to discuss it with their son. They often anticipate that, if they do discuss sexuality with him, questions will emerge that they can't answer, or questions will come forth about their own sexual behaviors.

---

2. The list of questions cited here is by no means complete. It is rather a sample of the types of questions that all parents should be asking themselves on a daily basis.

This situation can become ludicrous. Several years ago, I was "hired" by a physician of some twenty-five years experience to "handle this facts of life thing" with his son. At first, I thought it was a joke, but I soon discovered that the doctor was quite serious and terribly embarrassed over the whole situation, hoping that I could "just make it all go away." (See **CHESTER**, in chapter 4, for more on this case.)

Part 1

The "Who" of Sexual Abuse

1

THE SEX OFFENDER

The first and most important consideration in our attempt to prevent any more children or adults from being sexually abused is to gain some understanding of the type of individuals who perpetrate these offenses. They are complex persons who could be our next-door neighbors, people we work with, people we admire and look up to because of their titles or accomplishments, people who are in positions of authority or trust that are taken for granted, and so on.

The most important fact to remember about sex offenders is that they can be *anyone*. Sex offenders do not fulfill some stereotyped image of a deviant. Many people have an image of a sex offender as, for instance, a dirty old man in a long coat waiting behind a tree or building to expose himself or to kidnap a child for his own deviant purposes. The available literature and television dramas often added to this misperception, as did the misinformed press, until the late 1970s and early 1980s, when their stories of molestations and sexual assaults became more realistic.

In my experience in treating these individuals, I have found the most common demographic trait among them to be an inadequate personality (see the glossary of terms and the next paragraph for a definition). The only other commonality I encountered was that a majority of them had experienced some form of sexual trauma, active or passive, conscious or repressed. The active sexual traumas are easy to find and usually involve a direct sexual-abuse incident that is either remembered or repressed. The passive sexual traumas, on the other hand, are more difficult to uncover, and only specially trained therapists are capable of looking for and uncovering these events. In general, the passive sexual traumas involve an incident where sex itself is the traumatic factor even though the individual is not involved directly or molested in any manner. A simple example of passive sexual trauma would be a case where a child is forced to watch his or her mother being raped by an intruder. These events are usually repressed (forgotten and locked in the unconscious) until many years later when the life of the individual is grossly affected by the emotional content of the event. Girls may be unable to participate in sexual behaviors, and some may even be unable to bear seeing a man who is naked; boys may be impotent when they attempt intercourse and not know why.

A further word or two on the trait of inadequacy is necessary at this point. When I use the term "inadequate personality," I am not referring to inadequate persons but rather to individuals who perceive themselves as being less than any of their peers. These individuals feel that in all comparable areas, they are the least, the lowest, the smallest, the dumbest, the most nondeserving, and so on. This feeling has been there since they were children and usually resulted from their persistent inability to please an overly zealous, perfectionist, and demanding parent, who may have had the best motives but, nonetheless, severely damaged the child. After years of this situation, these children begin to agree with the parent that they will never amount to anything, that nothing they do is good enough.

What happens then is that they develop different *rulers* for themselves than for any of their peers. A ruler is a method of measuring ourselves against our peers on either a single personality trait or totally as a person. Rulers are based on learned values in early childhood. These values are usually imbedded in children by their parents but may also come from relatives or peer interactions. An example will clarify.

GLEN idolized his father for as long as he could remember. His father, **KNUTE**, was a college graduate who had excelled in both academic subjects and athletics. Wanting the best for his only son, he began unconsciously to put demands on little Glen, even before he was ready for preschool. Glen, on the other hand, was physically small and delicate, sensitive and easily hurt, and more passive than assertive. Each time that Glen did not live up to his father's expectations (rulers), his father would become angry or quiet and then ignore (reject) the little boy. By the time Glen was ready for school, he had adopted his father's demands and goals for himself, and whenever he did not live up to these goals, he would experience extreme guilt, feelings of unworthiness, and fears of the anticipated rejection that he would (and did!) receive from his father. As Glen grew older, he fully adopted his father's rulers and placed unrealistic and unreachable demands and goals upon himself that resulted in a constant cycle of failures. He was unknowingly (unconsciously) setting himself up for failure. This pattern lasted throughout his life until he finally could no longer stand the persistent, unending list of failures and attempted suicide.

Questions for Discussion

1. Why do you think that Glen's father imposed such strict measures or guidelines on everything the boy did?

2. When Glen had done the best he could but his father did not accept it as his best, what were his choices?

3. Can you name some areas of a child's or adolescent's life where the notion of "rulers" would apply?

4. What problems in relationships are attached to being a perfectionist?

5. How do you feel Glen's perfectionism and his "rulers" affected his adult sexual relationships?

Next, we need to look at some of the traits and demographics that make up a typical sex offender.

SEX OFFENDER TRAITS

- Physically, sex offenders come in all sizes, shapes, colors, and nationalities, and for the most part they fit the "boy/girl next door" or "good neighbor" profile.

- In terms of education, their profiles span the gamut: ranging from those who never completed grammar school to those with Ph.D.'s.

- In terms of employment, their profiles range from simple laborers to work supervisors, from professionals of every category to individuals who own and successfully operate their own businesses.

- In terms of economic class, the range spans from indigent to very wealthy.

- As regards social adjustment, they range from social misfits to social giants who are often perceived as the pillars of the community.

- As regards religion, all denominations are represented, including clergy from most of the denominations.

- As to marital status, it appears to have no bearing on the problem. Both single and married females and males sexually abuse.

Due to their inadequate personalities, sex offenders are repetitively looking for victims who are inferior to them in every way possible. Since the offender cannot deal with equals (peers), the potential victim is too often a child or adolescent with characteristics that pose no threat to the offender and who offers more than one opportunity for the offender to become involved with him or her. A list of some of the characteristics that sex offenders seek in victims can be seen in figure 1. In what follows, each of these traits will be defined and explained, and, where applicable, an illustration of the trait will be provided.

FIGURE 1: TRAITS OFFENDERS SEEK IN POTENTIAL VICTIMS

- Poor self-image coupled with low self-esteem

- A feeling that no one cares for them

- A persistent need for acceptance and approval

- A tendency to be loners and to isolate

- Being handicapped in some way: physically, emotionally, mentally

- Sexual naïveté

- Fear of adults and authority figures

- A history of abuse of any kind

- Being institutionalized ("Caretaker Abuse")

TRAITS OFFENDERS SEEK IN POTENTIAL VICTIMS

Poor Self-Image Coupled with Low Self-Esteem

How a child, an adolescent, or even an adult perceives himself/herself is often highly visible in that person's attitudes, behaviors, responses to others, and social life (or lack of it). Sex offenders look for shy, isolated, and withdrawn individuals who obviously have little or no self-confidence and who obviously rate themselves below their peers in all areas. These individuals rarely speak up for themselves, raise their hand in school to answer a question, or volunteer to lead a group, game, or program; they mostly sit back and wait to be called on or chosen for games, sports, or class activities. They "stick out" anywhere they go and are easily identified by their peers and by sex offenders.

Their strongest needs are for approval and acceptance, and they are willing to do anything to gain that approval or acceptance. This

makes them highly vulnerable to the seductions and approaches
of offenders and of more aggressive peers. **Rusty**, discussed in
chapter 2, is an excellent example of this type of individual.

A Feeling That No One Cares for Them

Closely related to potential victims' low self-esteem is their sense
that no matter how hard they try to conform to peer standards or
parental standards, they are not accepted or cared for. The two traits
are not mutually exclusive, however; individuals with strong self-
esteem and a highly positive self-image can also have a sense that
no one cares for them. People of this type have less a chance of
submitting to the seductions of the sex offender (although some do)
than those who have both traits. There is also a more positive prognosis for adjustment with minimal help or counseling by a friend,
relative, teacher, counselor, or anyone else whom they are willing
to *trust*. Trusting for this group is easier than for the other group;
however, they are still vulnerable, due to this need, to become the
prey of a predator-type sex offender. Once the offender identifies
their need for someone who cares for them, the offenders' scripting
of the seduction is automatic and simple since most offenders, as
children and adolescents, lived with this trait. (**Lew**, whom we will
meet in chapter 2, exemplifies this situation clearly.)

A Persistent Need for Acceptance and Approval

Both of the above-discussed characteristics are natural consequences of poor self-esteem and a negative self-image coupled
with the belief that one is not cared for. What distinguishes persons with a persistent need for acceptance and approval from their
peers (who also need acceptance and approval) is the degree and
intensity of the need. While their peers will modify their behavior
and go along to a certain degree with adults or stronger or older
peers and authority figures from whom they desire acceptance and
approval, there is a limit to what they will agree to. Potential victims, in contrast, have such an intense and almost desperate need

for this acceptance and approval that they will pay any price to obtain it. Sex predators seek exactly this type of individual. They will carefully test a potential victim over a long time to be sure that they have chosen correctly. This "testing period" might take as long as six months or even an entire year before any overt sexual move is made. Here, the sex offender's own inadequacy and insecurity become evident. His or her safety takes precedence over obtaining a new victim. (**MR. HOWIE**, discussed in chapter 4, is an exaggerated example of this type of offender.)

A Tendency to Be Loners and to Isolate

Loners who do not interact with their peers are prime potential victims for any older adolescent or adult sex offender. Isolation offers the offender the opportunity to become the loner's only true friend and to have the opportunity to spend plenty of time in the seduction process. The offender's attention will not be interrupted by the victim's friends or participation in sports activities, school clubs, or dating. The loner really has nowhere to go and nothing to do except be alone again at home. Loners are also sad and depressed individuals who will do anything to be part of their peer group, and they pray and fantasize constantly that they will be asked to join. The thought of asking on their own is unthinkable and produces such severe anxiety that the isolation is intensified. All social contact is considered dangerous and therefore to be avoided. Teachers, priests, ministers, Big Brothers, and scoutmasters all have perfect entrée to these children or adolescents as part of their jobs. (**KEIF** [see chapter 2] typically chose loners in his institutions to molest and was almost 100 percent successful in these choices.)

Being Handicapped in Some Way: Physically, Emotionally, Mentally

Sex offenders, weak and inadequate as they are, prefer victims who are weaker and more inadequate than they are. Handicapped individuals, therefore, are high on their preference list. It is also usually true, unfortunately, that these individuals are dependent on others and have a minimal number of friends with whom they associate. They tend to be onlookers at school and sports events and easy prey to the offender.

It is equally true, again unfortunately, that sex offenders are great at volunteering for organizations that deal with the physically handicapped. I have treated sex offenders who were bus drivers, Big Brothers, and volunteers at schools and facilities for the handicapped (for example, schools for those with cerebral palsy or multiple sclerosis, where many of the children or adolescents need to be taken to the bathroom, helped to dress and undress, and so on).

Where emotionally and mentally handicapped persons are concerned, the problem is just as great. Many of these individuals are institutionalized due to behavioral or management problems, and the staff, too often, is not properly screened. One such case involved KEIF (see chapter 2) who worked in several institutions of this type and in each molested a large number of male patients. Although he gave permission on his employment application for his credentials to be verified, they never were in the four institutions where he molested. In each, when the molestation was either suspected or reported, he was allowed to resign with no action taken. Two of the institutions actually gave him favorable recommendations for working again with handicapped children.

Sexual Naïveté

The sexually naive are easy to single out as targets. The rationalization "I was only teaching him/her sex education" has been used countless times by incestuous parents, school teachers, scoutmasters, Big Brothers, and other predators to justify their deviant behavior. The sex education that the sex offender teaches always fits his or her needs and leads up to some sexual act or involvement, usually beginning with a demonstration of one of the sex-education "facts" being taught. A child or adolescent who has had proper and detailed sex education either at home or in school will not, as easily, fall prey to the machinations of this type of predator. An example will clarify.

DON was a sixth grade teacher in a local community. Don was also a sex offender and had been involved with preadolescent boys several times without being apprehended. In fact, since he began his teaching career, he had been molesting anywhere from five to seven boys in his sixth grade class each year.

Don's seduction routine was both clever and simple. At the beginning of each new school year, Don would have the students write an essay about their families and their home life that included a list of changes they wished could magically be made.

From these essays, Don would look for boys who were not in a positive relationship with their fathers or who were from fatherless homes. From his classroom observations, he would look for boys who were loners, isolated from the rest of the children, and who were sensitive and obviously in need of attention, affection, and physical contact. The latter need was easily determined by having each of them come to his desk to go over some of their work, and, while there, he would place his arm around their backs or shoulders and "feel" for their reactions. If these reactions were positive and they enjoyed both the attention and the physical contact, Don would progress with his plan of seduction.

Next, Don would appoint one or more of these "chosen" boys his assistants and ask them to stay after class to help with whatever. Other boys on his list needed tutoring, and this was his entrée to personal contact and time alone with them.

In one way or another, the subject of sex would be brought up, and he would ask them questions he knew they could not answer. Thus, sex education began. Often, Don would call the boys' parents and ask permission to tutor them in his apartment after having dinner at McDonald's or some other child-oriented fast-food restaurant.[1]

---

1. Don was never refused this permission or the permission, once a boy was at his apartment, to have the boy spend the night, "saving his parents the trouble of picking him up and bringing him to school the next day."

Sex education would lead to the boy's watching Don's penis, erection, and ejaculation. Don would then teach the boy to masturbate, quickly taking over for the boy since he was "doing it wrong." From there, oral sex and, depending on the age of the boy, mutual sodomy would complete the "course."

One boy, punished by his parents for being in detention for some school infraction, revengefully told on Don. This boy later admitted in therapy that had Don not punished him and had his parents not been as upset as they were, he would never have told anyone about his molestation by Don.

Questions for Discussion

1. Why do parents so easily give their permission to authority figures with whom they have had no contact?

2. Why do you feel that Don was so successful in his sexual molestations?

3. Was the age of the boys in Don's sixth grade class a significant factor in his success? If so, why?

4. Why do you think that none of the boys reported Don for so long?

5. What does it mean when the boy who finally reported Don says that were he not punished, he would not have even mentioned his molestation?

Fear of Adults and Authority Figures

Children and adolescents who fear adults and authority figures are attractive and easy prey for sex offenders. Once offenders identify this trait, they slowly, carefully, and purposely initiate contact with the intended victim. Since many of the offenders themselves experienced this trait in their own childhood or adolescence, they are quite adept at choosing the correct approach to these potential victims. Here, again, the sex offenders' patience is vast, and they may invest six months to a year in establishing a relationship of trust with no sexual overtones or approaches.

Once the relationship is firmly established and the victim is "hooked" on the "trust" that has developed, a slow and methodical sexual contact begins with small touches to shoulders and back, ever so slowly advancing down the back to the buttocks. Sex offenders know whether the touch is or is not accepted by the tenseness of the muscles in the touch area. They will wait as long as possible before making the next move, which is often to say something like: "I've done all of these things for you, and now I need a favor too." An excellent example of this type of approach can be seen in the case of **BRUCE**, in chapter 2.

A History of Abuse of Any Kind

Sex offenders also look for those who have been abused. It does not really matter whether this abuse has been physical, emotional, or sexual; all of the individuals in this group, regardless of age, are vulnerable to seduction by the sexual predator. As with the handicapped group, the sex offender sees these individuals as needy, already damaged goods, and easy to seduce. As with many of the other trait groups, patience is the key, coupled with a keen analysis of what approach will work best. The first step is for the offender to uncover the exact details of the previous abuse and then to build on this knowledge. Providing the opposite needs is the usual approach. For example, if rejection (as in emotional abuse) was involved, acceptance of the individual as he or she is fills the requirement; if beating and physical abuse were involved, soft, soothing touch and massage answer the need; if forced sex, such as rape or forcible sodomy, were involved, then, at the right time, seductive, pleasant sexual arousal (usually begun with light fondling to erection or lubrication) is the choice. (The sex offender cases referred to in the sections above on handicapped and fearful victims apply here as well.)

Being Institutionalized ("Caretaker Abuse")

Institutionalized children and adults often have most of the traits discussed above, and the examples listed above apply as well. The main factor in this group is that all control is in the hands of the institutional personnel, and there is no parent, relative, or close friend available for protection. These individuals are vulnerable to both forced and seductive sexual molestation and their distrust of authority (both before and confirmed after the assault or seduction) usually precludes their reporting the incident. This group also tends to believe that all adults or authority figures side with and protect each other, so there is no use in reporting the event. This situation poses one of the most serious problems in society today.

❖

It is important here to look back to figure 1, which lists all of the traits that sex offenders look for in potential victims. I hope it is now clear and obvious that everyone involved with children and adolescents (parents, relatives, teachers, ministers, priests, and so on) needs to help them to develop traits opposite to those on the list. In my many years of treating both sex offenders and the survivors of sexual abuse, I have never encountered a case where several, if not all, of the conditions presented in figure 1 did not exist. Even in homes that *appeared* ideal, the picture became less than ideal once family values, family secrets, and parent-child relationships were explored and uncovered. A list of ideal traits would look something like the one in figure 2. It will, obviously, not always be possible to develop all these traits in every child or adolescent. However, the higher the number of these traits that are developed in a child or adolescent, the greater the chance will be for that child or adolescent to remain free from sexual abuse from outside the home. Where incest (see chapter 5) is concerned, the story is somewhat different.

Figure 2: Traits That Will Help to Prevent Child/Adolescent Sexual Molestation

- Feeling loved by parents, siblings, relatives, and friends

- Wanting but not needing approval and acceptance from others

- Being social and having many friends

- Being stable and age-mature on a physical, emotional, and mental level

- Having had age-appropriate sex education from a reliable source

- Relating to authority figures with respect, not fear

- Being free from past abuse or trauma

- For those who were abused or traumatized, having professional therapy with a qualified and trained therapist in this field

- Having a stable home (with either both parents or a single parent)

THE ROLE OF SEXUAL TRAUMA IN THE FORMATION OF THE OFFENDER

A major area of controversy among individuals involved in the treatment and study of sexual abuse regards the role that past sexual trauma (an emotional shock due to either an active or a passive sexual molestation that leaves a lasting mark on the individual) plays in the formation of the sexual deviate. While some professionals in the field insist that all sex offenders were themselves victims of sexual assault or molestation, others strongly disagree, myself included. Many complicated factors determine the permanent effects of a sexual trauma, and we will consider these as we progress.

I have met many adult males and females who were molested as children but who today are happy, emotionally well adjusted, productive, and sexually normal. Many of them are also good parents who are quite sensitive to sexual issues where their own children are concerned. I have also met hundreds of adults, mostly males, who were molested as children but who today are unhappy, maladjusted child molesters or sexually assaultive personalities. An example of this dichotomy occurring in the same home follows.

> **BENNY** and **BURT** are two brothers who, between the ages of eleven and fourteen, were masturbated and fellated on a weekly basis by a granduncle who supported the family, treated them well, and always brought them gifts. They went to their mother and reported the sexual abuse and were told: "Do what he wants you to because he's so good to us." (She also feared him since he was allegedly connected to the mob.)
>
> The molestations continued for over four years, when the granduncle disappeared. Years later, Benny married, had three children, and became an excellent husband and parent; Burt, in contrast, became a child molester, repeating the granduncle's rituals exactly. He is now serving a lengthy sentence in prison.

Questions for Discussion

1. If the boys' mother had told them the truth (that she was afraid of the granduncle), would the effect on them have been different?

2. Do you feel that the boys allowed the molestations to continue for over four years only because of their mother's seeming approval?

3. Does the granduncle fit the profile of the pedophilic sex offender?

4. What motivates elderly men like this granduncle to molest prepubertal and pubertal boys?

5. What differences in the personalities of the two boys might have brought about the radically different outcomes of this dual sexual molestation?

It is important, at this juncture, to compare figure 3, below, with figure 2, presented earlier. There are many essential similarities between the lists. As stated above, prevention demands that parents and all other individuals involved in the raising and training of children do all in their power to help each and every child develop these essential traits and conditions in order to give them the greatest possible weapons against being sexually assaulted or molested.

In order to understand more fully the difference between children who are abused and then become sexual abusers and children who are abused and do not become sexual abusers, I interviewed 125 of the latter. The results were the basis for figure 3, which I hope can help establish a preventive framework.

The confusion as to whether a sexually abused child will become an adult sexual molester appears to result from a misunderstanding of the concept of sexual trauma and its effects. There are two possible immediate reactions when an individual of any age is sexually assaulted or abused: either the blame, responsibility, and guilt are internalized, or they are externalized onto the offender, where they belong. Two additional concepts need to be discussed that may help to resolve any confusion regarding this matter.

DISTINGUISHING ACTIVE SEXUAL TRAUMA FROM PASSIVE SEXUAL TRAUMA

I discussed active and passive sexual trauma above, but it might be helpful to repeat the distinction here: (1) Active sexual trauma is well known and easily identified. It occurs when there is a direct molestation involving sexually explicit behavior on the part of the molester and also on the part of the child. (2) Passive sexual trauma

FIGURE 3: TEN FACTORS FOUND IN SEXUALLY ABUSED
MALES WHO DID NOT BECOME ADULT SEXUAL OFFENDERS

1. Their self-esteem was strong and positive.

2. They had a fairly good sexual knowledge at the time of the molestation or seduction.

3. There was an important adult in their lives with whom they could discuss anything without fear of repercussion.

4. Their religious education was along positive and forgiving pathways rather than the "sin and damnation" models.

5. They had several real friends in their peer group with whom they could discuss anything without fear of rejection or put-down.

6. Their personality structure was stronger and more positive than the usually quite inadequate sex offender personality.

7. They were successful in either school, sports, or some other area that produced pride, both for their parents and, more importantly, for themselves.

8. Their parents were more regularly involved in their lives and activities, attended PTA meetings and other school functions, spent as much time as possible with them on weekends, and so on. They also traveled and vacationed with their parents.

9. They believed in themselves and had enduring self-confidence.

10. They had long-term goals as opposed to the day-by-day orientation of the sex offender.

occurs when sex itself in some indirect way has a profound and traumatic effect on the child's life, without the child ever having been directly sexually molested.

When an active-sexual-trauma case appears in a therapist's office, the therapist already knows that there has been a sexual assault or molestation. Either the referring person, a parent or parents, or the patient has disclosed this factor when the initial contact for therapy was made. These are all cases where the sexual assault or molestation is consciously known and admitted to. Therapy begins directly on the problem and hopefully is rapid and successful. However, even in these cases, patients lie (usually by omission — that is, leaving some important detail out of the retelling of the event that they are too ashamed of or embarrassed by or that they feel guilty over, fearing rebuke and rejection from the therapist) or consciously decide to tell the story of the abuse in "little pieces or episodes," taking as long as a year before the entire story emerges. The latter type delays therapeutic progress much longer.

In contrast, when a therapist suspects a case of passive sexual trauma due to observed behavioral symptoms and asks the child or adult if he or she has ever been molested, those who have been traumatized in this way spontaneously and honestly reply that they have not. The therapist, if he or she believes the client, then usually looks for other causes of the presenting problem and may use the wrong treatment methods. Too few therapists that I have supervised were able to ask specific questions that would elicit details of passive sexual trauma, due to lack of training in this area and a lack of initiative on the part of postgraduate therapists to seek out specialized training and supervision before attempting to treat survivors. Two examples — the cases of Ralph and Herb — will clarify.

RALPH (whom we will meet in greater detail in chapter 4) is a severe case of passive sexual trauma. The trauma occurred when his mother came home from work early one day, due to illness, and caught his father in bed with his secretary. Ralph's mother threw her husband and the secretary out of the house (which was exactly what they wanted), and the father was never seen again. This changed the economic base of the family and totally changed Ralph's life for the worst. The most visible effect was Ralph's rage toward his mother, projected onto all women, which resulted in his referral for treatment. The sexual connection was uncovered in his statement: "Why does my life have to be ruined, just because of a little sex?" Ralph also eventually admitted to masturbating to fantasies of raping his mother for what she had *done to him.* While Ralph was never physically sexually molested, he was well on his way to becoming a sexually assaultive person, and only identification and treatment prevented it.

Questions for Discussion

1. How could Ralph's explosive reaction have been avoided?

2. What do you think Ralph's attitude toward girls and women was at the time of the father's exposure?

3. Where did this attitude come from?

4. Did Ralph's mother's personality play any role in Ralph's reaction?

5. Why did Ralph side with his father?

HERB came from an incestuous family where he was the only boy. He had four sisters, all of whom were repeatedly sexually molested by their father over a period of twelve years. In about the third year, Herb's oldest sister (the first to be victimized) revealed to him what was going on but swore him to secrecy. Herb later found out that the rest of the girls were being molested as well and, in fact, walked in on one occasion of the father's incestuous molestation. The father threatened to kill Herb and the whole family and also to use Herb as a girl if he ever said a word to anyone.

Some ten years later, Herb's oldest sister committed suicide, and he went into a deep depression, exacerbated by a deep personal guilt since he had never interfered or reported the problem to his mother or to the authorities.

As an adult, Herb was a loner and never dated; when he attempted intercourse for the first time, he was impotent. When he finally tried therapy, none of these facts was elicited, and he was treated for his impotence alone. Nothing worked. He became more and more depressed and eventually made a feeble suicidal gesture. With a new sex therapist, well trained in this area, the whole story emerged in a little over a month, and Herb then began to respond.

It should be noted here that this type of passive sexual trauma may be as severe in its effects as active or direct sexual trauma and may, at times, be worse.

Questions for Discussion

1. How did finding out about his sisters' molestations initially affect Herb?

2. Did the effects worsen when he walked in on an actual molestation by his father?

3. Why did the effects worsen?

4. How did his father's threats to kill him and the whole family affect Herb?

5. What connection existed between his sisters' incestuous molestations and Herb's adult impotence?

PATTERNS OF CHILD MOLESTERS WHO WERE THEMSELVES SEXUALLY MOLESTED AS CHILDREN

Several distinct behavior patterns employed by child molesters, both pedophiles (who choose prepubertal, preorgasmic victims) and hebophiles (who choose adolescent or postadolescent, orgasmic victims), need to be recognized and dealt with in treatment.

Projecting All Responsibility onto the Victim

In seductive molestation, incestuous fathers and other authority figures who molest their charges often make statements such as:

- "If you weren't so cute and seductive, this wouldn't have happened."
- "If you hadn't made your mother [or father] leave us, this wouldn't have happened."
- "If you didn't dress so seductively and sexually, it wouldn't have happened."
- "You don't have to do this, even though I do so much for you. It's your decision!"

In incest, the abusing parent cons the child into believing that he or she is protecting the family, siblings, the other parent, relatives, pets, and so on. Then, starting with the second time, the abuser puts all blame on the victim as wanting it. An example will clarify.

DARLENE and KAREN lived with their mother, JOYCE, and their father, BRAD. Brad was a longtime alcoholic who, when intoxicated, became verbally and physically abusive to anyone in sight. Often he had been arrested for simple assaults that were, in reality, bar fights that he had started. Unfortunately, he was physically quite strong and both frightening and controlling.

When Darlene was approximately twelve years old and Karen only eight, Brad began paying more attention to Darlene. He became more physically involved with her, touching her hair, rubbing her back, patting her on the buttocks, and so on. Early one morning (about 1:00 A.M.), Brad arrived home drunker than usual and feeling horny. His wife rebuked his advances and began crying, which Brad hated. She shouted at him, "Go bother your daughter since you're so interested in her lately." Brad did exactly that. He went to the girls' room, climbed into Darlene's bed with only his undershorts on, and began fondling her. She awakened and, in terror, tried to push him away. Brad slapped her hard across the face and asked her if she preferred that he went to her little sister.

The thought of her father sexually molesting her little sister, whom she loved and protected daily, was unthinkable. Closing her eyes, Darlene submitted to her father's incestuous assault, screaming with pain as he violently penetrated her (she was a virgin) and then passing out. When she awoke, she was still in her bed, naked, soiled, and bleeding. She called for her mother, who slept in the bedroom next door, but Joyce never came. She was too ashamed of what had happened and, yet, too terrified of her husband to take any remedial action.

This was only the first of almost a hundred sexual assaults by Brad over the next three to four years. (More on Darlene and incest in chapter 5.)

Questions for Discussion

1. Does Darlene's father's behavior follow the profile of a child molester?

2. Are there any differences?

3. How does incest differ from child sexual abuse?

4. How do you suspect Darlene's submission to her father to protect her sister affected her adult life and her values regarding men?

5. If Darlene married, what kind of a man do you suspect she would choose?

Creating Insurance

Child molesters frequently take photographs (usually Polaroids, to avoid film-processing firms) or make home videos of the children performing sexually or posing in the nude in a sexually excited state (for example, boys with erections, girls masturbating or touching their genitals) or make audiotapes of the children talking about how much they enjoyed having sex with the abuser and how they want to continue both the acts and the relationship. Of course, all of these methods of blackmail are carefully prepared and scripted in advance of the first molestation.

Psyching-Out Potential Victims

The offenders are constantly concerned about their own personal safety. They, therefore, choose passive-dependent-type children or adolescents who either are in conflict with their parents or have demonstrated that they want or need the molester's attention and acceptance. Both pedophiles and hebophiles prefer loners, needy kids, missing-parent kids, kids who are shy and timid, or, conversely, popular and outgoing kids (so that in his or her fantasies, the offender may become the kid that he or she never was: his or her ideal self).

The molester makes sure that he or she has the victim well hooked in wanting and needing the relationship and the benefits that the relationship provides (gifts, trips, "love," acceptance, and so on) before making the first, simplest test, sexual advance, or suggestion. As stated before, the offenders have infinite patience.

While the above three patterns of the molester apply to all sexual abuse, there are several distinct differences in cases of assaultive sexual abuse. In assaultive sexual molestation, the molester hurts the victim in many ways, not just physically. Not only is there a need for control, but there is also a need to make the victim suffer and experience pain, usually as the offender suffered and experienced pain as a child. If the victim appears to be enjoying the assault, the offender is either turned off and leaves or becomes so enraged that he or she may kill the victim. This factor makes offering suggestions on how to handle these assaults both difficult and dangerous.

Of extreme importance in treating survivors of assaultive sexual trauma is the need to be sure that all aspects of the assault are exposed, including a step-by-step account of the attack, but only when the survivor is ready to deal with this issue. Quite often, a survivor tells the police and the therapist only what she or he feels is necessary for prosecution. This is most often true in cases of aggravated sexual assault (rape), regardless of whether the survivor is a female or a male.

Associated behavior, preceding or following the actual rape, is often more important than the forced intercourse itself. An example will clarify this.

> JAY, a fifty-year-old psychologist, was a self-referral to my office for severe depression and sexual dysfunction. After the usual initial resistance and once he stated that he was ready to discuss the real problem, Jay related that while at a conference he had been raped in his hotel room. His story was that he had made a special presentation and when finished had offered to discuss his paper and its new therapy technique with anyone who so wished that evening. A young man, identifying himself as a graduate student at the local university, asked if he could see him in private and Jay, without thinking of the potential danger, invited the man to his room later that evening. When the man arrived, he appeared grateful and pleasant and, after the usual chitchat, asked if he could use the bathroom. When he came out, he was naked and wielding a large switchblade knife. Jay was shocked and asked what was going on. The demeanor of the young man changed from a friendly and polite individual to an angry, ordering, and threatening one. Jay was ordered to undress and lie on the bed or die. Jay complied, and the young man sat on his chest, reached back and placed the knife point at the base of Jay's penis, and told him he would definitely castrate him slowly if he did not do as he was told. After being forced to fellate the young attacker, he was ordered to roll over and was then raped with sadistic force and in extreme pain.

Questions for Discussion

1. In what way does the rape of a male differ from the rape of a female, and are there additional long-term effects?

2. What values come into play in the rape of a male that do not in the rape of a female?

3. Does Jay's professional background play an important role in the incident? If so, what role did it play?

4. Why did Jay assume all of the guilt for the incident?

5. What was Jay guilty of, if anything?

Throughout the ordeal, the assailant kept telling Jay that it was all his fault, since he had looked at him in a sexual manner during the paper presentation and had offered the invitation to his room in a seductive manner. Also, the attacker had continued stimulating Jay throughout the four-hour ordeal and had brought him to a climax more than once. The intruder's immediate and mocking interpretation of this was that Jay was enjoying the sexual assault and that he, the attacker, was correct in interpreting Jay's attitude toward him. When the four-hour ordeal was over, the young man told Jay that he knew his name and address and that if Jay made any mention of the assault, he would report to the police that Jay had raped him after luring him to his room, allegedly to discuss the paper. Since he was younger and a student at the conference, he assured Jay that he would be believed. He even boldly offered Jay the telephone, daring him to call the authorities.

Jay was traumatized and fearful of his colleagues' reactions and the reactions of his family, so he told no one. He left early the next morning, feigning illness to one of the leaders of the conference and to his family when he arrived home two days early.

For the next year (before calling for an appointment) Jay lived a life of fear and paranoia, anticipating a call from the assailant or possibly blackmail or extortion attempts. His co-workers sensed something was wrong, but he continued to place the blame on physical problems. Sex with his wife ended, and she accepted the fact that he was physically ill.

The above facts took over nine months of therapy to elicit. Each time the incident was discussed, something new was added. Eighteen months into therapy, Jay remembered being sexually molested at age twelve by a scoutmaster, over a three-year period, and then admitted, for the first time, that while his fear and shock were real, there was an element of sexual excitement in the recent rape and that he was now masturbating to the sexual incident with the young man but changing the fantasy to one that was friendly and compliant. Guilt was incredible at this point, and therapy became a real challenge.

No real progress occurred from that point on until Jay accepted the fact that he had a bisexual imprint from the time of the scoutmaster's sexual molestation. He gradually came to the realization that he never had had to act out homosexually because of his bisexual orientation and because he could choose to function exclusively in a heterosexual manner. In other words, he did not lose the ability to choose his present or future sexual preference.

Projecting Blame onto the Survivor

Jay's rapist did a really good con job on him, projecting all the blame onto Jay because he had an orgasm.[2] What the offender was unaware of was Jay's past sexual molestation and its connection to the fact that Jay did enjoy parts of the sexual attack. Also, in the assault on Jay, the issue of control, on the part of the offender, is more than apparent, though the offender was unaware that the control would last for years after the attack. Too often, new therapists, dealing with a case of this type, miss the fact that even though the incident is over, the feelings of control (Jay's fears of being discovered, contacted, or blackmailed) persist.

Almost all of the rape survivors that I have dealt with still feel the fear that the offender will find them again and that the rape

---

2. It should be noted here that it is not uncommon for victims of sexual assault to experience pleasurable sexual feelings and even to reach an orgasm during the molestation or assault. While the mind continues to reject what is happening, the body switches to "autopilot" and from past learned experience reacts naturally. Survivors of sexual assault should feel no guilt or shame should this occur, nor should they interpret it as an indication of either cooperation or blame for the assault.

will recur. There are even cases where this fear appears to cause the survivors to set themselves up to be assaulted again.

Altering the Survivor's Values about Sex

Seductive molestation teaches the distorted value that sex equals love. Sexual assault teaches the distorted values that sex equals hate, fear, pain, and degradation. These distorted values must be continually dealt with in the treatment of the survivor and changed to more positive and realistic values. The molester also attempts to convince the survivor that the molestation is normal and natural or that the molester has been given permission by parents, by position of authority, or even by God (see **KYLE**, in chapters 2 and 6).

Choosing Loaded Words for Use before, during, and after the Act

There are cases where what the offender says during the attack is more traumatic and psychologically damaging than the actual physical act. Several examples from my own experiences with survivors will clarify:

- The boy who is raped and then told that he was "better than any girl" that the abuser had been with. This can significantly damage the boy's self-image and self-esteem. Therapy must aid the survivor to understand and accept these words as part of the pathology of the offender and not the survivor's problem. **JOEY** (who will be discussed in chapter 3) is an appropriate example of this type of damaging pattern. His father, during a sexual assault on him, referred to Joey as his "boy pussy." That phrase stayed with Joey into adulthood and into his marriage. Needless to say, he was sexually dysfunctional with women.

- The young girl who is blamed by her abuser for causing the abuse because she was either "too pretty" or "too sexy." The effects on her will be similar to those for the boy in the previous example.

- The rape victim who is told that since she or he had an orgasm or became obviously stimulated that she or he "wanted to be raped and enjoyed it."

- The boy who has his first orgasm with a male abuser who then tells him "I knew you were a queer; I can spot them a mile away."

- The survivor, male or female, who is told by the police or his parents: "You must have given him some signal that you were interested or wanted sex with him!" or "You must have acted seductively or done something that stimulated him!"[3]

---

3. For more in-depth information on sex offenders, their etiology, dynamics, and treatment, see my first book, *Treating Sex Offenders in Correctional Institutions and Outpatient Clinics: A Guide to Clinical Practice* (New York: Haworth Press, 1991). For a differing viewpoint, see Nathaniel J. Pallone, *Rehabilitating Criminal Sexual Psychopaths: Legislative Mandate, Clinical Quandaries* (Rutgers University, New Brunswick, N.J.: Transaction Books, 1990). Pallone presents an excellent survey of both standard and aggressive methods of treatment for sex offenders and their legal constraints. He discusses such aggressive treatment modalities as bioimpedance measures, including surgical and chemical castration, and aversive modalities, including aversive behavior therapy, revulsion, electroshock, and pharmacologically induced aversion (nausea). Examples and studies are included for each type of therapy.

2

THE SURVIVOR

In chapter 1, in discussing sex offenders, I found it necessary to dwell at considerable length on the traits of ideal victims. I will not cover that ground again in this chapter, but there are a few additional, specific traits of victims and their families that should be elucidated before moving on to matters involving the settings for molestation and treatment.

ADDITIONAL CHARACTERISTICS OF IDEAL VICTIMS AND THEIR FAMILIES

Appearance

An important factor I did not discuss thoroughly in chapter 1 is appearance. When appearance is a factor in a sex offender's choice of a potential victim, it usually involves one of two scenarios.

In the first scenario, the potential victim must be the ideal child or adolescent that the abuser never was. Most sex offenders were inadequate personalities as children — they were shy, withdrawn, loners, and terrified of rejection on any level from both adults and peers. They saw themselves as ugly, too skinny or too fat, too awkward and uncoordinated, too anything that would bode rejection, laughter, or humiliation. When they become adults, their ideal victim must be the opposite, that is, the most popular kid in the class, the most attractive kid with the ideal body, the most assertive and outspoken student who excels in studies or athletics, or both: an intellectual giant or a "jock." In short, the victim must possess all of the exact opposite traits of the inadequate offender.

In the second scenario, the potential victim must look, act, and behave as identically as possible to the abuser at the time of his or her own molestation. In the former case (that of the ideal child or adolescent), many of the sexual behaviors provide a vicarious identification and/or incorporation of the victim's traits by the offender, and for that short period of time, the two become one. In the latter case (that of the search for the identical child or adolescent), the offender denies one of the most damaging effects of sexual abuse: the "I'm the only one" perception. A majority of children who have been seductively sexually abused over a long term believe that they are the only ones who would submit to the sexual demands of an adult over a period of time. When these victims grow older, they believe that by seducing and molesting a child whom they perceive as closely or identically resembling themselves as a child, they can rid themselves of the "I'm the only one" perception. An example of each type will elucidate the matter.

RUSTY was a tall, plain-looking, shy boy throughout his grammar and high school years. He was also naive, especially regarding sexuality. When other sixth-grade boys made sexual innuendoes in the boys' bathroom, Rusty made believe that he knew what they were talking about, but he didn't.

During that fatal sixth grade there was a scandal that affected Rusty's life in a dramatic and permanent way. Rusty belonged to a secret club, and the club had a tree house in the woods that only members knew about or could use. One day, **KARL**, the most popular, the most physically developed, and the most aggressive member of the club brought **SANDRA**, "the school slut" (unbeknownst to Rusty), with him, and Rusty learned a distorted view of the facts of life. Sandra first fellated the then five members of the club but not to orgasm. The club members then formed a "train" (a lineup of the members who took turns having intercourse with Sandra). Naturally, Rusty was the "caboose" (that is, the last in line). When his turn came, much to his embarrassment and humiliation, he was unable to get an erection.

The group members howled, and from that day forward his new nickname became "Limp Dick."

Almost compulsively, Rusty began hanging around Karl although he remained the butt of Karl's jokes. After a short period of time, Karl invited Rusty to visit him at night in the school's maintenance room behind the boiler room (Karl's father was the school janitor). Reluctantly and with trepidation, Rusty arrived at the appointed time and was pleasantly surprised at Karl's friendliness and offered camaraderie. Within five minutes or so, Karl switched the subject to sex and to Rusty's failure at the clubhouse. He then offered to "help" Rusty with his problem by showing him "what a real man should be able to do." Karl dropped his pants to reveal an erection of some nine inches. Rusty was amazed and, now, even more embarrassed since he had a very small penis and could only obtain about a four-inch erection. When Karl asked him to drop his pants and follow what he was doing, Rusty said he couldn't. Karl then quickly offered Rusty the use of his penis, and Rusty began his homosexual career.

Rusty was both thrilled and amazed to be masturbating such an enormous penis and instantly closed his eyes and fantasized that it was his. When Karl ejaculated a copious quantity of semen, Rusty was once more amazed, since he had, to this point in his life, never ejaculated. The wonder of it all and the *acceptance* he felt from Karl made him the "happiest little boy in the world." Naturally, Karl made Rusty swear an oath of secrecy and, in return, offered to be his mentor and his protector. He also offered him the use of his penis whenever he wanted it.

Less than two months into this relationship (the boys met about three to four times per week), Karl offered Rusty the opportunity to "borrow" other penises for his fantasy pleasure, assuring him of secrecy and additional friendships. He arranged nighttime meetings at the school with his cousins, uncles, and some other friends from his neighborhood for Rusty to have sex with. Within a short period of time, Rusty was compulsively looking for other large penises to "borrow" in public rest

rooms, parks, shopping malls, and so on. He now felt more popular and accepted than he had ever felt in his life. His fantasies
delusionally made up for his own felt gross inadequacies.

Questions for Discussion

1. What personality characteristics made Rusty vulnerable to being sexually abused?

2. Why do you think Karl felt comfortable and safe in seducing Rusty?

3. Would sex education by a well-trained professional have helped
   to prevent Rusty's sexual seduction and abuse?

4. Can you predict some of Rusty's traits as an adult?

5. Was Rusty's lack of communication with his parents and other
   adults a contributing factor to his molestation?

As an adult, Rusty failed in social relationships and became a
bookworm. He was an all-A student and consistently on the honor
roll. At home, alone, he was lonely and depressed, and whenever
these feelings emerged, he immediately set out to "hunt" for someone with a big penis. However, due to what he felt were his sexual
and physical inadequacies, he feared making adult sexual contacts
and so began a career of looking for emerging adolescents to seduce. To accomplish his new goals, he became a tutor in several high
school subjects and offered his services to several schools, with the
limitation that he would only work with boys, so that no accusa-
tions of improper conduct could be made against him by girls. He
knew that tutoring would introduce him to many new boys, and he
believed that he would have no problem finding plenty of penises
to vicariously fantasize as his own. Additionally, he believed that by
seducing his students and eventually giving them sexual pleasure,
he would gain their acceptance and hopefully their "love." Before
Rusty left for a university in another state, he had seduced and
possessed more than fifty teenage boys.

Another example of the first type follows.

LEW was a short and fat little boy when he entered grammar school. He had had very few friends or playmates during his preschool years except for his cousins. Lew tended to be shy, a loner who preferred reading and crafts that he could do by himself (doing coloring books, making potholders, reading comic books, and so on), and was totally lacking in either assertiveness or social skills. Lew was a very sensitive lad who was particularly vulnerable to name calling and slurs such as "fatso," "blubber," "Crisco" (fat in the can), and so on. The thought of going to school terrified him, and from the first day of classes, he either stayed alone in the play yard or clung closely to the teachers. He was never asked to join in group games and rarely raised his hand to volunteer to answer questions or to engage in classroom activities. The only area in which Lew was able to excel was in academic subjects. From day one, he was an A student and was admired by both teachers and students for his ability to learn new skills quickly and also for his excellent reading and mathematics skills. Students used Lew for help in academic work but still did not accept him or invite him for social or other group activities. His resentment was intense.

At age twelve, Lew joined the Boy Scouts and quickly became the "pet" of the scoutmaster. He was appointed as "troop assistant" and felt fantastic about himself for the first time in his lonely life. Since his father was an alcoholic and there was only an angry, negative relationship between them, this new-found father figure was a godsend. Less than a month after his joining the troop, a weekend camping trip was scheduled, and Lew was asked to go a day early with the scoutmaster to open and prepare the camp. He eagerly agreed. The camp was on a small island that could be reached only by boat. It was totally isolated: no electricity, no telephone, and no access except by the one boat.

The afternoon of their arrival went quickly: Coleman lamps needed to be filled, a generator needed to be cleaned and primed, food had to be stored for future meals, and sweeping and dusting of accumulated filth became a must. Finally, dinner and a brief period of talk about the upcoming weekend completed the first day. Lew chose one of the beds in the large dormitory-type room, and the scoutmaster went into the separate and private bedroom that was his alone. Lights out and sleep followed.

Lew was awakened sometime around 2:00 A.M. by someone removing his pajamas. It was pitch dark and he could see nothing. He then felt something poking at his anus, and the next thing he experienced was searing pain as he was forcibly penetrated (raped). He eventually felt a wetness on his buttocks, and then the assault ended. He felt himself being wiped clean and then felt his pajamas being pulled back up. During all of this time not a word was spoken.

As Lew lay there, unable to sleep from the shock and from the pain, he realized that whatever had been done to him must have been done by the scoutmaster since only the two of them were in the cabin.

The next morning, everything returned to "normal." Nothing was said by the scoutmaster, and Lew said nothing either. He so wanted the approval and acceptance of this "wonderful, ideal father" that he would pay any price.

About a month or so later, the scoutmaster again approached Lew and asked him if he would help him open the cabin by going to camp with him a day earlier than the rest of the scouts. Knowing what would happen, Lew, without a second's hesitation, accepted. This pattern continued for three years until Lew left the scout troop.

Years later, in treatment, after having been convicted of molesting some forty Boy Scouts in the troop in which he had once been a scout and was now the scoutmaster, Lew was able to clearly recall that in every grade of grammar and high school he was "attracted" to the worst-looking, least popular, shiest, and most inhibited boy in the scout troop. He could still name each of them and describe them in sufficient detail to be able to draw portraits of each one. His persistent masturbation fantasies were about seducing these individuals and thereby destroying his persistent belief that he was the only one who would have sex with his scoutmaster. It is interesting to note that at no time did Lew do anything about his obesity or his shyness nor did he ever discuss his feelings or pain with anyone. (More on Lew in chapter 3.)

Questions for Discussion

1. Why hadn't parents, family, or relatives noticed Lew's shyness and negative self-image before he was sexually abused?

2. What typical pedophilic techniques did the scoutmaster use to con Lew into doing whatever he wanted?

3. Why didn't Lew say or do anything to prevent the first rape?

4. What deep-seated needs influenced Lew's decision to go the second time?

5. When Lew became a child molester as an adult, what do you suspect were his methods of seduction?

If, as in the case of Rusty, the ideal self is chosen, then the potential victims' personalities must be outgoing, assertive, positive, and pleasant, and they must be one of the most popular individuals in their group; if, as in the case of Lew, the identical self is chosen, then passivity, shyness, inadequacy, loneliness, and often isolation dominate the traits that the potential victims must possess. Dependency and neediness, especially for affection and love that do not exist in the individuals' homes, are also primary qualifications.

Family Constellation

While fatherless children and adolescents are frequently the primary targets of male abusers, this is not always the case. Big brothers, scoutmasters, athletic counselors, teachers, and so on, however, all tend to prefer this group. Fatherless children, who resent their situation desperately, need a father-substitute. The male offender, once he discovers this situation (especially teachers like **DON** [discussed in chapters 1, 4, and 8] who have access to family information or who have students write essays on their families), uses it to his advantage and offers himself as that substitute and "perfect" father. This type of offender also ingratiates himself to the child's mother and often becomes a good friend of the family, thus gaining the necessary trust to find opportunities to be alone with the intended victim.

Children and adolescents with ineffectual fathers are also targeted since the molester can, once he uncovers this situation, fulfill the needs of the potential victim that are not being met at home, as in the case of **BRUCE** (see below), who was introduced in chapter 1. These are cases where the father has either rejected the child or adolescent or believes that working two jobs and providing for materialistic needs fulfill his parental responsibility. Written essays (for teachers), one-on-one counseling, and group rap-sessions can quickly provide this information to the potential abuser. A specific group of hebophiles informed me that, with a father living in the home, there is less danger of the abuser being suspected of anything devious or illegal should he choose to have a relationship with a child of that family. Several grammar school teachers, priests, ministers, Boy Scout leaders, and Big Brothers concurred in this philosophy and followed it "religiously." An example should help fill in this picture.

BRUCE, a twelve-year-old, good-looking, emerging adolescent, lived in a home with two working parents and no brothers and sisters. Although from an upper-middle-class home, Bruce was a latchkey kid; he was also an inadequate person who felt below his peers. He functioned in school basically as a loner and came home daily to an empty house where his loneliness and depression deepened.

His teacher, an insightful and caring Catholic nun, aware of Bruce's problems, referred him to the parish priest, who was assigned as liaison and counsellor for the parish school. **FATHER GEORGE**, thirty-four years old, knew Bruce because he was also in charge of the altar boys, and Bruce had just been chosen for that prestigious group. Father George began seeing Bruce three times a week and very quickly found himself attracted to the young boy.

After one of their counseling sessions, Father George walked over to Bruce and massaged his shoulders from behind. He told Bruce that he was rigid and tense and that he had the perfect solution. He led him to his bedroom on the second floor and told him to get fully undressed for a massage. Father George then told Bruce to lay on his stomach on the bed, and he then knelt over the boy and gave him an excellent massage (he had professional training in massage therapy). After about fifteen minutes, he told Bruce to turn over on his back so that he could get at his shoulders and biceps and then massaged him, moving lower and lower on the boy's body until he reached the genital area. He then, without a word, massaged Bruce's penis to orgasm and told him that his reaction and ejaculation were perfectly normal and not sinful under these circumstances. (This was Bruce's first sexual experience.)

Massage then became a regular follow-up to each of the three weekly counseling sessions. Bruce remained confused and ambivalent since his religious teachings told him that this was wrong and sinful but physically it felt fantastic, and Father George told him it was all right.

About one month into this pattern, after a Monday counseling session, without a spoken word, the two went upstairs to Father George's room, and Bruce undressed for his massage. This time, Father George sat on the edge of the bed and told Bruce of all the parish problems that he was encountering and how the pressures were getting to him. He then asked Bruce to return the favors he had been granting him and to massage him. He undressed as he spoke and before Bruce could answer was naked on the bed. He then said: "I'm ready when you are," and Bruce, almost like a robot, knelt over the priest's body and began to massage him. Within fifteen minutes, Father George turned over to reveal an erection, and Bruce again automatically performed the same ritual massage that Father George usually performed on him.

While confused, concerned, and emotionally distressed, Bruce could not make himself confide in his working, always tired parents and endured the relationship for the next year until Father George was transferred, without explanation, to another parish. Bruce's guilt increased when he confessed his sins to an elderly and old-fashioned priest who belittled him and made him feel that the entire affair was his fault. The damage to Bruce's self-image and self-esteem was extreme, and his isolation and problems with interpersonal relationships increased.

As an adult, not surprisingly, Bruce, at age thirty, molested his first twelve-year-old boy. After more than thirty molestations, Bruce was arrested and incarcerated.

Communication and Credibility

As mentioned in the preface, tragedy after tragedy occurs in situations where there is little or no communication between parents and children or where children are not believed. The sex offender thrives on and relies on both of these situations and attempts to ascertain their existence before attempting anything sexual with a victim. The offender also uses the credibility factor as part of the seduction and intimidation process. Offenders typically say things like: "If you tell anyone, including your parents, about what we're doing, they won't believe you. I'll tell them you're lying, and they'll believe me, not you." An example where this occurred follows.

KYLE, now an adult male, was sexually abused from age ten to age fifteen by a Catholic priest from his parish who was a close friend of his parents and who slept in Kyle's room whenever he stayed over for a weekend. The abuse began almost from the first overnight stay and consisted of fondling Kyle either in bed or in the shower. When Kyle found out that the priest was also molesting other boys in his parish school, he went to his mother and told her what was going on. His mother replied simply: "If it's going on, don't let it happen again!" and did nothing more. The following day was Friday, and the priest returned. Without hesitation, he once again molested Kyle, telling him that he had permission from God to do what he was doing and that if Kyle complained, he would be punished by God for eternity. The sexual abuse continued for several more years unabated and unchecked, resulting in extensive personality and self-image damage for Kyle that lasted until the present time. (More on Kyle and the effects of sexual abuse by members of the clergy later.)

Questions for Discussion

1. Why do think Kyle's mother reacted the way she did?

2. What additional effects do you feel sexual abuse by religious personnel add to the list of sexual abuse by nonreligious personnel?

3. Kyle reported his abuse by the priest to his mother only out of jealousy. Had he not discovered that the priest was involved with other boys, he would not have reported. Why not?

4. What effects do you feel this religious sexual abuse had on Kyle's adult life?

5. How could Kyle's parents have prevented this situation?

SETTINGS THAT PROVIDE AVAILABILITY TO THE MOLESTERS

Grammar and High Schools

Teachers play a parental-substitute role with their students as well as having authority and a strong influence over them. Teachers who are pedophiles looking for potential victims also have the ability to access personal and family information that enables them to make a safe choice and one that offers the most chance of success. Unfortunately, in most teacher-hiring situations, little or no psychological testing is utilized, and even where testing is employed, trained examiners who are capable of interviewing and weeding out potential abuser types are not used or even considered.

Of the hundreds of teachers I have interviewed or treated as sex offenders, most admitted that their choice of teaching as a career was motivated by their pedophilic or hebophilic needs. This factor also accounted for their choice of teaching level.

The rest of the school staff also have access to the children and are also capable of being sexual predators. I have seen custodians and maintenance staff, crossing guards, substitute teachers, food-service workers, and counselors, in both public and private schools, accused and convicted of child or adolescent molestation and, in schools, priests, ministers, and nuns also accused and convicted or plead guilty to charges of sexual molestation. Both males and females can be molesters, although reports involving males still outnumber those regarding females.

Youth Organizations

All youth-group settings offer an ideal source of potential victims for both pedophiles and hebophiles. As stated before, organizations such as the Boy Scouts, the Sea Scouts, the YMCA, the CYO, and boys and girls clubs offer a large selection of potential victims to molesters. As in the case of teachers, it is horrendous that so little professional and effective screening (if any) is used to choose workers in these groups. In a recent scandal in New Jersey, the leadership of a county Big Brothers organization was composed of pedophiles and hebophiles who had been actively molesting boys for several years before one of the boys reported. The number of victims is still unknown and may never be known.

Childcare and Adolescent-Care Institutions

Group homes, juvenile detention centers, reformatories, orphanages, special schools for the educationally disabled, private residential schools, and so on, are all magnets for the sex offender. What better place to find children who are already damaged to some extent and therefore more vulnerable than so-called normal children? These are our throwaway kids, both materialistically and emotionally deprived. Sex offenders are particularly expert in seducing and using these children and adolescents for their own deviant needs.

A major problem in this area is that many of these settings are not the most attractive, pleasant places to work, nor are salaries the highest. Therefore, staffing needs often necessitate less-stringent testing and screening of personnel. An even more dangerous practice in these settings is to utilize temporary personnel, about whom the institution knows nothing, to fill a temporarily vacant position (for example, to cover for a regular staff member on sick leave). This is an ideal placement for the sex offender looking to gain access to victims. An example will help dramatize this situation.

KEIF was a twenty-six-year-old, good-looking, well-built, six-foot physical-education instructor who worked in several childcare institutions throughout the country. He began his career in a Far West institution for emotionally disturbed children and after a seemingly brilliant career was asked to resign when allegations of sexual abuse were made by several boys in his gym class. Keif moved to the Midwest and again found employment as an athletic instructor in an all-male childcare facility for emotionally disturbed children. His former employee gave him an excellent set of references with no mention of the reason for his resignation. After two years, Keif was again asked to resign when caught in a compromising position in the showers with one of the younger, more passive boys who would not answer questions as to why the two of them were showering alone. Keif again moved, this time to the Northeast, and again was employed by a childcare institution for emotionally disturbed children. After Keif had been at this last institution for several years, a major investigation was launched regarding allegations of physical, sexual, and emotional abuse. The outcome was that Keif was arrested for sexually molesting over thirty young boys in his care and was sentenced to a treatment unit for sex offenders. In this latter case as in the former, the previous institution had given Keif an excellent reference with a recommendation that he be hired. How could this happen in today's era of litigation? I have no answer, but I certainly feel that both institutions that gave the recommendations should be held both legally and morally responsible for what happened to the children.

Questions for Discussion

1. What changes need to be made in the hiring practices of childcare institutions, and whose responsibility is it to see that these changes are made?

2. Why would an institution officer who knew of Keif's pedophilia not press charges against him?

3. Why would an institution officer who knew of Keif's pedophilia be willing to give him a positive recommendation to another childcare institution or agency?

4. Why do you feel that so many boys submitted repeatedly to Keif's sexual abuse without reporting it to relatives or institutional personnel?

5. What additional damaging effects do you feel institutional victims experience that are different from victims living at home?

PROBLEM AREAS FOR PROFESSIONALS INVOLVED IN SUSPECTED CASES OF SEXUAL ABUSE

Part of the reason that institutionalized children are continually being molested lies in the inadequate formal training that professionals operating these institutions receive regarding sex offenders and sexual abuse. In much of the supervision that I have provided both to new professionals to the field and to older professionals desiring to change the focus of their practice, a major missing skill is that of proper interviewing techniques. This is especially true in the initial contact. Over and over again, I have observed the following very serious errors.

Asking Suggestive Questions

Improperly trained individuals ask questions that either directly state or clearly imply the answer that the interviewer desires: for example, "He did threaten you, didn't he?" or "How did he hurt you?" or "It must have been terrible for you, wasn't it?" The first question implies threat where none may have existed and seduction was used instead; the second implies pain and injury while in many cases pleasure and orgasm may have been experienced; the third insists that the experience was negative and distressing when in many seductive cases the experience was either neutral or pleasurable and the child returned for another encounter. (See the section below for more on this type of sexual-abuse reaction.)

The damage here is that once the questioner implies the direction that the interview should take, no true knowledge of what really occurred is possible, nor can the survivor ventilate or deal with guilts accompanying perceived cooperation and/or enjoyment.

Accepting the Victim's Words Literally

Taking victims' words as stating exact facts may be a critical error when interviewing young children. In a recent case that I was discussing with a police official, the child was not believed when she stated that the man had "shot her in the stomach." Upon physical examination, there were no injuries to her stomach and no signs of a bullet wound (the assumption of the investigators). When a trained interviewer questioned the child correctly, the real details emerged. The molester was masturbating while kneeling over the little girl's body. He told her that his penis was a gun that he was going to shoot her with it, and he then ejaculated on her stomach. The little girl was totally naive about sex (she was only five years old) and thus described the abuse to the investigating police officer in the words of the molester.

Assuming Definitions of the Words Used by the Victim

Too often interviewers or investigators assume that they understand the words of the victim without asking for clarification. Survivors, especially young children, often either are ashamed and embarrassed by what occurred or are still in some form of denial. They persistently use vague, generic terms, especially in the initial interview. They offer answers such as: "He touched me"; "He made me do it"; "He had sex with me"; "He hurt my 'goolie'"; or "He rubbed me."

These and other generic phrases can be easily misinterpreted by untrained interviewers, especially when they are in a hurry or have heavy caseloads. Complacency plays a large part in the ensuing errors. A technique I call the "man from Mars approach" has worked well for me with young children, adolescents, as well as adults. I ask the survivor to imagine that I am from Mars, where people have sex by putting their index fingers together. (With extremely young children, no mention of sex is made. Instead I simply tell them that Martians do everything differently than people on earth, and thus I need a clear picture telling me what happened.) I tell the survivor that Martians like myself know nothing of human sexual behavior, and therefore each detail must be described in Technicolor, in wide-screen images, and with Dolby-stereo sounds. This approach saves a great deal of time, avoids having to interfere in the survivor's narrative with questions, and usually produces a clear and lucid picture of the assault or abuse. If the survivor becomes vague during the narrative, a simple cue-word ("picture") is used to inform the client that the interviewer is no longer able to clearly see what is happening. This simple cue-word does not break the concentration of the survivor or cause him or her to lose track of thoughts or memories.

Poor Timing

A hurried approach, expecting full and complete disclosure to a virtual stranger in the first interview, bodes failure. This critical error in approaching survivors of sexual abuse ignores readiness concepts. Readiness depends on many factors, including the emotional strength of the patient, the depth of the trauma ("nightmare") that occurred, the trust-level the patient has developed with the therapist (fear of being rejected, hated, or punished for involvement in the event must be resolved by this point), and the survivor's own willingness to remember the abuse and all of its fear, pain, and guilt.

Since control was a dominant factor in the sexual abuse, this control must be returned to the survivor as quickly as possible if normalcy is to be regained. Pushing for facts and disclosure too quickly guarantees poor communication, poor investigating, and poor therapy results.

The Sequence of Disclosure

In my years of experience in dealing with hundreds of sexually abused survivors, the usual sequence of remembering and/or sharing the full abuse is as follows:

- First, there are vague generalizations of what occurred, a sort of outline.

- Next, snapshots, without movement, return to consciousness and are related.

- Next, movement is added; plus words and phrases return to conscious memory.

- Finally, feelings and emotions return, especially those that occurred during the actual abuse. During this stage, a form of reliving the abuse often occurs, and the therapist/interviewer must be trained and prepared to handle this highly volatile and often physical session.

The time between each stage may be short or may be months or even years, depending on how deeply repressed the event is. A slow, careful, and considerate approach, always allowing the survivor to move at his or her own pace, produces the best results for both the therapist/interviewer and the survivor.

In reality, this simple and considerate approach to interviewing is too often replaced with a cold, clinical, stereotyped approach that wrongly assumes that all survivors are the same and that therefore a single, standardized interviewing approach will produce effective results.

Confidentiality Issues

Confidentiality is probably the most difficult and sensitive area in the entire process of dealing with survivors of sexual abuse, be they children, adolescents, or adults. A primary concern must be the agreement made between the interviewer and the survivor. There is no circumstance where lies and deceit are tolerable. This includes lies of omission: for instance, the interviewer not explaining certain rules and regulations (for example, in New Jersey, the law mandates reporting of any and all child abuse) until *after* the survivor has disclosed the abuse with the belief that what is being said is confidential. My practice has always been to discuss the rules and procedures that will be used in the interview *before* the survivor discloses a single fact. Considerations must include the laws (what *must* be reported and what is discretionary); parents', families', and significant others' rights to know the details of the abuse; and what the survivors wish disclosed to these individuals and what they wish withheld. This is especially critical where small children are concerned who do not want their parents to know what they did or what was done to them. Since this can be a conflictual situation, I usually discuss it with the parents *before* seeing the survivor or accepting the case. My policy has always been that *the child's rights take precedence over the parents' rights* and that *it is the child's task to inform the parents regarding what he or she wishes them to know and to what extent.*

When the child or adolescent is *ready* to disclose the matter to his
or her parents, this disclosure usually takes place in my office and in
my presence. Not all therapists will agree with my philosophy, and
each one must work in the most effective way that he or she can.
As long as the welfare and recovery of the survivor remain the primary considerations, the specifics of the techniques that individual
therapists use may vary.

Once we have a picture of the victim, it is important to discuss
the effects that sexual abuse has on all survivors and especially on
children and adolescents.

3

THE EFFECTS OF
SEXUAL ABUSE

The effects of a particular sexual assault or molestation depend on a large number of factors. The following factors apply to both male and female survivors:

1. The ego-strength of the victim at the time of the assault or molestation.

2. Where the blame or guilt was placed by the survivor: if on himself/herself, the outcome will be traumatic and negative; if on the molester, the outcome will be either neutral or positive.

3. The time between the assault or molestation and the survivor entering treatment: the longer this period of time, the more problems the survivor will experience; the shorter this period of time, the quicker the adjustment and return to normalcy.

4. The *amount* of direct support the survivor receives from his or her family, siblings, and peers/friends.

5. The *credibility* that family, siblings, and peers/friends attach to the survivor's description of the assault or molestation.

6. The *attitude* of the police investigators, attorneys, judges, and other authority figures involved either in the case or in the survivor's personal life.

7. The *outcome of the trial* (if one occurs). Probation or an ineffectual reprimand often sends the message to the survivor that
   what the perpetrator did was really not all that bad.

8. The *speed* of the survivor's return to school or work. There appears to be a direct relationship between this factor and the
   survivor's speed of recovery.

9. The *attitude* of school authorities and supervisory personnel and
   of schoolmates and workmates toward the survivor upon his or
   her return.

10. The degree of self-judgmentalism in which the survivor en-
    gages. The more guilt and shame, the slower the progress.

Six of the ten listed effects (those in italics) are out of the hands of
the survivor, and all six involve issues of control.

I have divided all of the survivors with whom I have had contact into three distinct groups. (1) The *deny-ers* are those who are so
traumatized by the sexual assault or abuse that they repress the event
and have no conscious memory of being molested; only the effects
of the abuse continue to prove problematic. (2) The *adjust-ers* are
those who rightly place all blame on the molester and have minimal
post-traumatic stress as a result. (3) The *accept-ers* are those who
believe, as the molester intended, that the molestation was all their
fault; they have the longest traumatic effects from their abuse, often lifelong, and need the most time and patience in counseling. See
figure 4 for a summary of these types and of all the most common
negative effects of sexual abuse.

A prime general consideration regarding survivors is the problem
of their becoming judgmental rather than analytic or curious about
their abuse. When the focus of the survivor, especially the accept-
ers, becomes judgmental, a series of consequences occur. These
consequences of self-judgmentalism are displayed in figure 5. In
those individuals who, following the sexual abuse, label themselves
dirty, evil, promiscuous, bad, used, untouchable, unworthy, unequal,
and so on, there will always be negative results.

FIGURE 4: NEGATIVE REACTIONS OF SURVIVORS OF SEXUAL ABUSE

A. DENY-ERS: tend to repress the event. Their behavior abruptly changes, but the true results of the trauma do not surface until later life, usually due to some triggering event (marriage, loss of employment, sexual failure, death of a loved one, and so on).

BOYS	GIRLS
• often become satyrs to prove manhood	• develop problems in their adult sex life, especially frigidity
• sometimes become sexually assaultive persons, especially if they were forcibly sodomized and interpreted this as being seen as a "girl"	• see sex as dirty or disgusting; may become physically abusive parents without knowing why; nudity is embarrassing, and any arousal produces shame and guilt
• end up referred for sexual dysfunctions, especially impotence and premature ejaculation	• end up referred for sexual dysfunctions, especially frigidity

B. ADJUST-ERS: usually have no negative effects since they

• put all blame and responsibility on the abuser

• vent appropriate anger onto the abuser

• discuss what happened with their parents and friends

• ask for counseling or therapy if they feel the need

C. ACCEPT-ERS: accept the abuse as deserved and their fault. As a result, self-image is damaged and the effects are long-lasting and sometimes permanent.

BOYS	GIRLS
• repeat their abuse behavior on a same-age child, almost ritualistically in order to reverse roles with the abuser	• tend to prostitute, become promiscuous, or develop other self-punishing behaviors
• now feel that they are the adult aggressor in control rather than being controlled	• tend to marry aggressive, battering-type (dominant) husbands
• may show no other visible problems in their employment or social lives	• tend to lose all goal motivation; isolate socially

FIGURE 5: EFFECTS OF SELF-JUDGMENTALISM
ON THE SURVIVORS OF SEXUAL ABUSE

1. Guilt and the attending emotions

2. Feelings of being inferior, different, sick or perverted, abnormal, relationally unacceptable

3. Isolation

4. Distrust of self and others

5. Fear of rejection

6. Depression (from mild to suicidal)

7. Activation of the classic defense mechanisms, especially denial, minimization, projection, externalization, and, if the trauma is severe enough, repression

EFFECTS OF UNREPORTED AND UNTREATED SEXUAL ABUSE

Let us now look at the different reactions that survivors have when the sexual molestation or assault is not reported or treated.

Forced Sexual Assault

Deny-ers constitute a group of survivors who cope with their molestation by denying that it occurred and through repressing the event. As in all cases of repressed sexual trauma, their behavior abruptly changes, usually for the worse, and in later life the full results of the trauma surface.

Since repression is a major defense mechanism in all cases of deny-ers, we need to first define the concept of repression. Benjamin B. Wolman writes:

Repression can be best understood as an unconscious exclusion from the consciousness of objectionable impulses, memories, and ideas. The ego, as it were, pushes the objectionable material down into the unconscious and acts as if the objectionable material were nonexistent.[1]

In forced sexual assault, the reaction of male survivors differs from that of female survivors and needs to be discussed.

Boys often become "satyrs" to regain the manhood that they feel they have lost as a result of the sexual assault. Feelings that they should have been able to protect themselves and thereby prevent the assault produce severe ego-damage and self-doubt. Feelings of inadequacy and inferiority often result. Besides all of the expected reactions discussed previously, if their behavior becomes pathological, they often become sexually assaultive persons, especially if they had been sodomized and perceived that act as their having been used as a girl. A striking example will clarify.

JOEY, whom we met briefly in chapter 1, now an adult rapist, came from a family of marital conflicts. When Joey was around twelve years old, the following set of circumstances occurred.

Joey's father began to take him out every Saturday, explaining to Joey's mother that he and his son needed more time alone to become friends and to get to know each other better, especially since Joey was entering adolescence. Joey's mother believed the story.

In reality, Joey's father was using him as an alibi to visit his secret paramour. After a quick lunch at McDonald's or Burger King, Joey would be given a game or some comic books to read and instructed to sit on the porch of the paramour's home while the father visited upstairs.

Joey was quite streetwise by age twelve and knew (or fantasized) what he felt was going on upstairs. However, as long as his father treated him well and bought him gifts and later took him

---

1. Benjamin B. Wolman, *Dictionary of Behavioral Science*, 2d ed. (New York: Academic Press, 1989), 292.

somewhere, such as an amusement park, a swimming pool, or a bowling alley, he really didn't care. He also wanted and needed the individual attention he was getting from his father and was unwilling to upset the situation.

These Saturday excursions continued for more than six months, and then a dramatic change occurred. One day, as Joey was reading a comic book on the front porch of the paramour's home, his father came down in his underwear and took him by the hand, leading him upstairs.

Upon entering the bedroom, Joey, now quite frightened, became aware of two things immediately: a naked woman, quite large, lying on a frilly bed and a strong odor of cheap perfume.

Joey's father ordered him to undress, and when he hesitated, the father undressed him, stating, "It's about time you became a man, if you're good enough!" Joey was then ordered to lie on top of the woman and to "show me what kind of a man you are!" Joey knew about sexual intercourse but was a virgin and, under the circumstances, was so frightened and confused that he could not get an erection. The woman (he never was told her name) put her arms around him, held him tightly, and whispered in his ear, "Be a good boy for daddy, Joey, and don't cry."

Joey, more frightened and confused than ever, felt his father climbing on top of him. The next thing he felt was terrible anal pain as his father forcibly and without lubricant penetrated him. Joey now was in shock, and the woman kept trying to calm and comfort him. When the father was finally finished, he said, "Boy, you've got the best and tightest pussy I've ever had!"

Joey was never to forget this phrase, which to him meant that his father had used him as a woman.

When they left the mistress's house, not a word was spoken between them throughout the ride home. Upon arriving home, Joey's father simply dropped him off and left. As he entered the house, Joey obviously was in pain, and his short pants were wet since he was bleeding quite a bit. His mother took him into the bathroom and treated his bleeding by forcefully packing cotton up his anus — a second rape. She never asked him a single question as to what happened. Joey, therefore, assumed that she knew what his father had done to him and that she really didn't care. When she was through tending to his injuries, his mother sent Joey to bed telling him, "You'll be all right in the morning."

Lying in bed but unable to sleep, Joey replayed the scene of being sexually assaulted by his father over and over again. He had to have an answer to his paramount question, Why? He suddenly remembered that whenever he showered, his father found an excuse to come into the bathroom and to open the shower curtains. Since he was often erect (especially if he had been masturbating), Joey would turn toward the wall so that his father could not see his erect penis. Each time, then, what his father did see was his bare buttocks. Maybe, thought Joey, his naked behind turned his father on. If that were true, then the assault was his, Joey's, fault.

From this point on, Joey became a real behavior problem both at home and in school. He was constantly disrespectful to his mother and to his teachers. Also, he was always getting into fights and doing all sorts of daring feats to prove his strength but more to prove his masculinity.

Less than a full year after his own rape, Joey committed his first sexual assault on a high school girl whom he so terrified and threatened that she never reported it. Joey was on his way to becoming a compulsive sex offender, and by the time he was finally apprehended, some eight years later, he had sexually assaulted more than twenty-five women, inflicting some type of severe physical injury on each one.

During his first year or more of therapy, he had no conscious memory of his own rape. Joey had repressed the entire incident. He had rationalized the rapes he had committed by referring to his difficulties in all relationships with women and the resulting anger and rage he felt at being ridiculed, rejected, or put down by them, regardless of age.

One of the most difficult problems in treating the survivor is to discover whether there are any repressions and, if there are repressions suspected, to bring them to the conscious level. I have developed the following rule or guideline in determining whether a repression exists in a particular case: whenever a compulsive behavior is discovered that has no logical explanation or etiology, I look for a repressed trauma.

Girls who have been sexually assaulted usually have problems in their adult interpersonal relationships, especially where sexual behavior is concerned. They often see sex as dirty, disgusting, repulsive, and so on. They usually end up being referred for a sexual dysfunction, the most frequent ones being frigidity, vaginismus, and sexual aversion. An example of this here will clarify.

> JULIE, a twenty-nine-year-old nurse, referred herself for severe depression resulting from a "screwed-up and unsatisfactory sex life" (her words). She had accumulated seven failed relationships, all due to sexual difficulties. While she insisted that she "liked sex," in each sexual encounter that she had experienced since she began dating, she would become "frightened, uncomfortable, and then nonresponsive," although each occurrence began willingly, happily, and excitedly. When asked to recall the latest "failure" in minute detail, the following picture emerged: "We returned to his apartment from an absolutely wonderful and enchanting evening. We dined at a new and marvelous restaurant, went to see the greatest top-hit play on Broadway, and then went for a romantic ride in a surrey in Central Park. At his apartment, we talked over after-dinner drinks, and one thing led to another. The next thing I knew we were in bed, naked. The moment I realized that he was going to eventually penetrate me, I began to get frightened, started sweating profusely, and stopped responding to him. I just laid there like a mannequin as stiff as a board. He realized something was wrong and stopped. The rest of the evening was an embarrassing disaster. I haven't dated since."

Julie, by this time in the story, was sobbing with her head down. Her shame and embarrassment were quite obvious and painful for her. I waited for several minutes until she had calmed down and was more composed. I then asked her to tell me about her childhood sexual molestation. She immediately began to deny that anything had ever happened, protesting that "that's always what therapists attribute sexual problems to." She appeared angry and quite upset by my inference. When she calmed down, I explained the need to remember what had happened to her as a child, and we ended the session without her making another appointment.

A month later, Julie called and asked for an "emergency" appointment, as the depression had worsened and she was now willing to do whatever it took to get better since she feared becoming suicidal. In the next session, after some small talk and time to relax, Julie recounted the following.

JULIE had been sexually molested and raped by UNCLE LOUIE, a maternal uncle who had lived with and supported her and her mother after her father's desertion. The first molestation occurred when she was nine years old, and further molestations and assaults continued until she was twelve.

In a pattern typical of seductive child molesters, Uncle Louie first befriended her, taking her to parks and amusement areas and buying her gifts almost daily. Her mother enjoyed watching the two of them developing a father-daughter relationship and trusted her brother implicitly.

Within a month of his arrival, the mother had to work late one evening and asked Uncle Louie to arrange for Julie's bath and to put her to bed. Instead of arranging for her bath, he gave her a bath, fondling her genitals and attempting digital vaginal penetration until she cried from pain. Uncle Louie then threatened to leave the family if she told her mother what he had done. He also assured her that her mother would believe him and not her (a typical caretaker abuser ploy).

Julie was devastated. She had begun to see her uncle as her father and trusted him enough to allow him to give her the bath. She concluded that "it had to be my fault that all of this occurred. God must be punishing me, just like he did when my father left, which was also my fault."

Uncle Louie continued his fondling at every opportunity and slowly but surely progressed. The next phase was to have Julie fondle and then masturbate him. In less than three more months, he completely lost control one night and raped her. The pain was terrible; she bled and was sure that she was going to die. The threats now heightened to include the promise that "he would have to kill me and my mother if anyone found out what he had done, since he was not going to prison for anyone."

From then on, Uncle Louie used Julie whenever he felt the urge. Her life became a constant frightening nightmare. At age twelve, her uncle was arrested for molesting another girl in the neighborhood but Julie, when questioned, denied that he had ever touched her, remembering the death threats against her and her mother that Uncle Louie had made.

By age fourteen, Julie had successfully repressed the entire period of time that her uncle lived in her home until I triggered the memories with the inference that she had been molested. Once the repression was brought to light, therapy was rapid and successful, with Julie experiencing her first really happy sexual encounter within a month. The man was someone she had always cared for and whom she brought to two of her last therapy sessions. They are now happily married, but Julie still needs an occasional booster session, as the nightmares sometimes recur.

Seductive Sexual Abuse

Accept-ers justify their sexual molestation and abuse and continue the learned behavior, or some form of it, on a peer level until they eventually fail sexually as an adult. They then tend to reenact, almost ritualistically, the molestation on a child who is the same age as they were when they were originally molested, thus reversing the roles so that they are now the aggressor. They attempt to justify this behavior by referring to their own original abuse.

Additionally, once they have sexually molested another child, they no longer need to deal with the obsessive fear that "I'm the only one!" Here again, the reaction of male survivors differs from that of female survivors and needs to be delineated. An example will help substantiate this process.

> **GARY** was eighteen years old when he molested his first young child, an eight-year-old boy. In tracing his own sexual molestation, the following story emerged.
>
> At age eight, a twenty-six-year-old uncle, **UNCLE PAT**, used to take him on outings, going bowling or playing catch in the nearby park. He began his seduction by teaching Gary how to wrestle (another typical pattern of child molesters). His uncle would lay on top of him, moving around in what Gary termed a "dry-humping" fashion. This excited Gary, and he got an erection and sometimes had an orgasm. While it felt good, he still felt guilty about it but didn't try to stop Uncle Pat since he was the only male friend and father figure that Gary had. His own father deserted the family when Gary was only five years old.
>
> The sex-play progressed when he stayed overnight at his uncle's house. Since Uncle Pat slept nude, Gary also slept nude, at his uncle's suggestion. They began wrestling, and once they were both erect, Uncle Pat fondled Gary, and Gary fondled him in return. From this beginning, they graduated to mutual masturbation. After an hour or so of sex-play, Uncle Pat carefully sodomized Gary, and Gary learned to "like it a lot." Their sexual relationship lasted until Gary was twelve and had just fully entered puberty.
>
> Gary cannot remember why the relationship ended. (It is quite possible that Gary was now too developed and too old for the uncle's tastes.)
>
> From age thirteen on, Gary had sex with girls and enjoyed it. However, he never stopped masturbating to fantasies of Uncle Pat sodomizing him. In fact, he now had to digitally penetrate his own anus to enjoy his masturbation and to reach orgasm.
>
> Eventually Gary became impotent with girls, and at age eighteen, he initiated sex with his eight-year-old male cousin. Gary repeated the identical behavior pattern with his cousin that

had occurred between himself and his uncle. Eventually, after molesting twelve or more young boys, Gary was arrested.

Girls who are accept-ers tend to become prostitutes or promiscuous; tend to marry aggressive, battering (dominant) husbands; and tend to lose their personal goal motivation. What follows is an example.

JANE is a twenty-three-year-old college student who has earned the reputation of being the "dorm slut." She was a self-referral for what she termed "an obsession with penises and wanting oral sex with males who treat me nicely." While, at first, denying that she was a victim of sexual abuse, she later revealed the following story.

Jane's early childhood was fairly normal. Her mother and father treated her and her three brothers equally. She had several close friendships with girls in the neighborhood who were her own age. The problems began when she and her friends entered adolescence, around age eleven. All her girlfriends became interested in the boys in school and in the neighborhood, while Jane did not. Part of the problem was that Jane was "plump and pimply" (her description), and boys tended to "avoid her."

Living next door to Jane's home was a retired teacher who befriended all of the neighborhood children and maintained an open-house policy. He was known to all as **UNCLE JACK**, although he lived alone, had never married, and was unrelated to anyone in the community. Uncle Jack was a good listener and also a self-proclaimed "counselor" for everyone: children and adults alike.

One day, lonely and depressed, Jane sat on the swing in her backyard, and Uncle Jack called her over to his yard. He was able to get Jane to tell him what was bothering her and soothed her feelings by telling her that "she would always be his special little girl and that he would be proud to be her boyfriend." Jane felt much better, and in the next few weeks spent a great deal of time in Uncle Jack's house, often sitting on his lap while they watched television. Uncle Jack slowly and carefully went about his seduction and eventually convinced Jane that she was ready for sex education. He would teach her the real way, by "show and tell (and do!)." He undressed to teach her about a man's body and how it functions and then had her undress, fondling her during the lesson. Next came a lesson on childbirth, and in explaining reproduction, Uncle Jack masturbated to erection and then asked Jane to bring him to orgasm "so that she would see what sperm are like and what makes babies." From here, Uncle Jack's speed of teaching increased, and within a week, he carefully and gently had his first intercourse with Jane. Jane felt that "something was wrong," especially when Uncle Jack insisted that this had to be their secret or "he would have to go away and leave her."

The sexual abuse continued until Jane was sixteen. The only reason it ended was that Uncle Jack suddenly moved out of the neighborhood. (Unbeknownst to Jane, he was involved with other neighborhood girls and was under investigation by the local authorities.) Jane felt abandoned and betrayed, and *blamed herself* for losing Uncle Jack. Her reasoning was that she must not have pleased him, especially since recently he had been complaining that Jane wouldn't orally satisfy him often enough. From this time until college, Jane lost herself in her studies and had few if any social contacts or experiences and remained sexually inactive.

Jane won a scholarship to a college some four hundred miles from home. With trepidation, she moved into a nonsegregated, unisex dormitory and was introduced into the "world of pleasures that college is all about," according to her roommate, **BRENDA.** Brenda was a typical twenty-one-year-old woman, quite world-wise and liberal in all areas including sex. After each date, Brenda would relate to Jane, in explicit detail, what had transpired, emphasizing the sexual aspects. Concerned about Jane's lack of social life, Brenda encouraged Jane "to loosen up and give the guys what they want." Brenda arranged a date for Jane with one of the dorm "hunks," and Jane reluctantly accepted.

After a movie and something to eat at a local eatery, the "hunk" took Jane to his room in the dorm. He undressed, revealing an erection, laid back on the bed and said, "OK baby, time to pay up if you want to see me again. Let's see how good you suck!" Jane immediately thought about Uncle Jack and fearing another lost relationship — she really liked "Mr. Hunk" — complied. When Jane told Brenda what happened, Brenda congratulated her on becoming "one of us," a phrase that meant a great deal to Jane.

By the time of Jane's return from classes the next day, the whole dorm had been told of her performance the night before by the "hunk." Soon the guys were lined up at her room wanting dates. Thus began Jane's life as the "dorm slut." Very quickly, Jane realized that the guys really didn't care about her and only took her out for the sex. She felt the same bad way she had after an encounter with Uncle Jack. Still, Jane felt she had no real choice, since anything was better than the loneliness. She continued being used for two full years of college before coming into therapy, depressed and presuicidal.

Therapy will be a long and difficult restructuring of her self-image and self-esteem as well as restructuring a new personality. Emphasis will have to be on positive traits. Assertiveness training will be essential. The fact that she referred herself for therapy indicates that there is a good probability of a positive outcome. Only time will tell.

Incest

Girls who survive incest typically

- stress being adult (this begins suddenly and is not necessarily age-appropriate).

- put on too much makeup and overdress to give the impression of being seductive (especially true where teenagers are concerned).

- start using their looks and body for gain (learned from their incestuous father).

- become a tease to boys and older men.

- become outrageous flirts.

- lose interest in school — want gifts, job, travel, and so on.

- consider their father their secret boyfriend and lover (an idea that he implanted).

- become physically, but not sexually, abusive parents in later years.

Boys, while displaying many of the victim traits and some of the offender traits, tend to

- repeat the offense either simultaneously with their own molestation or in the distant future in a ritualistic manner.

- become rapists — especially if forced sodomy was involved — in order to deny feelings of femininity and to project the rage they feel for their mothers for not protecting them (identical to forced sexual-assault cases).

- display a projected, generalized rage at females throughout their lives that they cannot justify or explain; often this rage is sudden and explosive.

- be aggressive in their sexual behavior and often cause pain to either sex that they are involved with; again, they cannot explain or justify this behavior.

- have unresolved bisexual thoughts, feelings, or tendencies that disturb them greatly since they do not understand these thoughts and feelings and have always considered themselves heterosexual.

An example that incorporates these reactions may help to dramatize them briefly. JOEY, whom we met earlier, is a perfect example of the incestuously damaged male. All the rapes he committed were motivated by his drive to "prove his masculinity" and deny his feminine feelings and traits (including wearing his wife's underwear); the rapes were usually "triggered" when he experienced urges or fantasies of being sodomized by a male that he was attracted to.

COMMON SURVIVOR TRAITS

All survivors of sexual abuse have several traits or effects of the abuse in common that need to be carefully identified and treated. Seven of these are listed below.

1. They all experience guilt ranging from mild to severe, which may produce self-punishment in the form of failure, feelings of unworthiness, and low self-esteem and may even lead to prostitution on the part of both females and males.

2. They tend to look for and find inappropriate mates. Girls tend to find controlling and battering males (similar to their abusers, especially in incest), and boys look for lovers or wives who are mother figures or the opposite: weak and submissive women who are easy to control and dominate.

3. They often develop a poor to defective self-image and lose all goals or the desire to change. This becomes a severe resistance problem in therapy.

4. If they have repressed the event, it will surface in later years in their relationships and particularly in sexual affairs or marriage. When a sexual dysfunction results, it usually manifests itself in girls in frigidity and in boys in impotence.

5. Sex, for them, becomes either disgusting, dirty, and to be avoided or becomes a payment for love, acceptance, and delusional belonging.

6. They feel strange, scared, anxious, and so on, and do not know why. They then become convinced that they are abnormal, sick, or crazy (emotionally disturbed).

7. They fear therapy since they see it as a betrayal of the abuser, about whom they often retain highly ambivalent feelings of both love and hate. This causes confusion and indecision. In therapy, this is an extremely important consideration. Should the therapist, out of sympathy, criticize or castigate the abuser, rapport may be permanently damaged.

PROSTITUTION

Prostitution is too often overlooked as a major consequence of sexual abuse. The dynamics are complicated and differ in each survivor who chooses this form of behavior but there is a commonality. The sexual predators all too frequently use "love" as the justification for their perverted sexual abuse. This is almost always true with the seductive pedophiles and hebophiles. When their victims believe that what is being done to them is "love," the danger exists that a pattern or need for this type of "love" can easily be formed. For many young survivors, prostitution then becomes the method of obtaining this desperately needed "love."

Once the relationship with the original predator ends for any number of reasons (the predator is apprehended or moves out of the area; the victim no longer meets the requirements or needs of the predator, and so on) the need for "love" remains, and unfortunately the survivor too often chooses another similar adult and similar or exact sex acts in order to obtain that "love." This easily leads to prostitution for both female and male survivors.

While the literature and research spend a large amount of time on female prostitution resulting from sexual abuse, male prostitution, especially by teenagers, is covered to a much lesser extent.

Becoming prostitutes further damages those already harmed by incest: for both males and females the prostitution causes severe guilt, ego-damage, low self-esteem, censure if exposed, and so on. Male prostitutes with adult male clientele suffer even additional emotional damage. Teenagers, as a group, abhor and fear homosexuality. Any suspicion of a male peer being "gay" results in immediate rejection, ridicule, and often physical abuse at the hands of his peers. For this reason, the male survivor of homosexual sexual abuse has even greater problems when he becomes involved in prostitution. These problems are emotional, psychological, and too often physical: rape, sadomasochistic abuse, sexually transmitted diseases, and even AIDS. As will be discussed later in this chapter, boy/male reporting-problems are common and serious even when prostitution is not involved. When it is, it is practically impossible to motivate boy/male survivors to come forward until they either are hospitalized with physical trauma, contract a sexually transmitted disease, or are caught in the act by the authorities. Even in these cases, denial and projection of blame on the adult are very common defenses, and the real problem, their prostitution, is too frequently never uncovered or treated.

There are also cases where the male prostitute is allegedly both happy and accepting of his behavior. These males, both boys and teenagers, do not see their prostitution as a problem but more as a means to express their own private sexual mores and values. One striking case will illustrate this point.

GEORGIE (a friend of LEW, in chapter 2) was abused by his scoutmaster when twelve years old. The abuse lasted, as in Lew's case, for approximately three years and consisted of both oral and anal sex performed on Georgie by the scoutmaster.

Unlike Lew, who repeated the sexual abuse on other young boys, Georgie went searching for adult males who resembled the scoutmaster in any way. His search began in public rest rooms in neighborhood parks and was immediately successful. His first day out, he was molested by three adult males whom, he announced to Lew, he had "proudly seduced into doing exactly what I wanted." What he wanted was an exact repetition of the acts that the scoutmaster had performed on him.

By the end of his first year of prostituting, Georgie had seduced some thirty-five men, and he was only fifteen years old. He had also accrued a large sum of money since he charged each person prior to any sex acts. During this same first year he had also acquired a "lover," a brute of a truck driver, whom he actually detested but from whom he could extract large sums of money.

During that first year, Georgie confided all of his adventures to Lew in vivid and exacting detail but would never have sex with him. This changed in the second year when quite unexpectedly he seduced Lew in his own home. The unusual fact about this seduction was that with Lew, Georgie reversed the roles, becoming the active partner and fellating Lew. He refused to let Lew reciprocate or even to see his genitals, exactly as the scoutmaster had done with him.

Georgie's prostitution continued throughout high school and into college. He amassed more and more conquests and more and more money, which he gave away to Lew, other friends, and his school for special projects. In all of his school attendance, Georgie played the clown, providing entertainment for all of his classmates, regardless of the personal cost to himself and his self-image. Eventually he flunked out of college and disappeared.

Throughout his life, Georgie had little communication or emotional support from his parents, who were strict, rigid, second-generation people. He often complained to Lew that he had never been hugged, never been told that he was loved, and continually felt that he did not belong. He became independent at age twelve and from then on refused all parental orders or demands. His parents did nothing about the situation. When he flunked out of college, Lew called to give them the news, and they did not care a bit. The distance between Georgie and his parents continued to widen after that.

Many years later, Lew read in the newspapers that Georgie's dead body had been found in a gutter in the skid-row section of a major city. No reason for his disappearance or slide into alcoholic oblivion has ever been found.

Questions for Discussion

1. What do you feel made the difference in the outcome of the sexual abuse of Lew and Georgie?

2. What part did the money play in Georgie's prostitution?

3. What effect did Georgie's negative relationship with his parents play in his prostituting, if any?

4. What role did Georgie's parents' coldness and negativism have on Georgie's behavior?

5. Was "playing the clown" and eventually failing at college connected to Georgie's sexual abuse by his scoutmaster, or to his negative relationship with his parents, or to his prostitution, or to all three?

Can you imagine being a parent of an abused teenage male or a close friend of one? Do you believe that he would share with you that he is or was prostituting? In all of my years of treating children and adolescents who were abused, I have never had one volunteer this information to me or to his parents. Even in cases where the prostitution had been exposed, it usually took a long time to establish a relationship of trust and a great deal of therapy to reach a point where this subject could be effectively broached and worked on. (Georgie was something of an exception to this in that he confided his prostitution to Lew from the onset.)

Even when the prostitution is exposed, the boy's or teenager's need for real love (which was usually not there at the time of or immediately after his molestation) remains as strong as ever, if not even stronger. Learning to love himself is essential because he will never be able to believe or accept love from others — from family or friends — if he cannot love himself. Also, the "sex equals love" connection, instilled by the sexual predator, needs to be broken and a new value on love established as a replacement. This is where professional therapy by well-trained therapists is necessary and where involvement by relatives or friends is critical to success. More will be said about this in chapter 13, on treatment issues.

CONSENSUAL RAPE AS AN EFFECT
OF EARLIER ABUSE

Consensual rape is another form of sexual abusing as well as a form of being sexually abused. Both males and females are involved in this experience. Consensual rape not only exists in sadomasochistic relationships but is frequently found in everyday teenage and young-couple relationships. In my experience this usually unreported sexual abuse is at the basis of many broken marriages, suicides, and drug-abuse cases. It is rarely the referring reason for treatment and is thus too often overlooked or unexplored. An example will clarify.

CALVIN is a twenty-two-year-old male who is currently serving time in prison for auto theft. This is his second run-in with the law. On the first offense, he served reformatory time for a similar auto theft.

Calvin comes from a fatherless home. His mother is not only an inadequate personality but also rejects and fails to care for her children. Calvin and his younger brother often are locked out of their apartment and either have to stay with friends or live on the streets.

A church minister befriended Calvin and became a father-substitute for the young man. He strongly feels that Calvin was sexually abused and states: "Calvin has all of the classic symptoms: his bed-wetting, his extreme shyness, quietness, and his castration complex (he holds on to his penis while he sleeps). One thing I've thought about too is that perhaps he has become a sex offender in a different kind of way. When he's talked to me about the sex he's had with girls, the way he has sex, the way he describes it is very forceful, almost rapelike. This one girl he was living with, after they had had a fight, called me and left a five-minute message on my machine. She talked about how she missed sex with Calvin. Basically what she described is that he was raping her. For him sex was rape. OK, it was a willing rape, but he did it with force and hardness and was trying to hurt her. In fact, he bruised her vagina, at times. Perhaps what he was doing was raping her with her permission. That's the only way he knows how to have sex, and I'm totally convinced that when he chooses obese girls, who remind him so much of his mother, what he's really trying to do is hurt his mother. He needs to hurt her to get back at her for the pain she's caused him. He does this through the way he treats these women and the way he has sex with them."

It appears not only that Calvin is a sexual-abuse survivor but also that the girls he consensually rapes were also survivors. This form of projecting feelings from one person (Calvin's mother) onto another is extremely common in unreported and untreated sexual abuse. These survivors choose either to become the aggressor (in imitation of the predator who abused them) or to remain a perpetual victim as they were in their original abuse. The former group are deny-ers and the latter accept-ers.

Calvin not only victimizes his girlfriends but also allows himself to become a victim by putting himself in unhealthy situations. He chooses girls upon whom he is totally dependent, and when they become angry with him (usually for stupid reasons such as his not smiling the way they wanted him to, or for visiting his minister friend, or for refusing to have sex with them), they throw him out and toss his clothes onto the streets. Calvin then, very angry, stays with a friend for a couple of days, always convinced that they will call him and beg him to come back, and they do!

When they do call him back, he tries to hurt them in any way he can. He makes them beg him to return, and when he does, the cycle begins all over again. That night, they will have the roughest sex that they ever had (brutal rape).

In this manner, Calvin continues his "Ping-Pong relationships" with women. Also, if he finds a positive and healthy relationship, he sabotages it ("I don't deserve this!") and thus remains unhappy, returning to one of his former sick relationships where he is "safe," in that he doesn't have to become emotionally involved and face the pain of rejection. On top of this, he is still rejected by his mother. Calvin remains a lonely, sad, and hurt little boy.

Questions for Discussion

1. Calvin was always in trouble in school. How could his teachers and counselors have helped prevent him from ending up in prison?

2. How can Calvin's cycle of abuse be ended?

3. Why do Calvin's women tolerate his behavior and always come back for more?

4. What traits does Calvin look for in the women he chooses?

5. What traits do Calvin's women see in him that makes him a desirable lover?

PSEUDO-POSITIVE EFFECTS OF SEXUAL ABUSE

While it may seem ludicrous to even consider that any effects of sexual abuse could be positive, there are instances where the survivor, at the time of the abuse and shortly afterward, feels and perceives the abuse to have been a positive event in his or her life. I have seen cases like this too often not to mention them in this discussion, with the caveat that "pseudo" must always be prefixed to the perceived positive effects. An example at this point will help clarify this point.

HANS, when five years old, lived in a duplex: on one side lived Hans and his family, and on the other side lived his aunt and uncle and their sons, KURT, age eleven, and JEREMY, age ten. Kurt used to spend a lot of time at Hans's house and would often sleep over in Hans's bedroom. Hans, to this day, has a vivid memory of waking up during the early hours of the morning, on one of these sleep-overs, to discover that Kurt was performing oral sex on him. At five, Hans knew nothing about sex, and because he trusted and liked Kurt, he said and did nothing and really enjoyed the experience, which ended in his first mini-orgasm. Kurt repeated this sexual behavior on many occasions and some time later, but while he was still five years old, Hans reciprocated. However, due to his inexperience and his age, he was unable to bring Kurt to an orgasm.

During this same year of Hans's life, his parents separated due to his father's alcoholism and physical abuse of his mother. Hans's mother would take him to visit his father's aunt, and on a couple of occasions his cousin Kurt was there. Kurt would take Hans to a wooded area at the end of his aunt's property, and there they would perform oral sex on each other. At this time, Hans was six or seven, and Kurt was now twelve.

At age eight or nine, Hans became involved with another of his cousins, **HANK**, age thirteen, and now was performing oral sex on them both, still enjoying the relationship and the sex as well. During these encounters, Hans was getting little to no reciprocation, but Hank would later buy him candy or ice cream. With no positive relationships or experiences in his home life, Hans would do anything to be with his cousins and to be allowed to associate and to play with them. The oral sex now became a form of payment for being allowed this relationship with his cousins.

During this period, Hans felt like he was an awkward, "dorky" kid (his term) and certainly did not feel comfortable with other peers in school or in the neighborhood. Thus, acceptance by his cousins became extremely important to him.

Beginning in the seventh grade, Hans began to seduce other boys, since his cousins had now moved away. He was always the seducer and cared more about pleasing them than being pleased. Feeling ugly, he always picked a good-looking kid (his ideal self) to seduce, and when he succeeded, the conquest made him feel acceptable.

In the eighth grade, Hans, now thirteen, began going to and seducing younger boys since his peer group were all now interested in girls and not in a relationship with him. He would buy these young boys ice cream and candy and, on the whole, role-reversed to behave toward them in the exact same manner as his cousins had behaved toward him. The only difference was that he was still the one giving pleasure and was only minimally concerned about receiving pleasure back.

This pattern continued into adulthood, when he became a teacher to be near kids. He soon began seducing his students. His pattern was as follows. First, he would choose the boys he felt were vulnerable and needy. Next, he would get to know the parents and make sure that they knew he was interested in their son. This worked especially well with single parents who were concerned about being able to do enough for their sons (especially mothers). From tutoring after school, he next began taking them to movies and McDonald's and would gradually work up to having them stay at his place overnight. (Amazingly, the parents of all of the boys Hans molested never objected to any of these activities, including the overnights.) He paid the boys a great deal of attention and used a great deal of physical contact and hugging in his contacts with them. In his apartment, he would suggest lifting weights to get the boys to take their shirts off (to see what they looked like) and after they lifted weights, he would tell them they needed to shower and then have a massage. Hans would shower first, coming out of the shower nude and encouraging them to do the same since it was perfectly natural. While massaging them in the nude, he would discuss sex with them, and, of course, he gave them his version of what sex should be. Hans would massage them in a manner to get them erect. If they were embarrassed about their erection, he would tell them it was OK and that he also got erections and would show them his to prove his point. He then had them turn on their backs in order to massage their chest and frontal leg muscles and worked his way to their penises, which he would then massage to orgasm. His persistent need was to be the one who made the boys ejaculate, the same way he had made his cousins "squirt."

He would wrestle in the nude with some of the boys (as he often had done with his cousin Kurt) until they became erect and "ready" for sex. Hans would tell them that there was a way to make them feel even better than when he masturbated them but that he did that only with special friends that he really cared for. Oral sex would follow. If they were willing to reciprocate, that was fine, but it was not necessary.

On one occasion, while Hans was playing with the buttocks of a thirteen-year-old boy, the boy asked him to put a finger in his anus, and this really turned both the boy and Hans on. This was a new experience for Hans, and he described it like being "free in a candy shop." Anal sex then began with the older boys and has remained his favorite sexual activity to this day.

Hans molested some thirty boys before he was finally arrested and sent to a treatment institution for compulsive sex offenders. In therapy, a persistent theme that has never been resolved is the possibility of his having been molested by his father. Hans's father slept nude, and Hans often saw his father's penis and fantasized about touching it. He still, to this day, also wonders if his father had been molesting the same cousins that he was having sex with.

Before therapy, Hans would insist that there was nothing wrong in what he and his cousins did nor subsequently in what he did with his students and other neighborhood boys. As long as they allowed (consented) him to have sex with them and as long as they reciprocated willingly, he was not harming them. Only when he ended up arrested, embarrassed before his family and friends in court, and institutionalized in a prison for sex offenders did he begin to realize that the molestations by his cousins eventually led to his deviation and downfall. In therapy, he learned that his negative feelings about himself (defective self-image) made him vulnerable and an easy prey to his older cousins. He also learned that the patterns he was taught became compulsive and remained with him as needs even after the cousins moved away.

Questions for Discussion

1. What type of communication do you feel existed between Hans and his parents?

2. When he entered grammar school, why was Hans never observed to be a loner with a poor self-image, and why wasn't something done about it?

3. In grammar school, when his focus switched to younger boys, why was it never noticed that he did not associate with his peers but preferred boys from lower grades?

4. Once Hans became a teacher and initiated his infamous overnights, why did the parents of these sexual victims communicate so little with them and show such little interest? Why did no one ask how the time was spent with this teacher?

5. Why are so many prepubertal and pubertal boys so willing to allow themselves to be used by older men?

Cases of pseudo-positive sexual abuse are occurring daily in our cities, in our schools, in Big Brothers organizations, in the Boy Scouts, in YMCAs, in religious organizations (between priests and altar boys or choir boys or students in parochial schools). This type of abuse also occurs with friends of the family, relatives (aunts, uncles, grandparents, cousins), neighbors, employers of children and adolescents, theater patrons, shopping mall customers in rest rooms, park goers, and so on. All seductive sexual abuse can and does occur anywhere and everywhere and is grossly underreported, especially by males.

BOY/MALE REPORTING-PROBLEMS

It is important, at this point, to focus on the problems that male victims of seductive sexual abuse experience.

The Macho Mystique

Males in our culture must always be strong, brave, courageous, and masculine (that is, heterosexual). They also must be able to defend themselves and not be passive or "wimps." Additionally, they must know everything about "girls" and "sex." Independence is another essential trait that a boy must have. Taking all of these traits into consideration, how does a maturing boy (prepubertal to adolescent) ask questions, ask for help, or admit to fear or to an inability to defend himself from older males or from adults who are pressuring or bullying him? On top of everything else, homosexuality bodes automatic ostracizing by his peer group and potentially by his parents, especially his father.

Boys (and girls as well) certainly were not born with these distorted and chauvinistic values; they had to be learned. While most of the basic values are learned at home from parents and relatives, all children soon wander away from home and pick up additional and often different values from neighbors, school personnel (especially grammar and high school teachers), law enforcement individuals, religious figures, and peers (who are major contributors). Hopefully, they eventually weigh and understand what they have learned and experienced and thus establish their own value system.

The period of puberty and entry into adolescence is one of confusion, strife, and wars. These wars occur with parents, authority figures of any category, and eventually within the adolescents themselves. The primary need at this time is to obtain peer acceptance, and thus conformity to peer values is essential. When this peer acceptance comes at the price of rejecting parental, religious, legal, and other associated values, the stage of confusion reaches its peak. Only the strength of the personality resolves the confusion. In children with weak or defective egos, the confusion does not end, and adolescence becomes a period of pure "hell."

Fear of rejection and the intense need for acceptance make all children vulnerable during this period. The weaker the child, the more vulnerable and the greater price he or she is willing to pay for the acceptance from anyone offering it. As noted above, sex offenders are keenly aware of this condition and use it to their fullest advantage.

Comparison of Demands on and Values for Females and Males

Girls are still, today, seen as the weaker sex (although in reality they are stronger in many areas than boys are). While women have made inroads into sports, all scholastic areas, and all professions, and while they have demanded equality everywhere, the old male chauvinistic attitudes and values prevail to a larger than believed extent. Many men will mouth the politically correct thing to say while secretly believing in male superiority.

Besides this difference in values, relations among females are different from those among males. An explanation is needed. If a girl is raped or molested sexually in a high school by a male teacher, the entire school will be behind her, and she will have incredible support from everyone. Were a boy to be molested by a male teacher and it became known, he would never again be able to return to that school (see figure 6). There would be little or no support, and even those males (students, teachers, administrators) who wanted to be supportive would worry about their image and would back off or keep their support secret or on a one-to-one level. A true case that I was involved in will clarify.

Several years ago, I was asked to accept the role of facilitator at a high school where a sex scandal had recently been exposed. The drama teacher had been sexually involved (seductive molestation) with several boys in his acting class. One boy when approached by this teacher told his parents, and a major disruption ensued.

Now that the story (in several exaggerated and distorted versions) had emerged, the school was divided between those blaming the teacher and those blaming the boys. Fights were breaking out daily, and friends were becoming enemies who would not talk or associate with each other. Teachers were arguing with teachers and students as well, and the administration was at wit's end.

FIGURE 6: COMPARISON OF EFFECTS OF MOLESTATION
ON ADOLESCENT BOYS AND GIRLS

BOYS

- If molested during stage 4 (see pp. 114–117), boys are usually rejected. The need to be strong, macho, and heterosexual dominates the male adolescent value system.

- A strong homophobic aura exists in male peer groups during this stage. My personal belief is that this is the stage where true and intractable homophobia develops.

- Boys molested by older men during this stage cannot seek support and comfort from their peers or from the majority of their male authority figures (coaches, gym instructors, and so on, or, most importantly, their fathers).

GIRLS

- If molested during stage 4, girls receive support, empathy, and protection from both male and female peers as well as authority figures that they are involved with daily (for example, their teachers).

- While the molestation is still traumatic, they do not feel rejected by their peers, nor are they labeled or blamed for the occurrence, as frequently as boys are.

- They tend to report more readily and are much more motivated to become involved in therapy and then to get on with their lives. Naturally, there are exceptions to these reactions, especially when a girl is chronologically an adolescent but emotionally still a much younger child.

I agreed to help on one condition: a general assembly of teachers, administrators, and the school board was to be held in the auditorium after classes. Angrily and reluctantly this large group assembled, glaring at me from all sides. What to do? I looked around and saw a large, burly, gym instructor in his shorts nosily greeting other teachers as they arrived. When everyone was present, I asked for an assistant and suggested that hopefully this popular gym instructor would volunteer. To cheers and applause, he strode down the aisle, raising his hands in a gesture of victory and bathing in the attention. Once he was next to me and the audience had quieted down, I asked him if he could do a simple task. I would say half of a sentence, snap my fingers, and then he was to respond immediately with the first thing that popped into his head. He responded that that would be easy, and I proceeded.

I waited for the group's attention and then stated: "You're the football coach, and you walk into the locker room and observe two of your football stars in the showers engaged in a homosexual act. What would you do?" I then snapped my fingers, and he instantly replied: "Kick the fuckin' fags off the team, and let the whole school know what they were up to!"

Silence overtook the auditorium, and the school board looked as if they would like to hide under their seats. I waited a reasonable minute or two and shouted to the whole audience: "Now do you know why the boys in Mr. X's class could not tell anybody what was going on after drama practice?"

Were these female students, this type of problem would not have existed. This difference in values was brought up in the assembly, and the majority agreed. We then had a thirty-minute interchange of ideas on how to handle the problem with the student body, and it was agreed that I would hold a discussion group with all of the male seniors, which I did the next day. All staff members left the auditorium in a new harmony that had not existed for several weeks.

The boys (survivors) returned to school in two weeks and graduated that year, although they were never again accepted in the same way by some males in the senior class. The senior girls were more understanding and forgiving (although there was nothing to forgive!).

Had a survey been taken at this upper-middle-class high school, none of the faculty or administration would have seen themselves as sexist or chauvinistic. In the abstract, this self-perception would have been honest and real, but when a concrete incident tested their value system, the old values surfaced that had never been changed, only suppressed.

Boys' Treatment of Each Other

Boys tend to be much more judgmental than girls and also are more prone to reject each other for the simplest infraction of peer rules. The almost automatic empathy and need to understand that are characteristic of girls do not appear in the average, male, adolescent personality and emerge only much later in a percentage of mature men. Boys upon hearing a rumor about a male peer (presented and accepted as fact) immediately judge the allegedly offending peer and rejection occurs in more than 90 percent of the cases.

In a case of sexual abuse involving a parent, a teacher, a Boy Scout leader, a Big Brother, a priest, or any well-liked authority figure, my experience has been that male adolescents side with the authority figure and not with their peer. This seems to contradict the adolescent code of siding together against adults and especially against authority figures, so it needs more explanation.

When a male authority figure is reported as having abused or molested an adolescent male, other adolescents who have been emotionally involved in some way with the man but have not been abused by him often experience homosexual panic on an unconscious level. They may have felt some strong emotional bond with the adult, bordering on love (which a large proportion of teenagers unfortunately tend to equate with sex), and now hearing that their hero, friend, or mentor has committed a homosexual act they are forced to instantly reevaluate their own relationship with the adult and to question the adult's motives in showing them attention, affection, friendship, and so on. All of this happens instantly and on an unconscious level. Rather than lose the friendship or admit that they may also have been a target of homosexual lust, it is easier to put all of the blame on their peer since this poses no danger to their own egos or self-image. This occurs more often than one would suspect, and I have heard concerns of this type from literally hundreds of prepubertal and adolescent males.

Sex offenders in treatment also are able to remember feelings of this type in their own adolescence, and although in the sex offender these feelings are often conscious rather than unconscious, they still are never expressed (unless by good fortune the person is in therapy with a well-trained therapist).

When a male adolescent survivor (victim) of seductive sexual abuse or molestation experiences this judgmentalism and rejection from his peers, the damage doubles because a prime need in adolescence is acceptance by peers.

Thus, in the example related above, one of the most difficult problems for me as facilitator was to deal with the male senior students. It was essential to help them to understand their own angry reactions toward their fellow students who were abused and to help them to place the responsibility and blame on the sex offender without judging themselves erroneously. When I met with these boys, I discussed how the other teachers as well as the administration and the parents of the survivors were all conned by this clever, manipulating, devious individual who, rather than being evil, had serious emotional and sexual problems. By meeting with the senior boys for several hours and letting them express their feelings and discuss the situation openly and in their language, an atmosphere was eventually created that permitted the survivors to return to school (the senior class president contacted them and asked them to return) and graduate with their peers and friends. Unfortunately, not all situations of this type end so well, and many of these survivors are permanently damaged.

A word must be addended regarding parental values in cases of this type. If the parents become judgmental, refuse to talk openly about what happened, change their attitude and relationships with their teenagers, or in any other way demonstrate rejection or judgmental behaviors, the adjustment discussed above will not and cannot occur. The therapist must always take time to allow the parents to discuss their feelings and to ask any questions that are bothering them, such as: "Does this mean than my son is homosexual?" or "Do we have to worry about our son molesting his younger brothers or the neighborhood children?" These are actual questions I have been asked by parents of sexually abused teenage boys.

Questions for Discussion

1. Had this abuse incident occurred in your school or to one of your teenage sons, what would have been your immediate reaction?

2. Have you observed the difference in male and female judgmentalism and rejection behaviors discussed above?

3. Had the desensitizing groups not been held with the staff and board of education, what do you feel would have been the outcome?

4. Had the discussion group with the senior males not been held, what chances do you feel there would have been for these survivors to return to and graduate from that school?

5. What do you feel was done wrong by the school authorities, if anything?[2]

2. For a more in-depth study of the survivor, see William E. Prendergast, *The Merry-Go-Round of Sexual Abuse* (New York: Haworth Press, 1993).

4

NON-ABUSIVE PARENTS

After discussing sex offenders and the victims (survivors) of their sexual abuse, there only remains to discuss the parents and their role in the prevention of sexual abuse upon their children. The topic of parents must be divided into two separate chapters: one on non-abusive parents and one on incestuous parents. The reason for this separation is that personality makeup, treatment techniques, and prognosis for change are essentially different in each group. In this chapter, only non-abusive parents will be discussed.[1]

PARENTAL CHARACTERISTICS THAT HELP PREVENT OR HEAL ABUSE

Based on my thirty-three years of experience in the field, I have sadly come to the conclusion that we adults play a major role in the sexual abuse of our children. The major area of failure lies in adults not communicating that they are accessible and will be accepting and nonjudgmental toward the sexually abused child, and especially a boy. This communication must begin in early childhood and include the following conditions.

---

1. A distinction is necessary. Based on my experiences, I have come to the conclusion that only birth parents can fit the incestuous parents pattern. In my opinion, foster parents, live-in boyfriends, and adoptive parents who molest or abuse come under the pedophile/hebophile classification. Because they are not incestuous parents, the latter group is thus dealt with in the present chapter.

Availability

Too frequently in my therapy sessions with abused children, adolescents and adults, their major complaint is that no one (parents, siblings, relatives, friends, teachers, co-workers, and so on) was there when they needed and were ready to talk about their abuse. Parents, of course, do the most damage when they are unavailable, saying they are "too tired" or "too busy" or offering other lame excuses that avoid their responsibility as parents.

The major problem here is that survivors are not always ready or willing to discuss their being abused, and for many it takes a great deal of courage to tell anyone. In my experience, this readiness (see chapter 13 on treatment issues) often occurs only once, and when that opportunity is missed, it may never come again.

Belief in the Survivor and Assurance of Nonpunishment

I have seen and worked with too many cases where children or adolescents were not believed by a mother, father, teacher, priest, or minister when accusing another adult of sexually molesting them. I have even had cases where the child was severely punished for "lying" about an adult authority figure. KYLE (in chapter 2), HANS (in chapter 3), CONNIE (in chapter 5), and many others throughout this work are excellent examples of this pervasive problem. This punishment can be verbal — taking the form of degrading and humiliating remarks — and can also be physical. With fear of such punishment, why should survivors admit to their sexual assault or molestation?

Especially in long-term sexual molestation cases (as long as four to five years) but also in cases of multiple occurrences, children, adolescents, and even adults assume that they will be blamed for their involvement with the predator. The predator has implanted this idea, and in families where little is tolerated and sex is never mentioned or discussed, this fear becomes paralyzing and is, in part, the reason for the delayed reporting.

Assurance the Survivor Will Have a Voice

The matter of the survivor having a say in any action to be taken can be highly controversial since in some states any adult who knows or suspects that a child is being abused (physically, emotionally, or sexually) must report it to a specific state agency or face legal sanctions. This includes therapists and may include the clergy (this point is still up for legal clarification).

In my opinion, the survivor should make this decision, especially in incest cases or in sexual-assault cases (rape) where they know the predator and their lives or the lives of their family have been threatened. Treatment is more important than revenge, and while the argument that reporting and incarceration could prevent another individual from being sexually abused has weight, in too many cases the predator gets away with the offense (because only two people were present when it occurred). This is especially true in cases where physical evidence does not exist (for example, fondling children or performing oral sex on them), and the survivor does not make a credible witness. Also many of these predators plea-bargain to a lesser offense and receive probation. Some even return to the same neighborhood or place of employment.

Assurance of Long-Term Love and Support for the Survivor

The importance of long-term love and support for the survivor is obvious, but it must be verbalized on a continuing basis, especially regarding acts for which the survivor may be experiencing guilt or shame. Survivors' sense of whether they will have long-term love and support is determined by their loved ones' behavior, values, attitudes, and/or reactions to prior problems or indiscretions. If the survivor's perception of these prior attitudes is positive, the survivor is more likely to disclose. If this perception is negative, the survivor is less likely to disclose.

MISSING TRAITS IN PARENTS OF
CHILDREN/ADOLESCENTS WHO ARE VULNERABLE
TO SEXUAL MOLESTATION

Physical Contact on a Regular Basis

All children and adolescents need physical contact from someone, especially in times of emotional turmoil or when they are feeling confused, vulnerable, lonely, isolated, unloved, or unwanted. When this physical contact is not present in the home, children and adolescents will seek it outside of the home. The sex offender is an expert at observing and sensing these needs and is more than willing to fulfill them since they are his or her needs as well.

Parental physical contact should begin at birth in order for the infant to bond with both the mother and the father. Too often, it is only the mother who performs this bonding ritual in the delivery room. The need for bonding with the father is important to all children but is even more important to boys and is a primary reason that fathers should participate in the birth process.

After birth and infancy, many, many parents shy away from physical contact with their children except to punish. This behavior is always more dominant in fathers than in mothers. When children become adolescents, this parental avoidance of physical contact tends to increase due to homosexual panic — the fear that an act or behavior will be considered by anyone witnessing it to be homosexually motivated; in reality, it is the adult's own fears and distorted values that cause the reaction.

In families where physical contact has been maintained on a regular basis from birth through childhood, this avoidance-reaction does not occur, and touching continues and remains even into adulthood. Touching in these families is considered normal, and since parents teach children the majority of their values, the normalcy-of-touching value becomes part of the emerging adult personality. An example will clarify.

GLEN, introduced in chapter 1, never had physical contact of any kind with his demanding, judgmental father. He once stated in therapy: "I'd even misbehave just so I might get spanked. At least if he had spanked me, he would have had to touch me." However, it never happened. Glen's father used isolation in his room as punishment, and Glen would angrily masturbate whenever he was punished this way, fantasizing killing his father and possibly his mother also not only for marrying his father but for tolerating the ways he treated Glen. Eventually this anger led to assaultive rape, and Glen accumulated thirty victims before being apprehended and sent to prison.

In therapy, where physical contact was encouraged (hugging, arms around shoulders, and so on), Glen could not get enough physical contact and identified several males in his group as father figures from whom he sought all of the missing physical love and attention he had never had as a child.

Questions for Discussion

1. How could Glen's becoming an assaultive rapist have been avoided?

2. What other recourse was open to Glen that he did not try?

3. If you are a parent, how do you feel about Glen's father?

4. If you were Glen, how would you have gotten the attention, physical-affection, and love you needed?

5. What lesson can all parents learn from Glen?

Failing to Assure the Child/Adolescent of Care and Love

A surprisingly large percentage of children and adolescents do not believe that they are truly cared for and loved. Why? The most common reason I could detect in the children and adolescents that I have worked with over the years was that there was rarely, if ever, a direct, open statement or a positive behavior, on the part of the parents, that said: "I care for you. I love you." Most of the parents I have dealt with, when confronted with this situation, defended themselves by saying things like, "She [or he] knows I love her [or him]!" or "What does my hard work, this house, their clothes and possessions prove to them? Doesn't that show them I love them?" The answer is an unequivocal no.

There are also the cases where the words are spoken, but there is no behavioral backup to prove or demonstrate that the words are true. There are even instances where the words are used in a perverted way, such as in corporal punishment to "prove how much I love you" or in incestuous "love," which will be discussed in chapter 5.

Children and adolescents, in fact all of us, need to hear the words or feel the hugs to truly believe that we are cared for and loved. Sex offenders are acutely aware of this since they also felt unwanted, uncared for, and unloved in their childhood and adolescence. They, therefore, go overboard to exaggerate the acceptance, care, and love that they feel for the intended victim and verbalize these feelings over and over again. As in many other situations, the child or adolescent and even the adults need these feelings and statements so much that they are willing to pay any price to obtain and then keep them.

Certainly **LEW** (whom we met in chapters 1 and 2) desperately wanted these reactions and verbalizations from his drunken father but never received them. This made him completely vulnerable to an older father figure, his scoutmaster, and resulted in his "paying the price" (submitting to the scoutmaster's sexual molestations) for this "caring" and "love" for over three years.

GLEN (whom we also met in chapter 1) also never received affection, physical contact, care, and love from his demanding, never-satisfied, judgmental father. He also became vulnerable to an older father figure whom he met at work, **NICK**. Nick, once he got Glen to describe his family life, easily met all of Glen's needs and then seduced Glen into a long-term relationship that Glen did not want but was afraid to say no to lest he lose his new "caring," "loving," father figure.

Lack of or Defective Value-Teaching

Great care must be taken by parents concerning the values they teach their children or adolescents either directly or by their own example. Young children are not only curious and willing to learn but also want to become adults, someday, and so begin imitating adults very early in life in their play and overt behavior. The old adage "like mother, like daughter" or "like father, like son" is more often true than not. Even when a child or adolescent is trying desperately to become the opposite of his or her parents, certain traits and values of the corresponding parent continue to appear. An example will clarify.

> **GLEN**, with all his anger at his father, perfectly adopted his father's trait of being judgmental and never satisfied and applied it not only to others (two wives in marriages that failed) but also to himself. No matter how well he did at anything, he was never satisfied, and this resulted in his leaving one job after another, even when his supervisors thought he was doing excellent work.

Parents teach values from the day a child is born. If a baby behaves the way parents wish it to, it is picked up, hugged, cooed, and sung to by happy, smiling parents; however, if the baby misbehaves, a frightening look of disapproval appears on the parents' faces, and the baby is put into its crib and isolated, left to cry by itself. The first lessons in right and wrong have now occurred.

Values regarding social behavior, manners, nudity and modesty, religion (for example, prayers before meals), privacy (closed doors to parents' bedroom), gossiping, race, status, ambition, money, and so on, are taught daily, mostly by examples but also by the do's and don'ts that are imposed on the growing child. An example will help substantiate this point.

> **MITCH**, a twelve-year-old, emerging adolescent has discovered the joys and pleasures of masturbation. He uses his newfound behavior for many reasons, including to help him go to sleep.

He also often awakes in a "horny" mood and masturbates before showering and dressing.

Mitch arrived home one afternoon to a visibly furious mother who demanded that he follow her to his bedroom. Once there, she held up his sheet and asked him to explain what the stains were from. Mitch froze in embarrassment and remained speechless. His mother then screamed: "I know what filthy, disgusting act you are doing in your bed. If you keep it up you'll run out of seeds and never be able to have children. Everyone will know that you are a pervert and not a man. The next time I catch you doing this sinful and unnatural act, I'll hang the sheet out of your window for all of the neighbors and your friends to see. Now take your pants off!"

His mother then beat him with a switch on the penis and testicles until they were swollen and Mitch was ready to pass out. He could not go to school for several days and had to remain in bed with cold packs on his genitals until he could once again bear to walk.

Questions for Discussion

1. As a parent, how do you feel about Mitch's mother's reaction to the stains on the sheets?

2. What would have been a more healthy and normal reaction for Mitch's mother?

3. In reality, did Mitch's mother have any need for concern?

4. How do you as a parent or teen feel about masturbation?

5. How could Mitch have avoided this confrontation?

The "value lesson" that Mitch's mother taught remained with him throughout his life. He was sexually abstinent and could not masturbate without experiencing severe pain in both his penis and his testicles. Urologists could find no reason for the pain and referred him to me for sex therapy. The above-related story came back to him after several sessions of therapy. Where value formation is concerned, Mitch never left stage 1 (see "Five Stages of Value Formation" later in this chapter) and now had to progress through all of the remaining stages before any significant changes in his life could occur.

Lack of Concrete Value-Teaching

Children and a large percentage of adolescents are unable to perceptualize or understand abstract concepts such as sin, good and evil, love, and perversion. They learn primarily through concrete perceptions and experiences. When a parent continuously attempts to teach or discipline in abstract terms, the child perceives this as preaching, and, as the old teacher's adage goes: "The material is passed from the parent to the child without going through the minds of either."

When values are effectively taught through the use of concrete examples or behaviors, they rarely are forgotten (that is, they are internalized). An example will illustrate this principle.

When I was a young psychologist in a diagnostic center for children and adolescents that is now defunct, I was assigned a most difficult eleven-year-old boy, **LANCE**, as one of my first cases. Lance had been stealing for the last year or so from almost anyone and anywhere, including at home from his parents and his siblings, at school from both classmates and teachers, from neighborhood stores, from his local church poor box, and so on. He was sent to the diagnostic center for evaluation and for a recommendation as to where and how to deal with him. Choices included a reformatory for children his age, a foster-home placement, or return to his own home with outpatient treatment.

From the first day of his arrival, Lance was a problem. He was big and strong for his age and could overpower most of the other boys on his wing (a floor of individual rooms, usually age-oriented, with officers in charge). Lance began stealing from the other boys the first day of his arrival, and no method that the officers tried appeared to have an effect on him. He accepted punishment readily (usually consisting of room restriction or restriction from television or outdoor recreation, including swimming in the pool). However, once the punishment was over, someone would have to pay the price, usually the boy or officer who made the complaint against him. His revenge was often worse than his original offense and was always destructive (spilling the officer's coffee on his uniform, urinating in a cup or bottle and throwing it on the offending person, destroying personal property that had emotional meaning to the other person, and so on).

One day, some three weeks into Lance's stay, his regular daytime wing officer called me. He was at the end of his tether. Once again, Lance had stolen a gift from another boy that was given to him by his father and had strong emotional meaning. The gift could be found nowhere, and Lance would not tell anyone what he had done with it. I asked for the wing's afternoon schedule, and fortunately the entire wing was to be at the pool from 1:00 to 2:30 P.M. I then asked the officer what Lance had in his room that was important to him and found that he had a teddy bear that his mother, now deceased, had given to him when he was five years old.

While the wing was at the pool, I went to the wing, entered Lance's room, and stole the teddy bear. When the wing returned and Lance discovered the theft, he went into a rage and threatened everyone, including the officer. I was called, and I had him sent to my office. I made him wait for thirty minutes in the waiting area and then ushered him in. I asked what he was upset about, and he stated: "Some fuckin' idiot went into my room and stole my teddy bear. When I find out who it is I'll kill him."

I then asked Lance to tell me how it felt to have an important possession stolen, and he simply cried and cried, saying, "It hurts like hell!" I then told him that I had stolen the teddy bear, and he rushed at me to punch me, but I help him tightly by the arms so he couldn't move. In frustration, he wept and slid to the floor in defeat.

When he recovered to an extent, he asked why I had stolen the teddy bear, and I said: "I had your permission." He looked bewildered and said, "What the fuck does that mean?" I then told him that since he was stronger than the other boys on the wing, he pushed them around and stole anything he wanted from their rooms without shame or guilt. I then said that I certainly was stronger than he was and that I wanted his teddy bear, so I took it. Silence ensued. After several minutes he asked how he could get his teddy bear back, and I told him that I didn't know, that that was up to him to think about. I then sent him back to his wing.

Two days later I received a note from Lance asking to see me. When he arrived, he was a different boy. There was no anger, no macho image, just a little boy who seemed frightened yet calm and polite. He told me he had been thinking about the boys he had stolen from and now understood how they felt. He also related this to outside instances at home, in school, and in the neighborhood. His tears convinced me that he was being sincere, and I opened my bottom desk drawer and offered him his teddy bear. He ran toward me and hugged me so tightly I could barely breathe.

Needless to say, Lance no longer stole from anyone, and while there were still arguments, fights, and disobediences, his overall behavior improved sufficiently to send him home at the end of his ninety-day stay with outpatient therapy for him and also for his family.

Questions for Discussion

1. How do you think Lance's stealing began and why?

2. What role did his parents play in his problem?

3. Why didn't punishment work?

4. What other concrete methods might have been used to curb Lance's stealing?

5. If nothing worked at age eleven, what predictions can be made about Lance's adult life?

Parents need to be creative in deciding how to teach values to their children and to be extremely careful that teaching by example or behavior does not do more damage than good, an example being the incestuous father teaching sex education by performing sex with the child (see chapter 5).

Further, as stated above in this chapter and in other places in this work, the teaching of sound values must begin as early as possible in childhood. If parents wait to begin teaching values until an adolescent crisis or conflict with the law occurs, then the teaching will be terribly difficult and unlikely to succeed without professional intervention.

At this point, a discussion of value formation is necessary since once the child ventures out of his or her home, value confusion abounds and comparisons begin.

FIVE STAGES OF VALUE FORMATION

Stage 1 — The Prisoner Stage (from Birth to Two Years)

- All values are learned from parents and other adults in the child's home.

- Absolute obedience is necessary for acceptance and love.

- No comparisons are made at this stage.

Stage 2 — The Neighborhood Stage (from Two to Five Years)

- Friends, neighbors, relatives, and others outside the home introduce new values.

- Comparisons by the developing child begin and result in confusion and the first negative perceptions of parents and self.

- The first blame and guilt for failures also occur during this stage.

- Inadequacy as a characteristic most likely begins in this stage.

Stage 3 — The Societal Stage (from Five Years to Puberty)

- School, religion, and the law introduce additional values.

- Teachers, ministers, priests, scoutmasters, policemen, and other authority figures become new parent-substitutes, and comparison intensifies.

- Value confusion is strong, especially when a behavior is acceptable at home and is not acceptable in school or the community or vice versa.

- The need to please adults appears strongest in this stage, and the child is therefore more vulnerable to seduction by the child molester, especially when the home is not fulfilling his or her needs.

- Interaction between parents and parent-substitutes is critical for the stable development of the child. Each needs to know what values the other is teaching and which values they are in disagreement about.

Stage 4 — The Peer Stage (from the Onset of Puberty)

- An abrupt psychological change occurs from the beginning of this stage until its completion, with the needs for acceptance and approval shifting from adults to peers. The initial result of this shift depends on the first three stages and how smoothly they were experienced.

- Parents are most upset and disturbed about their children during this stage since they do not understand what is happening. Their formerly wonderful, obedient, and loving child may now turn into a monster who is defiant, disobedient, argumentative, and a constant source of irritation or even embarrassment.

- In the quest for independence and personal identity, the child must now break away from the parents' protection and direction and develop his or her own values, behaviors, decisions, and even appearance (dress, hairstyles, and so on). The delusion that awakening adolescents experience is that these new decisions are their own, when in reality they are strongly influenced and dictated by peer standards and pressures. The fear of being different is greatly magnified in this stage.

- Parents who, for the sake of status, force their adolescent to attend high school in conservative clothes (shirt and tie for boys, dresses for girls) can expect problems of all sorts as a result, including defiance, torn or damaged clothing, separate clothing hidden at school to change into, and hostility (bordering on rage).

- For both the sex offender and the survivor, this stage is the most upsetting and leaves a lasting set of effects that must be dealt with in therapy. The following problems may occur for the adolescents: (*a*) Fears, self-doubts, confusion, shifts of loyalty, and body-image problems arise, and the adolescents constantly test themselves, parents, and others. (*b*) Communication abruptly stops and needs to be fostered on a regular basis. (*c*) Definitions of "adult" are fluid. Subtle help in deciding on a mature definition is needed but is feared and/or rejected. (*d*) Sexuality explodes and becomes a major focus. Indecisiveness and confusion about all aspects of sex dominate this stage. The sex offender takes great advantage of this situation. (*e*) A war between old values (stages 1, 2, and 3) and peer pressure occurs and adds to the confusion. (*f*) Guilt of all types flourishes and imprints although it will be denied to parents and other authority figures. (*g*) AIDS-phobia makes sexuality even more disturbing and confusing. (*h*) Boys' and girls' expectations and demands separate more widely here than in any other stage. (*i*) This is the gang stage, and gang loyalty supersedes loyalty to parents and all others. Proofs of courage abound during this stage and often involve antisocial behavior such as drinking, drug use, theft, assault, violence against rival gangs, and so on.[2]

Stage 5 — The "I" Stage

- All other stages and values are reexamined, and decisions for adult life are made in this stage. For example, the adolescent might say: "Mom and dad say drinking is all right in moderation. My school teaches me that drinking is bad for me, as does my doctor. Religion is strongly against drinking, but I see priests, ministers, and even nuns drinking in restaurants. My friends all say that drinking is fun and that adults just don't want us to have any fun. Now, I say that drinking is all right for me as long as I don't drink and drive."

- Most adults either never reach the "I" stage or continue throughout their lives to fluctuate between stage 4 and stage 5, depending on their emotional maturity and reactions to trauma, the intensity of their need for approval, and the strength of their ego.

- Adolescents who are prone to gang involvement during stage 4 need to be made aware of stage 5 as a goal (this should happen early in their childhood development) and must be encouraged to make decisions that will result in happiness as opposed to acceptance by their peers. Self-acceptance then becomes the primary goal and route to happiness for anyone.

OTHER KEY PROBLEM AREAS

Sex Equals Love

An especially insidious value, learned early in the lives of both the sex offender who was molested as a child or adolescent and the

---

2. For adults who never leave this stage, this is the "Keeping up with the Joneses" stage or syndrome.

child victim of sexual molestation, is that sex equals love. Too often, individuals use the challenge "If you loved me, you'd..." to get a potential sex partner to do what they want. I have met children, adolescents, and adults who have admitted to utilizing this ploy to get something they wanted from someone else, especially sexual favors or submissions.

The sex offender expands on this theme by explaining to the child or adolescent who asks what the offender is doing during a sexual molestation that "I'm showing you how much I love you!" All pedophiles, hebophiles, and incestuous parents use this rationalization of their perverted behavior.

One of my pet peeves that I tend to preach on in all of my presentations is the almost universal practice in the United States of referring to any sex act as "making love." As far as I have been able to ascertain, the reason for this horrendous practice is that people in the United States are much more embarrassed about discussing sex openly than are the people in many other countries of the world. Yes, even in our so-called days of sexual openness and enlightenment, this factor persists. Just look at the arguments over sex education being taught in the schools. While parents claim that it is their right to teach their children sex education when they choose to, it is painfully true that most parents are incapable of doing the job.

Certainly many parents can teach biological sex education with medical terminology that they have learned from a book and, with great discomfort, can convey this information to their children or adolescents. However, this is definitely not enough to prevent sexual molestation or abuse or, for that matter, to prevent a variety of sexually transmitted diseases from venereal warts (How many parents know about them?) to AIDS. Where more than missionary-procreative intercourse (man on top) is concerned, parents usually are unable to handle the child's or adolescent's questions. This includes questions about oral sex ("Mom, what's a blow job?" or "What's a sixty-nine"), anal sex ("Dad, is sodomy a good substitute for intercourse, and how do I do it?"), a variety of sexual positions ("Mom, is using the 'swing' for intercourse fun?"), or many other nonprocreative sexual subjects including contraceptive techniques, homosexual experimentation, ménage à trois, and mutual masturbation. I strongly disagree that the average parents with a high school education and most college graduates before the 1990s can handle questions about these areas that our children and adolescents are curious about. An example will help prove this point.

CHESTER, when thirteen years old, began getting into a great deal of difficulty both in school and in the community. He was hanging out with a delinquent-type group of older teenagers, and his parents were at a loss as to how to handle the situation. Ultimately, he was arrested for criminal sexual contact with an eleven-year-old girl and given probation with treatment as a requirement.

Chester's parents were upper-middle-class, his father a highly successful pediatrician and his mother, a highly successful commercial decorator. Neither, however, was a parent. Chester's mother was permissive and used money as a love-substitute while his father avoided him as much as possible (he secretly doubted that Chester was really his son).

I knew both of Chester's parents professionally from community service organizations that we all belonged to. At one luncheon meeting, Chester's father took me aside and asked if I could stop by his office after the luncheon to discuss an important, personal matter.

When I arrived, Chester's father related the problems he had been having with the boy and then, out of the blue, asked me: "How much would you charge to teach Chester sex education? I simply can't handle it!" I was stunned and shocked. Here was a professional man with several degrees who couldn't teach his son basic sex education. I agreed, and slowly but surely, Chester's father relinquished all of his paternal responsibilities and placed them on me. I changed from Chester's therapist to Chester's substitute father.

Today, Chester is a successful lawyer in a western state who has little, if any, contact with his natural parents but who remains in contact with me on a regular basis. All of my attempts to reconcile the family have so far failed.

Questions for Discussion

1. Could Chester's situation have been avoided?

2. What problems do you feel existed in Chester's parents' marriage?

3. What was lacking in Chester's mother?

4. What major problem was Chester's father experiencing?

5. Why do you think that this family will not settle their problems?

Parental Accessibility

In today's economy, homes in which both parents work are common. The children and adolescents of these parents must be made aware of the economic situation of the family and specifically why both of their parents need to work. They then need to be taught their corresponding responsibility to the family (cutting grass, cleaning, preparing dinner, laundry, and so on). Where this is not done, conflict can and will arise.

In homes in which both parents work, both parents come home physically and emotionally drained yet still have responsibilities toward the home, the children, and each other. Quality time must be made available for all family members on a regular as well as an emergency basis. One method that I have successfully proposed in families that I have worked with in therapy is that of the dinner meeting. In families who eat dinner together, I suggest that after dessert and the dishes are cleared that there be a twenty-to-thirty-minute family meeting with mandatory attendance. Anyone can bring up any topic that is of concern to them at this time, or a rotation schedule can be arranged for each family member to have his or her turn at discussing anything of concern to them. This is also the place where all important family decisions should take place — in the open. Financial problems, medical problems, school problems, behavioral problems, employment problems, and so on, all belong at this meeting. It is important for children and adolescents to know everything about their family and to understand that their parents are not superhuman but may have emotional problems, anxieties, and worries of their own. Parents asking for suggestions and advice from their children has a tremendously positive affect on the children and bolsters their self-esteem and self-image. Even if arguments ensue, the overall results of these meeting are positive for all. The best result of these meetings is that they avoid the "secrecy" in families that all children resent and that destroys closeness and understanding between children and parents. An example follows.

SHEILA, thirteen, and STAN, eleven, are brother and sister in a conflictual family situation. The parents have had to call the juvenile authorities on several occasions due to their children's poor behavior at school and their defiance at home. The situation has reached the point where the court has ordered family therapy as a last-ditch effort before placing both adolescents in either foster homes or a juvenile facility.

Our first meeting was a screaming match with each family member projecting incredible anger and blame onto everyone else in the family. I halted the battle and asked if anyone was interested in solving the family's problems rather than creating more. Silence followed. I then gave each member of the family five minutes to express complaints about everyone else and the family in general, with the stipulation that no other family member interfere.

Once I gathered the "laundry list" of each family member, it became obvious that the teens wanted only benefits and "goodies" from the family with no effort or responsibility on their part. Neither Sheila nor Stan could tell me their role in the family or their responsibilities toward the family. I then discussed the concept of "contracts" with the four individuals, and all seemed to accept the idea. A homework assignment was then given. Each family member was to draw up a contract of what his or her role and responsibility in the family were to be without discussing them with the other family members.

The following session, I made copies of all of the contracts and then passed copies of each one to all four family members. Silence and shock resulted. Even the two parents had never discussed their roles in the family and were greatly surprised by what their partners had written. The teens came up with some very mature and responsible ideas that impressed me as well as their parents.

With very few minor changes, each family member signed a copy of his or her contract to the family, and everyone was given copies of all of the contracts. I scheduled the next session for one month, as a trial period to see if the contracts needed any changes.

The next session was our last. There had not been a serious argument or fight since the contracts, which for the first time clarified the role of each family member and provided cohesiveness and a working partnership for them.

Questions for Discussion

1. What role did lack of communication play in this family's problems?

2. How would you characterize Sheila and Stan?

3. Where did the parents go wrong in their children's upbringing?

4. Do you feel further problems will occur? If so, what kind?

5. How do you feel about "contracts"?

While seeming too easy and too simple, what occurred was quite complex in terms of dynamics. An understanding of the role of each member of the family was presented. The father was the major financial contributor while the mother was an essential adjunct financial contributor. The children were benefactors of the labor and efforts of their parents. They also were students, and that was their prime function in the family — that is, to do the best they could with the talents they were given. Additionally, they owed the family time and effort to aid the parents who were doing the most they could for all of the family. Chores became easier when the children perceived them as part of their role in the family partnership rather than as slave service "because I said so!"

The contracts were changeable at any time and could be discussed at a family dinner meeting (which also was incorporated into this family's schedule). The willingness of each of the four partners in this family to make something work was an essential element in the therapy.

Imagine what a different outcome there could have been had this type of communication existed with **RALPH** (whom we met in chapter 1). Had the marital problems that were ongoing in his family been openly discussed with the children, had his father discussed his falling out of love with his mother, had both parents explained what would happen to the children when they divorced, Ralph may not have reacted the way he did, and his mother's fears of being killed might have been avoided.

Lack of Credibility between Parents and Their Children

By this point, the role and responsibility of parents should be more obvious. But there is more to consider. Why don't our children who are being abused go to their parents with this information and for help? Why are most cases of child sexual molestation reported to a school teacher instead of to the parents? Why are children and adolescents such easy prey to sexual molesters? One of the major problems concerns the lack of credibility between parents and children. This credibility must begin practically from the cradle.

When I finally have developed sufficient rapport with a child or adolescent survivor and ask this sensitive question regarding not going to his or her parents (or parent) for help, the most frequent response is, "I didn't think they would believe me!" When asked why this was true there was either silence, a shrug of the shoulders, or some answer that intimated that they had not been believed in the past. As I have stated many times above, many child and adolescent survivors whom I have treated reported actually being punished (beaten, yelled at, or given restrictions) for reporting a teacher, priest, minister, or other authority figure. The parents utter statements such as:

- "How could you make up such lies about Father so-and-so?"

- "After all that teacher has done for you, you make up vicious lies about him [or her]."

- "Disgusting!"

- "Your father pays the bills and takes care of us. Just do what he tells you to do!"

Teaching Blind Obedience

We teach our children from an early age to respect and obey all authority figures, including teachers, policemen, scoutmasters, and Big Brothers, all groups well represented among child and adolescent molesters. Children and adolescents see adults defending adults, a sort of us-against-them concept. Is it therefore so surprising that children and adolescents do not report sexual abuse, as a general rule, to their parents but to teachers, relatives, or neighbors? Is it also so surprising that we are having so many serious problems with adolescent gangs and criminal activity?

The sex offender takes full advantage of this teaching of obedience to all adults. Teachers, ministers, priests, Big Brothers, scoutmasters, policemen, crossing guards, and camp counselors all have authority over our children, given to them by us. We now need to teach our children when to say no and to give them the permission to do so even with an authority figure like those mentioned above. Here, especially, early moral and religious value instruction as well a sex education by parents or by professionals are essential. An essential additional prevention aid is "good touch/bad touch" training when begun in early childhood years (nursery school and preschool). This training should be for any and all parts of the child's body, not just the "private" areas. Even an arm around the shoulders, a rub of a hand, or a pat on the butt can be considered "uncomfortable" by a child and should be refused. We also need to include family members in the groups, not just strangers. Sexual molestation and abuse occur quite frequently with relatives, including uncles and aunts, grandfathers and grandmothers, older siblings, and, of course, parents.

Language Concerns

As part of communication-training by parents, children and adolescents should be encouraged to use their own language in reporting a concern they may have about an occurrence. This is especially true where discussing sexual molestation or abuse is concerned. If parents have not taught their child correct anatomical and sexual terminology and all that the child knows is "street language," then parents should encourage the child to speak in that language without fear of punishment or reprisal. Under these circumstances, the parent has to be careful not to appear shocked or traumatized by the use of street terms for sexual behaviors. An example will clarify.

> **NED**, age eleven, came home from playing in the park and asked if he could speak to his mother. It seems that while he was shooting hoops in the park, he had to use the public rest room and while standing at the urinal was approached by an older man who had been trying to see his privates. Ned then said: "The man offered to pay me ten dollars if I would let him suck my cock! Mom, what does that mean? It scared me so much that I ran, but if it happens again I want to know what he was going to do. Was he trying to hurt me?"
>
> Ned's mother was able to discuss oral sex with him in a simple and rudimentary way and to tell him positively he had done right not only in running but in coming to tell her what happened and to ask questions that were bothering him.

Questions for Discussion

1. If you are a parent, could you have handled Ned's question as well as his mother did?

2. If you are a teenager and this happened to you, could you have gone home and discussed it with your mother or your father?

3. What effects do you think the experience in the public rest room had on Ned, if any?

4. What would have been the effects had Ned submitted to the old man's request?

5. What else should Ned have done while still in the park?

Parental Denial

Sexual abuse is so horrible a concept and so terrifying to parents that a form of unconscious denial takes place with the resulting perception: "Not my child!" This perception has become prevalent in today's families. A number of scenarios and examples will help illuminate this.

Parent Teacher Association (PTA) Attendance. While PTA attendance has always been low, in the 1991–1992 school year, it was at an all-time low. I speak at many of these groups on the prevention of child sexual abuse, and audience attendance, even for this most-important subject, is less than 5 percent of the parents in the schools. Leaders of the PTAs inform me that the attendees are the "regulars" and that the subject of my presentation does not increase or decrease attendance, nor does it bring out new faces. Parents are simply apathetic and always too busy. It is easy to infer, then, that the subject of child sexual abuse prevention is of low interest to a frighteningly large percentage of parents of grammar school, junior high school, and high school students.

Day Trips, Camping Overnight, and Other Trip Permissions. As I have stated above, sex offenders who prey on children (pedophiles) and adolescents (hebophiles) consistently have reported to me that they never had a problem in getting permission to take children on field trips, either for a day or for a weekend, scouting trips of all lengths, overnight tutoring sessions at a teacher's apartment or home, or any other function. The amazing fact, as mentioned earlier, is that few if any of the parents signing these permission slips had ever met the teacher in person or knew anything about him or her except that the individual was their child's teacher. The most common phrase I have heard and continue to hear over and over again from the molesters is, "Parents give us their children to molest because they don't care enough to check up on who we are or what we are about. We become convenient baby-sitters for a day or weekend, and that is all that they care about." Of course, this is an attempt to project the blame for their deviations onto the parents, but there is more than a kernel of truth in what they say. A frightening example will help prove this further (see also the case of **Don**, in chapter 1).

VIC bought an abandoned Baptist church in an upper-middle-class area and opened his "Church of Satan Resurrected." He consulted a lawyer and had a specific parental-permission form printed that gave him the right to initiate preadolescent and adolescent children, mostly boys, into his new religion. There were some fifteen levels or degrees of initiation, a majority of them containing sexual acting out and behavior by the initiates both with Vic as high priest and with other members of the religion under the strict supervision and direction of Vic. Over a two-year period, some 550 preteen and teenage boys and some five to ten girls were inducted into this religion, all with legally signed permission slips, witnessed and notarized. Naturally, the details of the initiations were not listed in the permission slips "since they were secret."

One diabolical element of the initiations must be mentioned at this point. Each new initiate had to lie naked on a marble altar. Vic in full satanic regalia would chant an invocation and then drip hot, melted wax from a black candle onto the abdomen of the initiate, just above the navel. When the wax hardened it was ripped off leaving a scar ("Vic's mark") that signified that the initiate now belonged to Satan and personally to Vic. The rest of the initiation was sexual in content and ended in an orgy involving all present with the initiate.

Shockingly, none of the parents ever asked for the details of the initiations, and the religion continued along its merry way for several years until two of the boys reported the sexual activities to a teacher (note: not to their parents) at school who reported the abuse. Vic was tried only for the abuse with the two boys and given a minimal sentence in a treatment unit for sex offenders in his state. It was only after a long period of therapy that Vic began to realize the extent of the damage he had done and reported the larger number of victims to his therapist. Unbelievable? Yes, but documented fact.

Questions for Discussion

1. Do you believe that Vic was a real satanist?

2. As a hebophile, why would Vic choose satanism to obtain victims?

3. Did Vic's being a satanic minister fulfill any needs besides sexual needs?

4. Did sexual molestation under these circumstances add any traumatic effects to the survivors that would not have existed, say, if Vic was a neighbor? (Refer to chapter 6.)

5. Why do you feel that the majority of Vic's victims have not come forward for treatment?

Still another case involving childcare volunteers recently shocked the state of New Jersey. It follows.

The executive director of a local Big Brothers organization and several members of his board of trustees were arrested and convicted of sexually molesting several boys in their care. They would pick up the boys and take them home for an overnight or a weekend, shower with them, and slowly and gradually lead up to and engage in sexual behavior with them. While the case was still going through the legal process, I was asked to do a "consultation-training" session at the headquarters of this organization. What I discovered still shocks me. Little or no background checks were being made on volunteers prior to the exposure and arrest of the leaders. I was asked to look at their application forms and randomly picked one up that had just been approved but not activated. I immediately noticed that this volunteer had listed three other Big Brothers groups as references. Upon inquiry, I discovered that none of the references had been checked.

During a coffee break in the training, I asked the director to telephone any one of the other groups, and she did. Not to my surprise but to her horror, she was informed that this volunteer had been asked to leave after several boys had made informal complaints about his sexual hinting and his touchy-feely behavior with them. No formal complaints were made to the authorities in order not to embarrass the organization or the boys involved. Here was a hebophile being approved for his third Big Brothers assignment. The alibi given to me by one of the staff at this organization was that they were desperate for volunteers since there were more fatherless boys than there were volunteers. Couldn't they see that the molesters are aware of this situation through advertisements, television, talk shows, and so on? This was the time for more, not less, caution and screening. Of additional interest (and disgust) to me was the fact that board members were not screened at all.

Questions for Discussion

1. Why did this group of influential and wealthy pedophiles and hebophiles organize a Big Brothers chapter in their community?

2. Why was the community so blind to what was going on?

3. Why did these perverts choose fatherless boys to molest?

4. Would screening have totally eliminated the problem?

5. What distorted values are involved in filling staff needs without screening?

Anyone who comes into personal contact with children or adolescents and has power, influence, or control over them should be very carefully screened and continuously supervised if we are to decrease the continuously rising number of victims of child and adolescent abuse.

DEFINITIONS OF PARENTAL ROLES
AND RESPONSIBILITIES

As I have said above, in today's pressure-filled world with all of its economic problems and the phenomenon of the two-working-parent families, it is not surprising in the least that children and adolescents go looking for someone outside the home to help meet their needs for attention, affection, love, and understanding. In order for parents to fulfill their parental roles and responsibilities, they need to know all they can of the modus operandi of the abusers. In this spirit, let us consider the following true scenario.

> **MR. HOWIE** was a junior high school science teacher whom the children liked and who was good at his job. He was always more comfortable with children than he was with adults and so spent more time with them. On one weekend a month, he held a science-oriented, overnight camping trip at a local lake for "special boys" in his class who showed an intense interest in science. During these camping trips, each of four boys would be molested. Now let us look at an actual diary-verified trip in order to try to understand why none of the boys in over five years of these science trips ever complained or reported.
>
> The trip began on a Friday afternoon after school, at approximately 3:30 P.M. The group arrived at the campsite around

4:30 p.m., set up tents and other camping paraphernalia, and finally were ready for a skinny-dip in the lake. They all played around with Mr. Howie, who "tested" to see how far he could go with physical touch by lifting and throwing the boys around in the lake. An "accidental" grope, here and there, usually resulted in silly laughing and smiles, and Mr. Howie felt safe and assured. Dinner followed with the boys being allowed to cook and eat whatever they desired (contrary to what happened at home). They did not have to dress or could cook in their underwear. A campfire and ghost stories followed, and whoever told the best ghost story could sleep in Mr. Howie's tent with him. Mr. Howie suggested (never insisted) that they sleep in the nude to feel how great it was (again not allowed in most of their homes), and this gave him the opportunity to offer a back massage. During the massage he would see how far he could go, exciting and stimulating the boy in the buttocks area and between his legs and after five minutes of massage would ask him to turn over. Frontal massage led to massage of his penis, and masturbation followed rapidly. For many of the boys this was their first masturbatory experience and their first orgasm. Therefore, a positive imprint was formed. Mr. Howie would then thank the boy for allowing him to massage him, never mentioning the masturbation and never asking for any reciprocal behavior. The entire sexual molestation episode never lasted more than ten to fifteen minutes.

Saturday was spent on science activities, looking for plant and animal specimens, hunting for lake specimens, and so on. Playtime was a free-for-all and often included wrestling, either nude or in underpants. A skinny-dip followed in the lake and then an afternoon nap. Again, using some form of contest, one of the boys was chosen to nap with Mr. Howie and received his "massage." That evening, the same freedom of food choice and the same contest were utilized, and a third boy got to sleep and be massaged by Mr. Howie. Sunday morning was spent in a science class with actual specimens from the lake area utilized. Lunch followed and then a nap, and a fourth boy won a chance to sleep with and be massaged by Mr. Howie. When packing for the return trip was completed, Mr. Howie held a "meeting" with the group during which he emphasized how much he enjoyed this group of six boys and how special they were to him. He asked if they would like to go camping again and received a unanimous "yes!" He then instilled the need for secrecy of all of the details of the weekend since both parents and other teachers might disagree with Mr. Howie's permissiveness and physical contact, especially the skinny-dipping with his students. All six boys promised and swore an oath and agreed that their parents and the other old fuddy-duddy teachers would be jealous. No mention of the massage or sleeping arrangements was made.

Questions for Discussion

1. How would you characterize Mr. Howie?

2. What was the chronology of Mr. Howie's seduction technique?

3. Why did the boys do what Mr. Howie suggested?

4. Did Mr. Howie choose a certain type of boy to take on his camping trips?

5. Why did the boys remain loyal to Mr. Howie knowing of his intentions?

If we look at the time involved in the sexual molestation that Mr. Howie perpetrated, it totaled one hour, more or less, of a trip that took over fifty hours. The majority of what occurred on the camping trip was fun, interesting, and good learning material. This is how Mr. Howie justified his behavior, but it was also how the boys perceived and remembered the trips and became one of the reasons they never reported the abuse. None of the original six boys ever refused to go on one of Mr. Howie's science-camping trips, nor did other groups of six boys as the years progressed. In fact, had Mr. Howie not been a pedophile/hebophile, he would have been a real hero.

Good Touch/Bad Touch Training

In order to stop the Mr. Howies of the world before their first attempted abuse, children and their parents must have a relationship that offers opportunities for communication and more than a "Did you have a good time?" question when the children return from trips like these. This communication must also be used to instill values and morals and to discuss realistically but not frighteningly the possibilities of sexual molestation. "Good touch/bad touch" type games and discussions are one of the ideal ways to accomplish this teaching.

Quality Time

Replacing the one-question approach to a child's day at school or a three-day camping trip also must become a priority. We often take our children for granted and give them a very low priority in our time schedules. The materialistic attitude that I am a good parent if I provide a good home, nice clothes, and food and medical care for my children is absolute nonsense. Regardless of how tired a parent is after a hard day's work, time must be made for talking to (not at) our children. In working with families experiencing problems with their children, I have found, as I discussed above (see p. 120 for details), that the best time for this is when dinner is finished. This is a period when real quality time between parents and their children can be built into the day.

Quality time, however, means more than talking or discussing problems. Going to the park, playing baseball or football in the backyard, taking camping trips, taking in a movie or watching a rented VHS with some popcorn at home, attending a child's or adolescent's sports games or parade band event, attending honors awards presentations, vacationing together as a family, painting a room, and so on, can be quality time if the child or adolescent has some say in choosing the activity and receives equal time with others involved in the activity.

Teens, especially, prefer to share problems or discuss quandaries in a nonformal, relaxed setting, usually following some activity such as a swim in the lake or while fixing a car or cooking dinner or simply while walking in the park or the woods.

Even for busy parents, quality time is possible since it is not the amount of time spent that is important; rather, what is important is the content, openness, and communication during the time spent with the child or adolescent.

CAN PARENTS PREVENT ALL ABUSE
AND MOLESTATION?

The realistic answer to the question in the heading above is no. Both children and adolescents are independent human beings with minds and wills of their own. Simply being exposed to the best moral, religious, and ethical training that parents are capable of providing is sometimes not enough. There is a particular type of personality that learns only by doing and often by getting burned in the process. In other words, these people learn from experience and by making mistakes. This group will always be vulnerable to the more sophisticated and cunning sexual predators with infinite patience and skill to get what they want. I have treated offenders who seductively worked on a child or adolescent for a year or more, always with the goal of "getting into their pants." Unfortunately, with the group we have just discussed they are too frequently successful in their endeavors. An example will clarify.

WOODY was a thirty-three-year-old graduate student at a well known university, studying sociology. Woody had been molested by a neighbor from the time he was eleven until he was thirteen but had never told anyone or resolved the resulting problem of sexual confusion and a bisexual orientation. His only experiences, prior to entering graduate school, were heterosexual, although he persistently found himself attracted to other male graduate students and often masturbated to fantasies of having sex with them.

At the end of his first semester, his advisor suggested that he spend the summer doing an externship at a local military academy where he might find a suitable topic, as well as subjects, for his master's thesis. Woody agreed.

The school was happy to have Woody for the summer and offered him an additional way to make some money, by being a dormitory supervisor for the senior boys. This involved living at the institution with room and board provided, saving Woody about a thousand dollars. He readily agreed.

From the first night, as he was supervising showering activities, Woody was uncomfortably attracted to one particular fourteen-year-old cadet, **BIF**. The attraction seemed mutual, and Bif took any opportunity or excuse to talk to or to be with Woody.

Woody was sure that Bif reminded him of someone from his past, but he could not remember who. All that he knew was that he was sexually attracted to the boy and masturbated nightly (often two or three times) to fantasies of sexually seducing Bif.

Woody planned the seduction carefully and in minute detail. He found every possible reason to spend time with Bif: he assigned him as dorm adjutant, put him in charge of the laundry pickup detail, took him with him to purchase supplies for the school, assigned him to work with him cleaning the gymnasium and pool, and so on. For all of these tasks, Bif was given special privileges such as spending time in Woody's room after lights-out, having special nighttime snacks, watching extra television, and getting extra gym and swim time with Woody. Bif became emotionally dependent on Woody, and when his parents did not show up for a scheduled leave (which was quite often), he and Woody spent the weekends together.

During all of this time, Woody solicited information from Bif that would aid the seduction. He chose Bif's strong interest in scuba diving, which he had never experienced. Woody promised to buy a complete scuba outfit for Bif and to allow him to practice in the school's pool. Bif was elated. Woody decided that Bif was hooked and asked him for a "favor." He told him that he was "horny" and had no outlet and badly needed, at least, to be masturbated. (He had caught Bif masturbating in the showers on several occasions and simply smiled saying: "Have fun and take all the time you need.")

Bif, desperate for the scuba gear and frightened of losing Woody's attention and affection, agreed and thus began a relationship that Bif believed would last forever. Woody had taken his time (some three months after choosing his victim), and eventually his patience and persistence paid off. Only when Woody returned to college in the fall and failed to contact Bif or to purchase the scuba gear did Bif realize that he had been manipulated and used. He was too ashamed to tell anyone and some ten years later was arrested for attempting to sexually molest a thirteen-year-old boy in the public rest room of a public park. Only in therapy did the story of Woody emerge and, even then, only under an agreement of confidentiality.

Girls are equally at risk to the patient, seductive molester. An example will clarify.

LESLIE, a fifteen-year-old high school student, was enamored of her science teacher, MR. DEXTER. In September, at the beginning of the school year, Mr. Dexter had chosen four of the girls in his new science class for possible or probable seduction. In the last five years, his "scoring" record had been quite good, and he had averaged two to three girls from each class for sexual molestation, a "special privilege" in his egomaniacal mind. Safety was a prime consideration for Mr. Dexter as he was married, had daughters of his own (whom he had fantasized about but could not conceive molesting, as it was against his morals), and was a well-paid teacher in an upper-middle-class area. Pleasure was his primary goal in all of his activities, and he felt that he had reached the ideal home and work situation, so caution was a primary consideration.

He began his careful weeding out process of the four potential victims through essays that would tell him more about their
character, family life, social involvements (especially if there was
a boyfriend), sexual knowledge and experience, and so on, all
of which he somehow included in his science (biology) class-
content. No one questioned these essays, and they were an
important tool to help him meet his needs. Leslie had been chosen since she had a minimal relationship with her two working
parents, lived her life quite independently, did not have a steady
boyfriend, and had remained a virgin. For Mr. Dexter's needs,
Leslie was ideal.

He made her a lab assistant, a prestigious position for a student in his classes, which entitled her to extra time to work on
special projects with Mr. Dexter after school. Mr. Dexter used
these special periods to begin touching, carefully seeing how far
he could go. Leslie responded positively and liked both the special attention as well as the physical contact, which did not exist
in her home with her parents.

Next, Mr. Dexter chose reproductive biology as a special topic
for her to research and to report on in class. Beginning with frogs,
Leslie was to advance up the biological chain until she reached
human beings. Each stage of the research had to be rehearsed
with Mr. Dexter in the lab after school the day before it would be
presented to the entire class. Mr. Dexter chose these times to try
to excite Leslie erotically by comparing the animal reproduction
to that of humans and by asking probing questions about Leslie's
own experiences (for example, Had she ever seen an erect male
penis?). When Leslie replied that she hadn't, Mr. Dexter offered
to show her his own whenever she wanted; all she had to do was
ask. (In this way he could put all the blame and responsibility on
her for whatever happened.)

At midsemester, Mr. Dexter and Leslie had spent a great many
hours after school together and were at a hugging and kissing
stage upon arrival and leaving the laboratory. The topic of human
reproduction would be the next class project after midsemester
break, and Mr. Dexter felt that this subject needed additional

effort and time to prepare during the break when no other students would be at school or be using the lab. Leslie agreed, and Mr. Dexter asked for drawings of both the male and female reproductive anatomy as well as an insemination drawing to be made for presentation to the class. Leslie said she didn't know how since she had never been involved sexually, and Mr. Dexter simply smiled and replied: "I'm sure you can find a male model." During their next session, Leslie asked Mr. Dexter if he would be the model, and in triumph the seduction occurred and progressed to full intercourse.

Unfortunately, Leslie thought she was in love and therefore never reported what had occurred but remained "available" for Mr. Dexter, whenever his need arose. There were three more Leslies over the next three years before Mr. Dexter was finally exposed and incarcerated with a "score" of nine virgin students, although he was charged with only one count of sexual molestation. He spent some five years in prison, manipulating everyone including his therapist and the administration and was released early on parole for "excellent therapy progress and behavior." Where he is today only God knows.

Next in our discussion is the other type of parent, those who abuse, the incestuous parents.

5

INCESTUOUS PARENTS

As stated in the last chapter, in addition to non-abusive parents, there are unfortunately parents who are incestuous and sexually abuse their own children. While the damage from any sexual assault or molestation is horrific and can have lifelong effects, the damage from an incestuous molestation is doubly serious. There is, first, the same sexual traumas that result from sexual molestation by a stranger, and then there is, second, the added trauma of betrayal of the relationships of love and trust, dependency, and identity that exist only between parents and their children. This double trauma makes reporting, confronting in a courtroom, and then treatment twice as hard as in any other sexual trauma, including forcible rape.

LIMITING THE CATEGORY TO ONLY
NATURAL PARENTS

I limit incest to natural or birth parents because I have found an essential difference between sexual abuse by natural parents and that by a second parent-substitute group including foster parents, adoptive parents, common-law parents, and live-in parents. Even though states or counties charge the latter group with incest, I label this type of abuse *caretaker incest*. Throughout interviewing and treatment of this second group, the dynamics and characteristics of pedophiles or hebophiles are usually uncovered, and the essential dynamics of true incest parents are glaringly missing.

An understanding of the dynamics of the incestuous parent is necessary to explore the depths of this increasing form of sexual molestation. One attitude or belief that is always present in the incestuous group but never present in the caretaker group is: "I own the child, and therefore I can do whatever I want with him/her!" With this statement, incestuous parents differentiate themselves from all other parent-substitutes and provide themselves with the seemingly perfect rationalization for their perverse behavior. Incestuous parents insist that they have a "natural right" to have sex with their children.

Incestuous parents do not consider themselves as abnormal or as being child or adolescent molesters or sex perverts. In fact, they harbor strong feelings and "principles" against sexual molestation, considering the child or adolescent sex molester "the lowest form of scum on the face of the earth." They make statements such as: "How could anyone molest someone else's child or adolescent?" "What gives these sick individuals the right to touch someone else's child or adolescent?" "If I were the father of one of the victims, I would kill the bastard who touched him [or her] and not in a pleasant or easy manner either."

An example of an incestuous father who made all of the above statements will help concretize the matter.

GENE, a forty-four-year-old police chief of an upper-middle-class community, is an incestuous father who, over a period of some ten years, molested all of his three children, a daughter, ELLA, fifteen years old, who reported the incest to her guidance counselor at school, and JORDAN, eleven, and JAMIE, fourteen, her two brothers who were not known as Gene's victims until this fact emerged in his treatment some fourteen months after his arrest and incarceration.

Gene was a pillar of his community. He was involved in every community organization and held office in most. He was also considered as the "best police chief that this city had ever had." No one wanted to believe Ella, and she became known as a "lying bitch, an ungrateful daughter, a troublemaker, and so on." Her life was miserable.

The denial and disbelief were so great that the city council made a bus trip to the treatment facility where Gene was housed to meet with the administration and the therapist to tell them that Gene was innocent and that Ella had lied. What the city council did not know was that by the time of their trip, Gene had already confessed not only that he was guilty of molesting Ella but that he had also molested Jordan and Jamie for several years.[1]

Gene's seductive pattern was quite typical of incestuous parents. He told Ella that her mother was no longer attractive or sexually stimulating to him and that if she did not cooperate, since he was only showing her how much he loved her, he would have to find a lover outside the house and that would mean divorce, loss of their expensive home, diminution of their lifestyle (changing from a wonderful high school to a public school in a poorer section of town, and so on), and shame and embarrassment in front of all of her friends. When this ploy did not work, he would then threaten to go to her brothers, especially to Jordan, the youngest and her favorite. If he did that, he said, "It would be her fault." For all of these reasons, Ella submitted to Gene for some ten years before attending a sexual abuse seminar in her school and realizing that what her father was doing was wrong. She then reported the incident.

Where Jordan and Jamie were concerned, no charges were filed, but by former agreement I saw them in individual and then joint therapy. The boys were ashamed and terribly embarrassed to discuss what occurred, and it took almost two months before Jordan told me the following story. Whenever his father came home frustrated and "horny" and Ella was not available, he took one or both of the boys to the attic, made them strip, then put on a training bra and panties and talked in a falsetto voice while he stimulated himself. He then made them lie on their stomachs and forcibly sodomized one while the other was made to watch and to massage his back, buttocks, and insert a finger into his anus until he reached orgasm. The boys, if they had not reached

---

1. As in too many cases of incest, only Ella, the complainant, was interviewed and questioned; the remaining siblings were not. This often occurs when a girl reports and her siblings are males. As will be discussed below, the adage of "any port in a storm" woefully applies to many incestuous parents.

orgasm by this point, had to bring each other to orgasm while Gene watched.

Gene, when finished with the boys, would tell them what beautiful girls they made and that he knew that they enjoyed the sex with him. He warned them that if they ever mentioned what happened, even to Ella, he would tell all of their friends that they were fags and that he had caught them having sex with each other. This assured their silence since he added that no one would believe them and that his word as chief of police would always be believed.

In the beginning of therapy, Gene rationalized his behavior: "After all, they're my kids; I created them; I've clothed and fed them and given them a fantastic home and the best schools and vacations possible. I certainly deserve something from them in return." It took several months for this attitude to change. The change was triggered by a special occasion. I had agreed to run a group with a female therapist in the community who treated female victims of sexual abuse, primarily incest victims. The group was to meet in the treatment center[2] with a group of offenders who had volunteered. This group was composed of rapists and incestuous fathers, and Gene was one of them.

One of the women was an incest survivor, and she sat opposite Gene and confronted him for the two hours that the session ran while emoting quite heavily. She told him how her father had made her feel and how she still lives with that feeling daily, how it has ruined several potentially wonderful relationships with men and how often she contemplates suicide. Gene sat stunned and, for the first time since I had known him, was speechless.

Several days after this group, Gene asked to see me and told me how powerfully he had been affected by that young lady. He said that it was the first time since he had been in therapy that he could understand how Ella, his daughter, felt. He felt even worse about his two sons and fairly accurately predicted the

---

2. The Adult Diagnostic and Treatment Center, Avenel, New Jersey, where I was then the Director of Professional Services.

kinds of negative emotions and negative self-judgments that they were experiencing. He cried for the first time and then asked if I could arrange for him to talk first to his daughter and later on to his sons. (There will be more discussion of these meetings in chapter 13, on treatment.)

Questions for Discussion

1. What defective "values" made Gene's molestation of his children easier?

2. Who would you, as a parent, have believed, Gene or Ella?

3. Who would you, as a teenager, have believed, Gene or Ella?

4. Why didn't the boys report their abuse to anyone? Was it simply because they felt they would not have been believed or were there other reasons?

5. Why didn't the children's mother become suspicious of what was going on or do you believe she did?

The case was taken from my files on incestuous parents and their perceptions, beliefs, rationalizations, and feelings. Surprisingly, I believe that such parents sincerely believe what they are saying and do not see what they are doing as wrong. Even when they are "training" their child or adolescent to submit to their sexual seductions, they make statements that secrecy is necessary only because other people do not understand them, or that what they do in their families is private and nobody else's business, or that exposure would mean a poorer lifestyle for them and loss of friends, schools, and so on.

Too often, the guilt that the child or adolescent feels is by itself sufficient to assure silence. This is especially true of adolescents in stage 4 (see chapter 3) where a need for acceptance and approval from peers is paramount.

REASONS FOR INCEST

While the reasons for incest are as varied as the incestuous parents, I have found a list of common reasons, traits, and dynamics that differ from traits found in the nonincestuous pedophiles and hebophiles.

The Incestuous Parent Was a Victim of Incest

In over 95 percent of the cases of incest that I have treated, the perpetrators were themselves survivors of incest and offered as rationalizations for their actions the common survivor fear of being the "only one" and the "principle" that because their parents committed incest with them, they believed it was fine to do the same with their children. Further, in many cases the incestuous parents of a multiple-child family give an older child or adolescent the "permission" to molest one or more of the younger siblings. An example will clarify.

> **PETER** is an incestuous father who victimized all of his eight children (six girls and two boys). His sexual abuses remained a "secret" and went undiscovered for over forty years until one daughter under hypnosis remembered. He is now in his eighties and comes to treatment under pressure from his daughters, who threaten to make his incest public if he doesn't show up.
>
> Peter himself was molested by his father from age five to nine in preparation for his being initiated into the secret subgroup of a well-known service-oriented organization, which practices satanic rituals and uses the children of their members for sex in these rituals. Peter's father sodomized him on every possible occasion and rationalized his incestuous behavior on his needing to prepare his son for this great honor. During the four years of molestation, Peter's father shared with Peter that he had been molested by his father, Peter's grandfather, and that the grandfather had been molested by his father, and so on, back some five or six generations in Europe.

Peter's favorite sexual behavior was sodomizing his sons as frequently as possible. He always told them that sex with males was so much better than sex with a woman and that they pleased him more than his wife or any of their six sisters. Peter was totally unaware of the damage that this statement did to the two boys and only discovered it in later years.

As a "perk" and in preparation for becoming fathers themselves, Peter, when he was finished with the boys, stated: "Now that I've taken your manhood from you, why don't you get it back by fucking one of your sisters." He thus encouraged the two boys to molest their sisters *with his permission and under his supervision.* They agreed and did so on many occasions while Peter taught them different techniques and masturbated as he supervised.

A major difference in the incestuous molestations of the sisters by their two brothers was that they were always sensitive, warm, caring, and loving as opposed to the father's coldness, cruelty, and treatment of the girls like objects rather than people. When I asked the boys about this in therapy, they explained that they were trying to give to their sisters what they had never gotten from their father.

Needless to say, all of the family is in treatment with many problems and sexual dysfunctions, suicide attempts, bulimia and anorexia problems, prolonged depressions, and child-rearing difficulties. More on this family in chapter 13 on treatment.

Questions for Discussion

1. How could this incredible molestation of eight children have gone on for so long without being detected?

2. Where was the mother during these lengthy episodes?

3. Why do you think that none of the eight children ever told their mother what was happening?

4. What do you feel the relationship between the mother and the children was and also between the husband and the wife?

5. Do you feel the influence of the secret organization was a real motive or only an excuse for Peter's deviant behavior?

The Incestuous Parent's Values on Love Are Defective

As can be easily understood, "love" for the distorted parent is equated with sex, obedience, submission, slavery, and all other proofs that meet his or her needs. This distorted value is taught to the children both verbally and by example. The old adage "If you really loved me, you would do this or that for me" readily applies to these parents; however, where the children of these parents are concerned, there is no choice involved. If the use of pressure and force is necessary, that also becomes another parental right in this group and will result not only in sexual assault but also in physical assault and brutality. For these parents to state "I was a strict disciplinarian" describes only the surface of their behavior and the rationalization for it.

The Incestuous Parent Uses the Parental Right to Teach Sex Education as a Justification

I have heard, over and over, from this group of deviates the "principle" that "It is the parents' right to teach their children sex education in any way they choose and when they choose." This includes teaching by example, with the parent sexually demonstrating on his or her own child. This type of behavior is not isolated to father's alone, as is commonly thought. The following example will clarify.

OLIVER was incestuously molested by his alcoholic mother from age fourteen. His father, a truck driver, was never around, and his sister was only five years old and very timid, weak, and dependent.

Whenever Oliver's mother was drunk, it was his job to care for her. One night as he was putting her to bed, she pulled him to her, undressed him, played with his penis until he was erect, and then pulled him on top of herself and forced him into her. Oliver says that when he realized what she was doing, he pushed her away and ran out of the room and out of the house.

When Oliver returned and his mother had sobered up, he asked her why she had sexually molested him. She replied: "It's about time you knew what sex is all about, and I don't want you learning from the kids on the street."

Oliver's mother continued to seduce him whenever she was intoxicated, but he usually ran out of the house and stayed away overnight, mostly at a friend's house.

Oliver also had and continues to have recurring nightmares about his father coming to his bed at night and fondling his penis to erection and masturbating him. However, while his memories of his mother's molestations are conscious, his suspicions about his father molesting him exist only in nightmares.

Oliver was also abused my a male teacher when he was either fourteen or fifteen years old. The teacher took him into his office, pulled his pants down, and masturbated him. When Oliver tried to get away, the teacher threatened him, so he submitted. This incident (a one-time occurrence) happened prior to his mother's first molestation and "imprinted," remaining a problem even today. (More detailed discussion of "imprinting" will be included in chapter 13, on treatment issues.")

There were many other occasions over the next three years when Oliver and his mother had sex. They showered together, and he would touch her all over, especially on her breasts. She would then perform oral sex (fellatio) on him, which he enjoyed immensely but then felt severe guilt over to the point of attempting suicide.

When Oliver was sixteen, the following incident occurred. He had had a bad day at school, came home depressed but also "horny," and found that his mother had passed out. He heard the shower running and saw his sister in it. He quickly undressed, entered the shower with her, pressed himself against her, and played with her breasts with one hand while inserting a finger into her vagina with the other, all the while fantasizing that he was with his mother. His sister thought that he was raping her, and she was seriously traumatized. She was then only seven years old.

For the next thirteen years, the guilt increased, especially after his mother died with the incestuous issues left unresolved. Oliver again attempted suicide. His sister told her father what Oliver had done in the shower, and he reported it to the police. Oliver pled guilty to protect his sister from having to testify and was given probation with intensive therapy on a weekly basis.

Presently, Oliver is in treatment and suffers not only from recurring depression (severe) but also from sexual desire-phase dysfunction. Having sex is traumatic for him since, when he is aroused, he cannot control his mental thoughts and fantasies of the sexual acts that he was involved in with his now-deceased mother. Treatment will be a long and difficult task involving "letting go" of the guilt and accepting his role in the adolescent incest both with his mother and then with his sister.

Questions for Discussion

1. Do you believe Oliver's statement that he pushed his mother away when she was molesting him?

2. Why do you think Oliver was molested by both his teacher and his mother (and possibly his father, as well)?

3. Is it possible that his seven-year-old sister mistook his finger for his penis while in the shower? Do you believe Oliver's version of this incident?

4. Do you feel that there is a difference in detrimental effects when a child, especially a boy, is molested by his mother rather than by his father?

5. In your opinion, was "not being the only one" involved in Oliver's molestation of his sister?

Cases like Oliver's are probably one of the least reported and cause the most traumatic damage in later life. The cases that are most often reported involve fathers incestuously molesting their daughters. It appears that, in our society, mothers are considered "sacred" and not to be criticized or even considered capable of incest. Today, this attitude has begun to change.

Survivors of incest suffer from all forms of sexual dysfunction: in males the most common problems are impotence, desire-phase dysfunction, and premature or retarded ejaculation; in females the common sexual dysfunctions are: dyspareunia, vaginismus, desire-phase dysfunction, and anorgasmia. In both sexes there tends to be a sexual aversion problem that seriously affects all adult relationships. Additionally, in males who believe that they are heterosexual but who were incestuously assaulted by their fathers, older brothers, or other older males, there are ongoing homosexual attractions and erotic reactions (resulting from the imprinting) that produce shame, guilt, and fear of being abnormal and that can be treated only by qualified sex therapists trained in this area of survivor treatment. I will cover some of the specific techniques used in these cases in chapter 13.

The Incestuous Parent's Partner Does Nothing to Stop the Incest

In the cases of **GENE** and **OLIVER**, the partner of the incestuous parent did nothing. Gene's wife, also a pillar of the community and involved in many social functions, liked her lifestyle and the fact that she and Gene could send their children to the best schools, dress them in the latest fashions, and take them on trips all over the world. She did not want anything to change. Therefore, even when she began to suspect that something was wrong and that there was a problem between Gene and the children, she did nothing. She never discussed with any of them what their day had been like while she was away at some social gathering and Gene was home. She never asked why Ella had red eyes from crying or why the boys cowered in Gene's presence. She also did not question the boys when she discovered bloodstains in their underwear, nor did she take them to a doctor, although the thought crossed her mind. She saw her marriage and her family through rose-colored glasses and, since the children did not complain about their father, preferred to believe that all was well.

Oliver's father, when he was home, noticed a strange closeness between the boy and his mother and that she was constantly touching his hair, rubbing his back, and showing other physical signs of affection to him that were more than "motherly." He also noticed that the two of them appeared to have "secrets" and would stop talking when he entered the room. There were winks and smiles between them that he could not comprehend, but he never questioned any of these disturbing signs. He liked his job and the money it brought him, so he did not want to find any problem that might demand he be home more often, meaning he would have to leave the truck driving he loved. As a result, the molestations continued unimpeded and unexposed.

It is important to note, at this juncture, that there are also partners of an incestuous parent who are aware of what is going on and who do nothing about it. When they confess to this fact, some of the reasons (excuses) they report are:

- "I was afraid that he would harm either the children or me."

- "I had nowhere to go and no skills to find employment that would care for the children and myself."

- "I've never been on my own and would not be able to handle all of the pressures, the children, and the bills."

- "I really didn't believe that the sex was harming the children. They seemed to be enjoying it."

- "Who would believe me? The children were too afraid to tell anyone, so it would be my word against their father/mother."

The list goes on interminably. The one common thread in these cases is self-concern rather than concern for the children. True, many of these partners of an incestuous parent are inadequate, passive, frightened, and helpless, but there are almost as many who are concerned only about their own needs, careers, friends, and lifestyles rather than being truly concerned about their children.

Some partners of incestuous parents simply do not want to know what, if anything, is going on. They never question their partner's behavior or handling of the children. If one or more of the children come to them to discuss the offending parent, they are either too busy, change the subject, or refuse to listen to anything negative about the parent "who is so good to you and who takes care of all of us." Children, in these situations, quickly get the message that there is at least tacit approval of the offending parent's behavior and that their only choice is to submit. Running-away behaviors, suicide attempts, passing on their anger to other adult authority figures (teachers, ministers, salespeople, and so on) or onto younger children (younger siblings, classmates, neighbors), and imitative sexual molesting of other innocent but inadequate individuals all occur in these survivors before exposure and treatment. These issues are an essential part of the treatment process if, and when, these survivors become involved in therapy.

The Inadequate Parent Uses Incestuous Conduct for Revenge

I have seen a considerable number of cases of incestuous conduct on the part of a parent that did not fit into any of the above categories. The majority of these cases involved men (the case of **OLIVER** and his mother was a definite exception) who were grossly inadequate, controlled and bullied by their partners, and never able to express either anger or disagreement with their marital partner.[3] A sexual

---

3. I am using the term "marital partner" rather than either "wife" or "husband" since I have seen this phenomenon in homosexual relationships as well where one of the partners had previously been married and had children (usually as a cover-up for his or her true homosexual preference) and in some way had retained custody of his or her children.

"trigger" usually precedes the first incestuous assault or molestation and usually, although not always, involves some criticism either of his or her body or sexual performance. Refusal to have sex is also a common "trigger" in these cases. Men in this group who are told they have small penises believe that their young daughter or son (usually prepubescent on this first occurrence) will not see their penis as small since they have had no other adult to compare with as their mother "must have."

In therapy, these individuals, both males and females, are conscious of the revenge element in their behavior and often blame their partners for the incestuous acts. They say things like:

- "If she hadn't made fun of my penis size, I wouldn't have molested my daughter."

- "If he weren't always drunk and impotent, I wouldn't have gone to my teenage son."

- "If he hadn't died (or deserted/divorced me), I wouldn't have had sex with my son."

- "If my wife wasn't cheating on me, I wouldn't have screwed my daughter."

These and other such rationalizations are common in this group, as is the fact that no matter what the criticism of the partner was, the molester never confronted him or her with it. It was suffered in silence, and, internally, the anger seethed and often became rage. An example will clarify.

ARNIE was a short, thin, boyish-looking, thirty-two-year-old male who had been frightened of women and interpersonal relationships for most of his adolescent and adult life.

Once a week, Arnie bowled with a group of men from work and then went with them to a local bar for a few beers. One night he was approached by TERRY, a thirty-five-year-old divorcée who told him he was "cute" while feeling his leg. Arnie panicked and just sat there smiling and said nothing. His friends laughed over the incident and encouraged Terry to "take Arnie under her wing" and to steal his "cherry."

Terry was amazed that Arnie was still a virgin and instantly decided that he was going to be hers. This way, she wouldn't have to undo bad habits as she had tried with her husband, and she could teach Arnie to perform sexually the way she wanted and liked.

Arnie was no match for Terry. Within a week, she had him in bed, where he was terrified and lost since he knew relatively nothing about sex. After "teaching" and humiliating Arnie for hours (he had had a premature ejaculation before Terry was ready), Terry finally inserted his penis into her and "coached" Arnie in how to have intercourse (her way: female on top). Arnie couldn't wait for it all to be over and was sore for a week afterward. He much preferred masturbation to this first intercourse experience. He also detested oral sex with Terry as she was not exactly hygienically oriented (that is, she smelled).

Within a month, Terry coaxed Arnie into marriage, and while intoxicated Arnie said "I do!" at a nearby justice of the peace. A marriage in hell had begun.

From day one, Arnie was made into a servant. Upon arriving home from work, he changed clothes, did all of the housework, and then cooked dinner while Terry watched television and relaxed after her hard day's work as a receptionist.

Sex was at Terry's discretion, whether Arnie wanted it or not. Sexual acts were chosen by Terry, and quite often Arnie's pleasure was not part of her scheduled performance. All Terry wanted was to get pregnant, and she orchestrated that condition in less than a month. For the next nine months, Arnie was allowed sexual freedom. Over the next ten years, the same pattern emerged, and the couple ended up with three girls.

Terry no longer cared about sex with Arnie. She had gotten what she wanted. To add insult to injury, Terry began having affairs. She brought men home and had sex with them overnight in their bed while Arnie was made to sleep downstairs on the couch. Arnie's fury mounted, but still he said or did nothing.

One night when Arnie was horny and needed sexual relief, Terry, intoxicated and angry (as usual), told him to undress and then humiliated him to a point where he wanted to crawl under the floorboards. He just stood there naked and took Terry's evaluation of his body and of his genitals, which she degradingly compared to those of an eleven- or twelve-year-old boy. Inside, Arnie raged and fumed, but not a word came out of his mouth. Terry finally stopped when she fell asleep, leaving Arnie standing there in tears of rage and hurt.

Arnie walked out of the room and into his oldest daughter's room. LINDA, thirteen, was asleep, and Arnie, still naked, uncovered her and lifted her nightgown. He began fondling her legs higher and higher until he reached her genital area. Linda awoke at that moment and asked her father, in shock, what he was doing and why he was naked. He told her that it was time for her to have a sex education lesson and that he was going to be the teacher and show her by example.

When Linda refused, Arnie threatened to go to her younger sister, Eileen, age eleven, whom Linda loved and usually protected. Linda submitted to Arnie to protect Eileen, and a four-year incestuous relationship began.

When Linda became seventeen, she met a boy in high school whom she liked a great deal and decided to leave home and live with him. Remembering her father's threats to go to Eileen, Linda finally reported Arnie to the police through a school counselor (not through her mother). Arnie was arrested and spent the next five years in a prison treatment program but made absolutely no changes. His therapist doubted that he ever saw anything wrong with what he did.

In prison he met a "daddy" (an older, more aggressive inmate who offers protection to younger inadequate inmates in return for sexual favors). At the end of his sentence, he "maxed-out" and is on the streets again with no supervision, living a homosexual lifestyle.

Questions for Discussion

1. How do children become adults like Arnie?

2. Should Arnie's parents share any of the responsibility for Arnie's incestuous behavior?

3. Were Arnie not an inadequate personality, what might he have done about his wife and his marriage?

4. Was sex simply sex for Arnie, or do you think it had other meanings and significances?

5. Do you think Arnie still poses a threat or danger to society?

SIBLING INCEST

It is important at this point to discuss an often overlooked and very infrequently reported form of incest, sibling incest. There are essentially three different types of sibling incest that need to be differentiated.

The Normal, Developmental, Experimental Sex-Play Group

This group includes two subgroups of children. First, there are the young children, close in age, who share the same bedroom, change clothing in front of each other, and often bathe together. Curiosity about differences in body structure, especially in the genital area, occurs normally, and no trauma results from this "checking each other out," or from a child's form of "playing doctor," or from masturbating in front of each other. Trauma, however, may result if a parent or other authority figure catches these children in these behaviors and reacts angrily, hysterically, judgmentally, or punitively.

The second group is composed of young male children and prepubertal or barely pubertal adolescents. This group tends to be impressed with the boasting or braggadocio of their peers, especially regarding their amazing and frequent sex conquests (most of which are fantasies). When they are "virginal," they thus feel "different," and in order to catch up to their peer group, they talk a sister who is close in age (younger or older does not matter) into "experimenting" with them. These occurrences are usually consenting and nontraumatic unless, again, the children are caught in the act by parents or other adults and judged, punished, or labeled. Trauma may also occur should there be some unfortunate result such as a sexually transmitted disease or a pregnancy. A very disturbing case will clarify.

PHILIP, age seven, returned home from a Sunday visit to his next-door neighbor and caught his mother and father in bed, nude and in the midst of having intercourse. He stood there and watched, unnoticed for several minutes. When his mother glanced over and saw him, she simply said something like, "Oh, hi!" and asked why he had come home so early. After explaining that his friend's parents had to go shopping, young Philip asked what his parents were doing and was told: "We're making love, but it's private, so please leave and close the door." Philip left and went to his room.

The following day, Philip's mother heard a commotion coming from the children's bedroom with a great deal of laughing and giggling and went to investigate. It should be no surprise to learn that she found Philip and his six-year-old sister, **RACHEL**, nude and "making love." His mother screamed, became hysterical, began beating Philip, and called him derogatory names including "pervert," "sickie," and "bastard." Nothing was said to his sister.

When his father came home, Philip was severely beaten on the buttocks and on his genitals and, once again, called every derogatory name and four-letter word that the father could think of. All of this for "making love" as he saw his parents doing.

The effects of this trauma lasted throughout adolescence. I first met Philip following his arrest for an attempted rape on one of his schoolmates.

Adolescents Sexually Abusing Younger Siblings

There appear to be two types of adolescents in this group. The first are those who are severely inadequate, are far behind their peer group both socially and sexually, and have a desperate need to be "normal," defined as being like the rest of their peers. To admit virginity in the locker room brag fests becomes impossible. Due to their naïveté, inadequacy, and immaturity, they believe everything that their more assertive and aggressive peers tell them. When there is a younger sibling at home of the opposite sex, in desperation, they too often "use" this sibling for sexual exploration in order to be able to say that they have been with a girl or boy and that they have had sex. Trauma here occurs when the used sibling hears about society's views on incest and all of the social taboos against it.

The second group, made up of both girls and boys, abuse their younger siblings as a means of undoing or normalizing their own abuse by their parents. Boys predominate and rationalize: "If dad [or an older brother, an uncle, and so on] can do it to me or my sister, then I can do it to them too." This group of boys identifies with the male, even though they were abused by him. Most of them were sodomized at one time or another in their abuse and perceived their father's action as "using me as a girl." Too often, the incestuous father bluntly tells them that this was the case (see **JOEY**, **JORDAN**, and **JAMIE**, above). The boy victim then decides that he may victimize his female or male siblings in an attempt to regain his masculinity.

This rapidly growing group remains highly unreported. One reason is that families do not want this "secret" known since an investigation would eventually lead to the incestuous parents (or parent). This group is also undertreated (at least until they become dysfunctional adults) since families do not want relatives and neighbors to know that one of their children is seeing a "shrink" and especially do not want the reason known. One case that I have treated lived over seventy miles from my office and traveled this distance weekly to ensure that no one in their local area would find out.

Reactive sexual molestation of this type does not occur exclusively in an incestuous manner, nor does it occur only with boys or girls who were molested. There are hundred of cases of inadequate, immature, inexperienced boys and girls who panic when they enter adolescence and hear sexual bragging from peers. Many, in desperation, molest any available child, either boys or girls, simply to be able to say that they have had sex. A current case will clarify this.

JARED, a seventeen-year-old, small, and physically younger-looking male, sexually abused his two female cousins, ages eight and fourteen. He was in his third year of high school and was captain of the wrestling team. Although small in build, he was strong and had won several championships.

In the locker room and showers, the persistent adolescent topic was sex and "getting it on" with girls. Jared was a virgin and, one day, let this slip. From that time on he was known as "Virg" no matter where he went or what he did.

Jared's self-esteem was low and his self-image quite negative. He had compared himself to the other team members and insisted that he had the smallest penis of them all. He was quite embarrassed by this fact and equated it with his lack of masculinity and aggressiveness (except when wrestling).

Jared often baby-sat his two female cousins, as his aunt and uncle double dated with his parents on a regular basis. After playing Scrabble one night, the three of them all sat on pillows on the floor and watched television. He began rubbing the leg of his younger cousin and slowly moved up to her genital area. She pushed his hand away, but he put it back and rubbed her for a few minutes while fantasizing intercourse with a girl at school.

Before the night was over, Jared did the same thing with his fourteen-year-old cousin, who did not push his hand away and let him do what he wanted. From that night on, "touchy-feely," his name for this behavior, continued and always ended in his running to the bathroom to masturbate.

One day Jared came home from school and a detective was waiting to interview him. He confessed to fondling his cousins and was given probation with therapy as a stipulation. Today, Jared is no longer a virgin, and his values have dramatically changed.

Questions for Discussion

1. What could Jared's parents have done to prevent his self-consciousness about his physical size?

2. Did communication problems contribute to Jared's problems?

3. Does Jared's behavior fall into the category of "sibling incest"?

4. How often do you feel that "penis size" causes problems for emerging adolescent males?

5. How could the discovery of Jared's sexual behavior with his cousins have been handled without involving the law?

I have treated many cases of this kind where cousins, neighbor's children, children in a park, schoolmates, and so on, are "used" to help an immature, inadequate teenager feel "normal" and equal to his peers. Most are unreported, but many of these adolescents end up in therapy as a condition of the victim's parent not reporting to the police or by their own parents' insistence.

Sibling Incest Provoked, Encouraged, or Taught by Parents

A surprisingly large number of incestuous parents that I have dealt with involved their children as co-offenders in incestuous abuse on other children in the family. This most often, in my experience, occurs with male incestuous abuse survivors. An example will clarify.

JIMMY was incestuously abused by his father from age nine to age sixteen. His father perpetrated every possible sex act with his son, promising him that, if he cooperated and told no one, he would eventually be allowed to have intercourse with his mother (an obsession with Jimmy).

In order for Jimmy to "practice" and become good enough to sleep with his mother, he was both taught and encouraged to have sex with his younger siblings, both male and female. Sexual molestation by his father was allegedly to "show you the way you should behave sexually with your mother. I'll be you and you'll be your mother."

Even though the incestuous molestations by his father continued for over seven years, Jimmy never got his wish to sleep with his mother. He branched out from the family and began molesting neighborhood children, including a boy only fifteen months old whom he masturbated while he baby-sat him.

Jimmy was eventually caught, as was his father, and I met both of them in the treatment unit while they were serving lengthy sentences.

Questions for Discussion

1. What do you feel contributed to Jimmy's obsession with his mother?

2. Do you feel that most teenage boys and girls go through a stage of "falling in love" with a parent of the same or opposite sex?

3. Why do you feel that the mother is so conspicuously absent in the story? Does that say anything about her personality?

4. Why do you feel that Jimmy never told anyone about his father until after he was arrested?

5. Why did Jimmy choose a fifteen-month-old infant for his first out-of-family victim? What values were involved in the sexual assault?

As stated above and as will be stated again and again, there are many, many cases of this type that are never reported, and so they do not become public knowledge.

THE LONG-TERM IMPACT OF THE WORDS
OF THE MOLESTER

It is essential to emphasize the potential damage that can be done by the words that the offender uses both during and after the sexual molestation. While this factor is pertinent to all sexual abuse and will be referred to in other sections as well, I strongly feel that the impact in incest is even greater since it is a parent's statement and judgment that are involved. Statements of this type in cases already cited include:

- "You're the best 'pussy' that I've ever had! No woman has ever made me feel this good!" (Told to **JOEY** [see chapter 3] by his father as he was raping him.)

- "You're better than either your mother or your sister!" (Told to **JORDAN** and **JAMIE** by **GENE,** above.)

- "If I'd known how good sex with you was going to be, I'd have left your mother and your six sisters alone. From now on, you're my favorite girl!" (Told by **PETER** to his son [see above in this chapter].)

- "Whenever you wiggle that butt of yours or walk around after a shower wrapped only in a towel, you turn me on to the point of no control! If you didn't do that, I wouldn't be doing this!" (Told to **DARLENE** [see chapter 1] by her father as he was forcing himself onto her.)

- "See that! You came just like I did, and that means that you wanted me to do this and were turned on as much as I was! Who do you think you're kidding, you little sex fiend?" (Told to **OLIVER,** above, by his mother on many occasions.)

Every sex offender that I had interviewed, diagnosed, or treated uses words of this type to transfer blame and guilt from himself or herself onto the victim. It is unfortunate that the majority of survivors of sexual abuse allow the molester to get away with this deception and manipulation. I have even had cases where this worked in a violent rape because the victims (both females and males) moved their hips or had obvious orgasms or, in the case of males, ejaculated. These cases were never reported, and many years later came to therapy for some severe depression or sexual dysfunction or for consistent interpersonal conflict and failure. **PETER**, mentioned above, is such a case. It took some thirty years before he admitted to his molestation and sought treatment.

REPORTING-PROBLEMS REGARDING INCEST

While reporting-problems exist in all types of sexual molestation or assault, there are specific problems that are involved for the survivor of incest. Five specific barriers come to mind.

Betrayal

In no other form of sexual assault or molestation are the feelings of betrayal as strong as when a child or adolescent has to report a parent or sibling and then be directly responsible for his or her arrest and incarceration (or, amazingly, in some cases probation).

Values about whose rights are primary are involved in this serious conflict and dilemma. In all incestuous homes, children are taught that the parents' rights dominate. Sometimes this is mistakenly called a value of respect, but in reality it is a value of control and domination. Children brought up in this type of household find it very difficult to develop self-respect or to differentiate their rights from those of their parents. The persistent "You owe me!" attitude of the dominating parent tends to overshadow development of individual rights unless these rights are learned from relatives outside the home, in the neighborhood, in school, or from strong and close friends. The latter scenario, however, is not the case for the majority of children and teenagers that I have treated for incestuous molestation or assault.

I'm positive that when well-meaning parents object to sex education being taught in the schools with values, they do not understand that they are playing into the hands of incestuous parents who want parents' rights to be the focus of this issue. Normal parents do not understand that they are supporting these perverted parents and aiding them in keeping their secret.

Ambivalence

In nearly 100 percent of the survivors of incest that I have treated, ambivalence (regarding love and hate) existed. These survivors were emotionally torn between loving the parent and hating him or her at the same time. No one had ever taught them that they could continue loving the parent and hate what the parent did.

Ambivalence plays an important role regarding other negative parental behaviors, including physical and emotional abuse, alcoholism, drug addiction, criminal behavior, lying, cheating on a spouse, and other problems that the child or adolescent becomes aware of. Ambivalence is usually present in all of these instances, and due to their embarrassing or shame-producing nature, children and adolescents hesitate to talk about them to anyone, fearing that somehow the shame and guilt will rub off on them and/or that they will be rejected and ridiculed as a result.

Incestuous parents are here again responsible. The persistent rationalization that they use on their children or adolescents is their love for them. Unfortunately, this is a love that is desperately wanted and needed, a love that the child or adolescent is willing to pay any price for.

Shared Guilt

In incestuous behavior of any type, more than in any other form of sexual molestation or assault, offenders insist that the sexual behavior is mutual. They make sure that the child or adolescent victim receives some form of sexual gratification either directly or indirectly — if nothing else, masturbation or oral sex to an orgasm.

Once the incestuous offender is sure that the victim has reached orgasm, it is easy then to instill the concept that the victim must have enjoyed the sex as much as the offender did and is, therefore, equally guilty or responsible. The fact that incest of all types rarely, if ever, occurs only once increases the amount of this guilt and responsibility.

Because victims tend to view themselves as sharing the guilt, it is critical not to make the common error of degrading the offender through labeling or name calling in order to be supportive of the victim. I have experienced this reaction in the nonoffending parent, parents of sibling incestuous behavior, detectives and investigating police officers, and even with untrained therapists. The effect is disastrous because whatever is said about the incestuous offender (or any child/adolescent molester for that matter) in a long-term relationship is automatically being said about the survivor. Rarely will the survivor tell the offender what he or she is feeling as these judgmental put-downs are being said, and any chance for rapport or substantive information is lost.

Discovery or exposure of an incestuous relationship does not scratch the surface of these most complicated relationships. Asking the survivor how he or she feels about the incest is far more productive and less suggestive of what the questioner wants to hear.

This issue of guilt and responsibility will be discussed more thoroughly in chapter 13.

Fear of Personal Consequences

An important and often not considered barrier to the reporting of incestuous molestation or assault is the survivors' fear of what will happen to them. Primary fears in this category are:

- Will my other parent hate me and reject me?

- Will I be taken out of my home and sent to a reformatory or a foster home?

- Will I be expelled from school or transferred to another school away from my friends?

- Will we have to move and leave my school and friends?

- Will my other parent find out what I did during the sexual encounters?

- Will my friends find out what I did? (This is especially important to males, who are more often rejected by peers than girls when incest is exposed.)

- Will my family hate me for embarrassing them in front of everyone or by changing their lifestyle? (See the next section.)

These and many other such fears and questions keep incestuous victims from reporting and result in serious adult adjustment problems, especially in marriage and in sexual relationships.

The "Bigmouth" Label

Of all of the barriers to reporting, the "bigmouth" label is one of the greatest fears. When a child in a multiple-child family is the only one molested (or is the only one concerned about the molestations) and reports the incest to a teacher (the most frequent source of reporting) or another adult and criminal sanctions result, the socioeconomic status of the family changes for the worse. The nonoffending parent and the remaining sibling(s) often are uprooted, lose their home, school, and friends, and have to move to a less desirable neighborhood. Why? All because of "bigmouth!" The survivor then becomes the offender where the family is concerned and is ostracized and even physically abused as a result. An example will clarify.

ART is a thirty-five-year-old, married male with two girls, CONNIE, age fourteen, and her twelve-year-old sister, HELEN. Art is a carpenter who remodels kitchens and other rooms in people's homes in the community where he lives. He is active in many community groups and spends a great deal of time at the local bar. He therefore has a large cluster of friends who all like and respect him.

Art molested Connie, who did nothing about it until she attended a special seminar in her high school on sexual abuse and its effects. Considering that someday her sister was bound to be her father's next victim, Connie reported her own abuse to a school counselor. The alleged molestations were reported to the authorities, and a major investigation began.

When news of the allegations by Connie against her father were learned by her mother and by her father's friends and associates, all hell broke loose. Nobody, including her mother, believed the story, even when Connie's sister, Helen, confirmed it. (She had not been asleep one night and saw her father molesting Connie.)

Connie was rejected and harassed at school, on buses, at shopping malls, and everywhere else she went. She was called a "slut" and "liar" and an "ungrateful daughter with a wonderful father." Connie became not only depressed but also suicidal and was referred to a community family counseling center where I worked part-time.

A dual session with her mother resulted in her mother attacking her and accusing her of "trying to steal my husband." She again was labeled a "slut," and the depression increased. It was impossible for Connie to remain in the community or to attend school. Even the teachers (many were customers of her father) rejected and verbally abused her.

Fortunately, Connie had a grandmother in Florida who agreed to let her live with her. She attended school there and slowly, with professional help, recovered to an extent. She will never forget what happened and how she was treated as the offender rather than the victim.

Today, Connie is attending a local college in Florida, is an honors student, and has a loving and caring boyfriend. Without her grandmother's help, I shudder to think of what would have happened to this bright and beautiful girl.

Several years after Connie moved, Helen was abused by her "wonderful father" and successfully reported him. He was given a twenty-year sentence in the state treatment facility.

Questions for Discussion

1. Why do you think that everyone, including Connie's mother, refused to believe her?

2. Did ambivalence play any role in Connie's not reporting? If so, what role and what effect did it have on her rejection by everyone?

3. Why do you think that Helen, after witnessing Connie's abuse, never went to her mother or anyone else?

4. What relationship do you think both girls had with their mother?

5. What role, if any, did the mother play in the incestuous process?

Incest has always been and continues to be one of the most damaging and long-lasting types of sexual abuse. When I first began working with sex offenders in 1961 and then when I opened the first sex offender treatment unit in New Jersey, the Rahway Treatment Unit,[4] there were no incest cases incarcerated. Some five years later the first incestuous father was sentenced to the unit, and slowly but surely with better reporting the number of incest cases rose until incestuous fathers became the fourth largest group that the unit treated. Hopefully this increase in reporting will continue until every child, boy or girl, who is or has been incestuously abused comes forward. Only then will the true statistics emerge and the enormity of this "secret" be revealed.

It is our responsibility as adults and parents to get the message to even the youngest child that he or she does not have to suffer this

---

4. The Rahway Treatment Unit (RTU) was opened on May 15, 1967, at the then Rahway Prison in Rahway, New Jersey. Although in a correctional facility, the RTU was operated under the direction and budget of the Diagnostic Center at Menlo Park, New Jersey.

abuse and that he or she is not the guilty party. Children need to be taught that these are sick parents who need help. I prefer to use the term "love sick" in attempting to explain this sickness to young and even older children who do not understand this horrific behavior. These children also need to know that we can help their incestuous parents and eventually return them to society.

I do not really believe that incest will ever be eradicated, but I do believe that we can dramatically lessen the number of incidents and the impact on the lives of the children and adolescents who fall prey to this offense.

6

THE TRIPLE DAMAGE OF RELIGION AND CULTS

When religion or a cult plays a role in sexual abuse, the effects are multiplied. This occurs especially when the priest, minister, rabbi, or other religious authority figure either directly or indirectly adds elements of the supernatural — "God," the devil, or any other religious entity — as the authority for the abuse, as the punisher should his or her wishes not be complied with, or as the vindicator should the survivor dare to tell anyone or report the abuse to the authorities. The addition of religion and cults in matters of sexual abuse actually triples its effect, as will be made clear below.

RELIGION

Before we can discuss this topic any further, we need a definition of the term "religion." The *American Heritage Dictionary* (1989) defines religion as "an organized system of beliefs and rituals centering on a supernatural being or beings." For any growing and learning child, religion can be a highly positive or a highly negative experience, depending on the perception and focus of the particular religious sect. In my experience, the sin-and-damnation type religions do the most serious harm to children, adolescents, and adults under the guise of doing something positive and of the highest good. Absolution-type religions, on the other hand, which focus on acceptance of human beings as imperfect and offer forgiveness and hope, offer the best hope of attaining happiness. The latter type of religious background provides the best therapeutic and effective aid for all survivors of sexual abuse.

There is a highly positive correlation between the type of religious upbringing a survivor of sexual abuse has been exposed to and the outcome of his or her treatment, especially where the abuse was perpetrated by a religiously connected authority figure such as a priest, a minister, a rabbi, or any other religiously identified personnel. This positive correlation indicates the following:

- Survivors from a religious background that is positive and forgiving appear to adjust the fastest and appear to be the least permanently damaged by their sexual abuse.

- Survivors with a religious background that preaches "hell and damnation" appear to be the ones most seriously and permanently damaged by their sexual abuse, and they have the most problems "letting go" of any residual guilt feelings associated with their perceived cooperation and/or willing participation in their sexual abuse. If their parents are deeply involved in a negatively oriented religion, the effects are even greater and longer lasting. Two cases will help to clarify this.

DAVID, a forty-one-year-old incestuous father, molested his seven-year-old daughter over a period of several years before being discovered. When he was offered treatment in lieu of a prison sentence, he chose treatment, and the court asked me to be his therapist. The two traits that were immediately evident on his first visit were guilt and a severely damaged self-image. While he was anxious for therapy, these factors indicated that treatment would be both difficult and long-term.

David was brought up in a stern and punitive Roman Catholic home, where he could do no right. He was constantly criticized and put down for the least thing. "Sin," "damnation," and "hell" were words he constantly heard in his parents' incessant lectures that occurred almost daily. The harder he tried, the more he seemed to fail, with criticism and condemnation the usual result. He could not remember being understood or forgiven.

At forty-one, David had no formal religion and had not practiced his Roman Catholic faith for almost twenty years. His philosophy was humanistic for everyone else but himself. David worked as a highly successful computer troubleshooter and program designer for a major, well-known corporation.

While David intellectually understood that he must let go of the guilt and all of the self-punishing behaviors that resulted from it, he stated that emotionally he could not but didn't know why. Self-hate, self-recrimination, severe self-criticism, and judgmentalism resulted, and David saw himself as a sort of "Satan incarnate." His negatively oriented religious upbringing had indelibly imprinted on him and prevented any real therapeutic progress. Although fifteen months have passed in therapy, David's guilt remains as strong as ever.

At work and with friends, David feels "unworthy" (his term) and persistently finds a way to destroy any real friendships "before the new friends find out what a real rotten piece of shit I really am!" The result is isolation and loneliness, revolving depression, and every escape defense possible. For example, he recently volunteered to be the first person to be fired in an upcoming cutback in his company.

David's plans are unrealistic and escape-oriented. He says that he will buy a motorcycle and spend a few months traveling around the country, possibly joining a bikers' group with a reputation for meanness and evil "since that's where I really belong."

Periodically, David has made religion the topic of a therapy session. His mood changes abruptly, his attitude toward himself becomes hypercritical and completely negative, and depression takes over. It usually takes an hour or more to break these moods and to bring David to an emotional state where it is safe to allow him to leave.

Although David is forbidden to have contact with his daughter without another adult present, I have recently seen him with her on his new motorcycle. This is another example of David's self-destructive behavior and bodes poorly for his daughter.

Questions for Discussion

1. What might have been the major factors that motivated David to go to his daughter for sex?

2. How might the molestation have been prevented?

3. Why do you think that David could not give up the guilt he felt?

4. What role, if any, did the little girl's mother play in this molestation?

5. Are any public agencies being neglectful of their responsibilities in this case?

A good general rule, for me, has been that the longer the negative religious indoctrination has existed and the more severe the form of this indoctrination has been, the more difficult it will be to help the survivor of sexual abuse to find forgiveness and happiness. "Letting go" becomes nearly impossible, regardless of the external support that the individual has. This has been true for both female and male adults who fell into this category. Another case will help elucidate this.

> **KYLE**, whom we first met in chapter 2, was a case of triple trauma since his abuser was a Catholic priest who was a long-term family friend and visited on regular weekends, sleeping overnight in Kyle's room, where the molestations took place. The "tripling" involves, first, the sexual abuse itself; second, the fact that the abuse was perpetrated by an adult authority figure whom both he and his parents trusted and befriended; and, third, the fact that the molester, as a priest, added a supernatural element. This third factor operated as follows.
>
> When Kyle asked the priest why he was fondling and masturbating him, the priest answered: "I have permission from God to do these things to you." The priest then cleverly added: "If you tell anyone, God will protect me, his priest, and punish you."

When Kyle went to his mother and she did not believe him and scolded him for lying about a priest of God, all of the priest's predictions appeared to come true, and this was confirmed by the priest in his next molestation when he said: "I told you if you told anyone, God would protect me and punish you, and he did!"

As an adult, while Kyle has made tremendous gains and has reached a fair degree of success, he remains in therapy since he is never totally guilt-free, happy, or secure. He still anticipates more punishment from God for betraying one of his priests and never fully accepts any of the praise for positive accomplishments in his life. (He is a practicing therapist, specializing in treating boys who were sexually abused, and is highly successful in this field.)

Kyle constantly has to be convinced that he is a good person or that he is worthy of anything positive happening in his life. He is married to a wonderful, supportive young lady who knows about his past and fully accepts it, but even here Kyle is insecure and feels "undeserving." These negative feelings affect his motivation to go on for advanced degrees, to run conferences, to speak at those that I conduct, and so on. Recently, he accepted my offer to write a chapter or section of a chapter for this book, and now, some eighteen months later, I have heard nothing from him.

How long will it take for Kyle or David to fully let go of their guilt feelings and the feeling that they are undeserving of praise, happiness, or simply peace of mind? Therapy cannot produce miraculous change in these individuals. I am firmly convinced that change must originate inside of these individuals, not from an outside source.[1]

---

1. While both of these cases involved Catholic priests, I have also treated Protestant ministers from several denominations and clergy from other religions as well. Most religions are represented in the literature on either abusers or survivors of abuse, and I have met Catholic priests, Baptist ministers, Methodist ministers, Episcopalian priests, and even a Jewish rabbi who all were involved in the molestation of either children, adolescents, or adults under their authority and/or supervision.

CULTS

A Definition

The *American Heritage Dictionary* (1989) defines a "cult" as "a system or community of religious worship and ritual"; or "a religion or religious sect generally considered to be extremist or bogus." There are a variety of "religions" that call themselves cults, including satanic cults, nature-worship cults, witches' cults, the infamous Manson cult, the Masons, the Branch Davidians, and so on. A few common factors are found in all of these cults, including mandated secrecy, secret rituals (sometimes including animal sacrifice), membership signals (usually a secret handshake), special clothing (usually robes), symbols, and, finally, an origin based on ancient legends, beliefs, books, or scriptures.

Most sexual predators are clever and psychopathic in the devices, manipulations, and lies that they use to accomplish their goals, that is, the sexual molestation of a victim. When indirect means are necessary, clubs, special membership groups, and cults are the most frequently used devices to hide the true, devious intent of the molester.

Sexual molestation, under these circumstances, is commonly referred to as "ritualized abuse." This phrase was coined by Lawrence Pazder in 1980 at an American Psychiatric Association annual meeting in New Orleans. Dr. Pazder wanted both to understand this phenomenon and to distinguish it from other forms of sexual abuse since he felt that the treatment techniques for ritualized abuse were distinct and different from those used with other forms of sexual abuse. The definition he presented follows: "Ritual abuse involves repeated physical, emotional, mental, and spiritual assaults combined with a systematic use of symbols, ceremonies, and machinations designed and orchestrated to attain malevolent effects."[2]

---

2. Lawrence Pazder et al., "Michelle Remembers," paper presented at the American Psychiatric Association Annual Meeting in New Orleans, 1980.

Satanic Cults

Of all of the topics in the area of sexual abuse, that of satanic cults is the most widely debated. There are two opposing groups: the first insists that satanic cults sexually victimize scores of people every year; the second insists that people who report being sexually abused in a satanic cult are delusional and hysterical or that their therapists suggested that they were abused by a satanic cult.

When a survivor comes to me and tells me that his or her molestation took place in a satanic cult setting, and if I feel that they truly believe that this is what happened, then it does not matter whether the cult existed or not. I treat them as if it did since the effects and treatment are more complicated and different from all other forms of sexual abuse. The tripling effect of religious sexual abuse exists in all of these cases, plus a firmly entrenched paranoia and seemingly unending fear of future abduction and molestation by the same cult. An example at this point will fill in this picture.

VIC (whose case was briefly described in chapter 4; a fuller description of the entire case is given here), at age twenty-three, had a diploma naming him an ordained satanic minister by the infamous Anton Levay in the Church of Satan Resurrected, originally based in California. Vic settled into a wealthy and cultured city and founded a satanic church in an abandoned Baptist church building.

Being legalistically oriented, Vic obtained written consent and permission from the parents of more than fifty teenagers, forty-eight boys and two girls, to join his flock and to undergo secret, physical initiations into his satanic religion. Without ever having met Vic or knowing anything about him, these parents signed permission slips permitting the initiations, in essence, permitting their sons or daughters to be sexually abused and physically scarred.

The initiations were tests of pain tolerance and had many levels, beginning with "a paddling on the bare buttocks" during which the initiate was not permitted to whimper, cry, or make any sound. Masturbation, group sex, and anal-receptive sex all followed in successive stages until stage 25 was reached. Stage 25 was the final stage and consisted of a full satanic ritual. Vic entered the chamber wearing black robes, as his title of "high priest" demanded. The initiate was tied naked on a flat marble table or altar. Vic then lit a black candle and dripped hot wax onto the stomach of the new member, inscribing his "permanent mark," symbolizing that the new member now belonged to Satan and to Vic. When the wax cooled and Vic ripped it off, it left a scar in the secret image he had inscribed.

Vic now owned the member of his cult and could do with him or her as he pleased. Vic held private sexual rituals with two and three other cult members and, in these private and secret rituals, sexually molested the victims in any manner that "fit his mood at the time" (his words).

After more than six years, one boy finally reported Vic to the authorities, and he was arrested and charged with only two counts of sexual molestation. In treatment, after some six months, Vic, guilt-ridden, showed his therapist his "black book" (a log of all of the rituals he performed). The log contained more than six hundred names of boys and girls who had been initiated by Vic and the level that each of them attained. Some 98 percent of the survivors were either adolescents or preadolescents. Since only first names were used in the log, most of the victims were never located, and the boy who reported Vic refused to expose any of them. The authorities visited all of the schools in the area in an attempt to locate some or all of the victims with no success. Without treatment, many of them could become sex offenders as adults.[3]

---

3. For further information on the effects of this and other forms of sexual molestation, see William E. Prendergast, *The Merry-Go-Round of Sexual Abuse: Identifying and Treating Survivors* (New York: Haworth Press, 1993).

Questions for Discussion

1. Why was it so easy for Vic to get signed permission slips from parents for their children to be initiated into a satanic cult?

2. Why do you think that 598 of the 600 victims that Vic molested were boys?

3. Why did so many preadolescents and adolescents submit to the initiations, all of which contained either pain or humiliation or sexual abuse?

4. What do you feel will happen to the 598 survivors who were never found and who probably never received treatment for their abuse?

5. How can incidents like this one be prevented in a community?

Cult leaders are clever and manipulative. They carefully choose their intended members (victims) following a careful list of guidelines. Usually they choose only young people who

- have or had problems at home with parents;

- appear and act weak, passive, and dependent;

- are looking for an authority figure as a parent-substitute and guide;

- instantly obey the orders and commands of the cult leader (this can be determined through simple testing);

- believe or are willing to believe that magical and supernatural forces have power and control over them, forces that, if obeyed, could provide power, money, happiness, security, and a solution to all of their problems; and

- are in the throes of adolescent rebellion against all authority, rules, and regulations in their lives.

Not surprisingly, Vic used these guidelines, which are similar, if not identical, to those used by both pedophiles and hebophiles, except for the belief in magical and supernatural forces. The dangers of long-term games like "Dungeons and Dragons" becomes obvious.

THE PROBLEM OF RECURRENCE OF THE ABUSE

Recurrence is a strong and definite possibility in these cases, especially during treatment and shortly thereafter. The vulnerability of this group of survivors is far greater than any other group discussed thus far. So is the guilt that they continue to experience for the deviant acts they "willingly" (their conditioned perception, placed there by the deviant cult leader) performed for the "master" or high priest. If publicity was involved in the exposure of the cult, other deviants with the same proclivities will come out of the woodwork looking for ex-cult members to recruit for their own sexual purposes. This danger must be avoided. Early discussion of this possibility and the dangers inherent in succumbing again to a similar influence by another satanic cult leader is the best method of preventing this possible recurrence. Parents, friends, other group members in a stronger position or more advanced in their own treatment, teachers, and other authority figures should all be involved in this area and made acutely aware of the dangers.

For at least the first month or two of treatment, the survivor should be left alone as little as possible, especially when in public (traveling back and forth to school, gym, community activities, and so on). The survivor should also have someone sleeping in his or her bedroom (but not in the same bed!) due to nightmares and night-terrors.

Prevention of recurrence is the major focus with this group. Some of the cult activities and behaviors will maintain a perverted attraction-potential for the survivor for several months after therapy begins. This is especially true where sexual activities and drug use are concerned. These areas need to be thoroughly explored, discussed, and resolved with the survivor and then discussed with all significant individuals involved in the life of the survivor including parents, siblings, close friends, school counselors, and church leaders.

CONCLUSIONS

While the subjects of religion, cults, and satanism had to be included in this book, my personal experience and knowledge in this area are new and very limited. In my travels around the United States and Europe, I have begun meeting more and more survivors of satanic abuse as well as more therapists involved in this field. I continue to accrue facts, case histories, and treatment methods being used that will eventually reach book-length. What I have gleaned from these experiences is that the damage is *long-term* and the effects *insidious*.

I have evaluated or treated people involved in all manner of sexual and criminal offenses, but I have never heard of more loathsome and deplorable acts than those foisted on innocent human beings by satanic cults. I recently met an eighteen-year-old female survivor with seventeen years of satanic cult abuse, both at home and outside the home. Her abuse began at birth. In fact, the reason the girl was conceived was for her to become "an instrument to be used for the greater glory of Satan and his minions" (a direct statement made to the authorities by her own parents). As her memories are brought into consciousness through hypnosis and regression techniques, the rituals and acts that she was subjected to throughout her life continue to surface. The majority of these acts are so horrible that I would not consider retelling them here or anywhere else. The fact that she is a survivor and existing is a miracle since she has already made many suicidal attempts. Treatment will be a long-term battle requiring courage and stamina on the parts of both the survivor and the therapist.

Society does not want to know or to believe that these kinds of sexual and physical abuse exist. Authorities often call what few reports are made the products of the imaginations of children and adolescents who are looking for attention and/or revenge on parents and other authority figures. In this way, they do not have to face the horrors that really do exist in their areas of responsibility. Even when presented with incontrovertible evidence such as being taken to the cult meeting room where ritual sacrifices have taken place and being shown the skulls and bones of the many victims, they find excuses and rationalizations to sweep the incidents and reports under the carpet. Why? The reason is obvious. The membership of these cults is composed of influential and authority-oriented individuals in society, who suppress evidence as well as hinder or block investigations or even order them stopped. In the case of the girl discussed in this section, that is exactly what occurred.

Could these reports be hysterical manifestations or manifestations of a deeper underlying pathology? Of course they can. However, the consistency of the survivors' stories and descriptions of the ceremonies and practices of the satanic cults is too exact to be explained away with a theory about a global unconsciousness of some type or other.

Are there individuals and groups of individuals who use the trappings of cult worship to justify and excuse their deviant behaviors? Of course there are. "Vic" (chapter 4) admitted that although ordained a satanic priest, he really did not believe in the powers of Satan since he never profited from them and was not protected from being sent to prison as he was told he would be. Yet he persisted in his deviant need for sex with teenage boys.

The reader is strongly advised to find more literature and discussions on this topic if presently involved with survivors of this type. The subject of cults and satanic cults in particular could fill many volumes. For our purposes what we have covered is sufficient, and the reader interested in more material on this subject is referred to the reading list at the end of this book.

Part 2

Prevention

7

PARENTAL BEHAVIORS

Before getting to the topic of this chapter — parental behaviors — it may be helpful to say a few words about the overall structure and focus of part 2. In part 1, I discussed the major types of sexual offenders, concentrating on the seductive-molestation types. Part 2 focuses on prevention measures regarding both assaultive-abductive offenders and seductive-molestation offenders and makes a distinction between these two types, though they do overlap in some categories. This distinction is necessary because the seductive-molestation offenders as far more insidious, cunning, and damaging, at times, than the assaultive-abductive offenders.

There are five basic factors involved in permitting and, at times, aiding sexual molestation. These are: parental behaviors; parental teachings; peer teachings, suggestions, and influence; the role and pressures of society; and self-imposed rulers. One chapter of part 2 will be devoted to each of these problem areas and suggested solutions for most will be offered. By no means does this discussion intend to be absolutely total or complete. It will focus on the situations and causes that I have experienced in my practice.

PARENTAL MISTAKES AND SOLUTIONS

As I noted earlier, hundreds of convicted or exposed sex offenders have repeatedly stated to me that parents are their best allies in their efforts to seduce and sexually molest children. What they are referring to are the many glaring errors that parents make that contribute to their child or adolescent being a potential victim of sexual abuse. I will discuss what I consider the major ones.

Believing Only Strangers Molest Children

More and more child and adolescent sexual molestation cases indicate that the child or adolescent, and often the parents, knew the molester. Family members (including siblings), relatives, neighbors, teachers, policemen, scoutmasters, priests, and ministers, all known by the family, have been among the many exposed and convicted sex offenders.

Suggested Solutions

Parents and other authority figures need to listen to children saying: "I don't want to go [someplace]." "I don't want to ride the school bus. Will you drive me to school?" or "I don't want to stay alone with [someone like a relative, neighbor, or baby-sitter]." Parents tend to send their children — often alone — to places "to get rid of them," and they usually choose places where sexual predators go to look for potential children to molest. These include malls, movie theaters, fast-food restaurants, YMCA pools, and parks. It's not surprising that sex offenders consider parents their allies.

Parents need to investigate these places first and even to check with local police departments on the number of sexual incidents that have occurred in them. Also, the people who operate these places need to take some responsibility for the safety of children and adolescents, especially in their public rest rooms.

Recently I took my two nieces and my nephew to a matinee at a local multiplex theater in a large shopping mall. I escorted my nephew to the men's room and, sure enough, there was a man "hanging out" there, just staring at and smiling at the boys as they entered. After leaving, I reported this to an usher, who stated: "It's not my problem!" I then walked to the manager's office and told him what I observed. He couldn't have been less concerned, stating, "I'll look into it." I waited in the lobby in view of the men's room for ten minutes, and no one came to check on the man, nor did he leave the men's room. When I returned to the theater, over the next two hours I observed many little children leaving on their own, either to go for refreshments or to use the lavatories. Either they were alone at the theater or their parents and grandparents considered it perfectly safe. Is this denial, naïveté, stupidity, or simply lack of concern? Here again, sending children *in groups* is always safer than sending them alone.

Knowing Too Little about Excursions

In the hundreds of cases of child and adolescent sexual molestations that I have treated, a predominant cause is that parents knew too little about an excursion they sent a child on, a practice vehemently defended by the parent or parents involved. I have uncovered several trust-factors, presented below, that could have prevented many, if not most, of these sexual molestations, abductions, and/or assaults.

As I discussed earlier, a particularly glaring aspect of this problem is parents' tendency to casually sign permission slips for day or overnight trips. Again, too many sexual molestations that I have worked on, either as a diagnostician or a therapist, for either the offender or the survivor, occur on seemingly legitimate school, scouting, Big Brother, or other day or overnight trips. A majority of the parents signing permission slips for such excursions had never met the teacher or other authority figure who would be in charge of the children. Trusting someone because they have a title or are a member of a particular profession, volunteer group, or religious organization can be disastrous unless care and concern are exercised by the parents. **DEXTER, HOWIE, DON**, and **VIC**, in chapter 4, are all excellent examples of this type of misplaced trust in authority figures that resulted in their sexually molesting many children and/or adolescents. Too often, signing permission slips for activities at or after school with an unknown adult is paramount to giving our children and adolescents to a child molester to be victimized.

Suggested Solutions

Be Sure There Is More Than One Supervisor on a Trip or for Other Activities. This is one of the easiest solutions since sexual molestation is a covert behavior, and the molester does not want any of his peers, for example, other teachers, priests, or ministers, to know that he or she is a pervert. When financial concerns or staff limitations prohibit more than one supervisor on a trip or when this is impossible due to the nature of the organization, such as the one-on-one arrangement of the Big Brothers organization, then it is the parents' responsibility to do the following:

1. They should learn all that it is possible to know about the teacher, Big Brother, and so on, and should ask for references about the particular supervisor from other parents regarding his or her character and past reputation.

2. Where references do not exist, the parents should ask to meet with and interview the prospective supervisor. During these interviews, parents should question:

    a. the motives of the individual for volunteering,

    b. his or her prior experience in the proposed activity (for example, supervising children on trips, handling emergencies of any type, etc.),

    c. his or her training and experience in the proposed activity, and

    d. where a one-on-one activity is proposed, the individual's particular interest in their child or adolescent.

This last factor (d) is probably one of the best potential indicators of potential danger. Sex offenders will exaggerate their interests, focusing on the potential of the child or his or her "special" (one of their favorite terms) personality traits. When allowed to talk on and on, they eventually go too far and become unbelievable. They also will get more and more nervous and anxious as the interview continues. Their discomfort in justifying their behavior to another adult will become clear. Eye contact is either poor or nonexistent.

Naturally, there are the more clever and psychopathic offenders who can "con" almost anyone, and the parent will have to rely in these cases on the old adage: "If it's too good to be true, then it probably isn't true." This "too good to be true" guideline works for the volunteer organizations and schools as well. A case that I was involved in personally will clarify.

MR. JOHNSON, a local high school teacher, eagerly accepted the additional chore of being the advisor for the drama club of his school. This meant working extra hours daily with little or no compensation. The main focus of the drama club was to end the school year with a dramatic presentation to which parents, relatives, and the public were invited.

This particular high school was one where I annually spoke to the senior class on the topic of sexual abuse and victimization. This was one of my favorite presentations, and I would usually end up with five to six of the seniors asking to talk to me. One by one they eventually admitted that they had been or were presently being sexually abused. I would then offer to help them to get into treatment, if they were willing. What may be surprising is that while girls readily agreed and were looking for treatment, boys rarely, if ever, agreed.

On one of these annual occasions, following my presentation, five girls remained behind in the auditorium on my left and four boys on my right. (They always separated into distinct groups by gender.) I first saw the girls individually. All were incest cases either involving their father, an older brother, or a cousin or uncle. All agreed to follow up with therapists I had suggested, and they then left the auditorium.

The four boys were obviously frightened, anxious, and hesitant to come over to where I was seated. When they finally did, one at a time, I discovered that all four of them were being molested by a male teacher in the school, either during or after an extracurricular activity that they refused to specify. While they realized that they needed treatment, none of them agreed to seek a therapist since they feared that either their parents or

their peers would somehow find out about their long-term involvement with an adult male in mutual homosexual acts. The
old double standard of how their peers and the other teachers
would react to exposure of their homosexual behavior reared
its ugly head once again. (For more on this see "Boy/Male
Reporting-Problems" in chapter 3.)

How could this be going on without someone in the school —
other students, faculty, or the administration — knowing about it?
Many, many clues that something was wrong were apparent but
overlooked either through nonconcern, apathy, or ignorance.

One bothersome memory immediately came to mind. I knew
many of the boys at the school and had discussed their school
lives with them on several occasions. From their conversations
and reactions (evasion, loss of eye contact, change in emotional
demeanor, and so on), I had suspected that something was
wrong with the drama teacher, Mr. Johnson, for several reasons.
To begin with, the "too good to be true" factor was more than
obvious. Mr. Johnson volunteered for this extra assignment and
then put in as many hours on it as he did teaching. Often, he and
the students could be found at the school "working on the play"
until eleven or twelve on school nights.

Even when rehearsal was over, he would often invite one to
three of the boys out for pizza, and at the restaurant he would
discuss his personal life with them in the most intimate detail,
looking for sympathy from the teens for all of his woes and the in-
justices that befell him. Until I had the occasion to talk to one of
the drama club members about Mr. Johnson, no one ever asked
any of the boys what the topics of these pizza talks were or why
they lasted until one or two in the morning on a school night.

None of the other teachers or the school principal ever saw
or heard of Mr. Johnson dating, and he never attended any of
the teacher- or administration-sponsored school functions for the
staff. Two more warning signs overlooked.

No one knew anything personal about Mr. Johnson. Where
did he live? Did he "moonlight" like most of the other teachers
did? Did he like sports or play any or attend a gym or health club?

Why was Mr. Johnson so private? Why did Mr. Johnson associate only with students from his drama club? He ate with them in the cafeteria, although the teachers had their own lunchroom; he sat with them in assemblies and in presentations, including mine. Why did Mr. Johnson associate only with male students and choose plays that were mostly composed of a male cast? Why didn't Mr. Johnson attend any of the school functions like football or basketball games, wrestling meets, or school dances, and why did he never volunteer to be a chaperone at any mixed school functions?

When I reported what I had discovered to the school principal (without divulging the names of the four boys), he was shocked, in disbelief, in denial. It was only the mention of a law suit and/or a police investigation that stirred him to some action. He promised to "look into things." Some three weeks later, nothing had occurred, and Mr. Johnson went about his merry business as usual.

I had the opportunity to attend a dress rehearsal of his next play and after it was finished went backstage to talk to him. Mr. Johnson was sitting in the electrical-panel control area with a younger boy (a freshman) on his lap and a couple of others milling about. When I asked to talk to him, he refused to look up and stated, "You'll have to make an appointment." I asked the boys to give me a couple of minutes in private with Mr. Johnson, and, knowing who I was, they all agreed and left us alone. I walked over to Mr. Johnson and shook his hand stating, "You've done a good job, and I'm sure the show will be a success." Then while holding onto his hand, I added, "You're a sick son of a bitch, and either you go for help or I'll make sure that you get it! Have a nice night." I then left.

The next morning I received a call from a staff member at the school stating that Mr. Johnson had not been heard from, that he never even came to empty his locker or his desk, and that he did not show up for his paycheck. The principal then admitted that he was wrong and that there apparently had been problems in the drama club that he was unaware of. He defended himself immediately by adding that his busy schedule did not permit him the time to visit all of the extracurricular activities. Sound familiar?

Unfortunately, the four boys never received treatment, and after graduation all left for colleges out of state. Will they be normal adults? It is impossible to tell. The depressing part is that all of this could have been prevented with a little more training for the school administrators and the rest of the teachers on the warning signs of potential staff abusers. It probably also could have been prevented if more than one supervisor had been engaged with the drama club. Additionally there could have been annual presentations to all of the student body on the subject, not only near the end of their senior year.

Ascertain What Criteria Are Used to Screen Supervisors. Where volunteer organizations are concerned, it is the parent's right and responsibility to ascertain whether potential volunteers have been screened for criminal records and what admissions testing was administered and by whom.

As discussed earlier, it has been my sad experience that many of these organizations have no such admissions-testing program. Where no criminal check and no testing is used, my *strong* suggestion is that the parent refuse the offer of assistance and also that the parent make known his or her objections to the organization's policies regarding admission into the program.

Discuss All Details of the Excursion When the Child Returns. Parents are negligent when they fail to discuss, in detail, the events of the hike, science trip, tutoring session, play practice, baby-sitting, and so on, when the child or adolescent returns home. Parents need to observe the behavior and demeanor of the child or adolescent, looking for any new behaviors, especially negative ones, that will occur if there had been an attempt or an actual molestation.

This does not mean a cursory "How was the trip [or tutoring, play practice, baby-sitting...]?" but a detailed, sit-down discussion indicating a sincere interest in the activity rather than assuming a prosecutorial approach. When this parental interest occurs consistently about all of a child's activities, an atmosphere of suspicion, distrust, or paranoia will be avoided, and instead the child will perceive it as simply the parent's true interest in the child and his or her activities. This parental interest is especially important when indicators of trauma are present. (These indicators will be discussed fully in chapter 12 in the section on recognition.)

Trusting Children Too Much and Allowing Them to Go Anywhere

Children and adolescents who are sexually assaulted, abducted, or molested are usually "picked up" when they are alone. Sex offenders rarely attempt a seduction or molestation of two or more children at a time unless they are his or her own children or are his or her charges. **HOWIE**, discussed in chapter 4, is one of these exceptions.

Part of the safety that sexual predators need is the one-on-one approach to a child or teen whom they feel is vulnerable or defenseless. I have treated victims of molestations and abductions that took place within a block or two of the child's or adolescent's home. In a recent tragic case in my state, a child was on his way to a friend's house to play, and the friend lived only one and a half blocks away on the same street as the victim. He was never seen again, and his mutilated, sexually abused body was found in a nearby wooded area several days later. This boy had gone to his friend's house on many occasions without incident, but on this particular day there was a predator waiting in a parked van that no one paid any attention to. It is important to note that this assault took place in an upper-middle-class neighborhood where nothing like this had ever happened before. Parents there had become complacent, and the result was a tragedy. The old belief that this will never happen in one's family or to one's child is simply a *denial* of conditions in society today and an excuse to avoid daily parental responsibility.

This same situation can occur in shopping malls, especially in the men's rest room, a favorite place for male sexual predators to "hang out," hoping for a victim to enter alone. Many incidents have occurred in this situation including fondling, masturbatory attempts or acts, and even cases of sodomy. There are very few such incidents reported as having occurred in the women's rest rooms, probably due to the fact that girls and women tend to use these facilities in twos and threes rather than alone. There are also less public, predatory female sexual predators than male predators.

Suggested Solutions

When it is impossible or impractical for the parent or another adult to accompany a child or adolescent, one of the easiest and least problematic solutions is to arrange for there to always be more than one child on these trips, visits to the bathroom, and so on. This will prevent the creation of a paranoidal atmosphere and will not produce unnecessary fear and distrust in the child or teen. Both children and adolescents enjoy being in the company of their friends and should be encouraged to make this a daily way of life: walking to and from school, playing in the playground or park, going to the malls to shop or just to "hang out," playing in the video arcades, going to the movies (another favorite haunt of sexual predators, especially during the "kiddie matinees"), going to Boy Scout meetings (especially at night), and even attending tutoring sessions.

When parents meet a great deal of opposition from the adult leaders who are operating whatever activity the child or teen wants to attend, this, in itself, should be a warning sign that something is not right. The normal adult involved in child or teen activities will have no problem in allowing and even fostering this "buddy system" not only as a protective measure but also as a positive social training effort.

Too much agreement with or assurances to parents concerning a child's safety at a particular event or activity by the leader of that activity should also be considered a warning sign. Sexual predators are quite adept at "selling" their sincerity and the "absolute safety" of their proposed activity to parents and other authority figures. They will do anything to gain access to potential victims.

It is easy to see that these possibilities result in a "damned if you do and damned if you don't" situation. In reality, all that these possibilities imply is that parents and other authority figures responsible for the safety of children and adolescents must take particular care regarding whom they place in charge. Here again careful screening and testing by trained professionals in this area are essential and should always take priority over simply filling a position or need.

Finally, driving the child or teen to any of these activities is well worth the effort and interruption of the parent's activities. "Better safe than sorry" certainly applies here. An example will clarify.

VANCE is a forty-nine-year-old psychologist friend of mine with two teenage daughters. His oldest daughter, **ANDREA**, is a fifteen-year-old, highly intelligent, honor student who often brought other girls home from school in order to tutor them in subjects that were causing them difficulty. Andrea enjoys helping her friends in this manner, and it became an almost daily occurrence.

One afternoon, Andrea brought **SHELLY** home with her to help her with her math problems (geometry was simply a mystery to Shelly). The tutoring was going so well that Shelly stayed for dinner, and the girls didn't finish working and studying until almost nine o'clock. Andrea came to her father to ask him if he would drive Shelly home, but he told her he was too busy with work from the office and that Shelly could easily walk home. (In reality, Vance never liked Shelly and thought she was a bad influence on Andrea.)

Shelly agreed that she could walk home without difficulty and left. On her way home, a car pulled up and a good-looking young man asked her if he could give her a ride since it was late and she shouldn't be walking alone on such a dark street. Without thinking, Shelly agreed since the man was friendly, seemed concerned about her safety, and was a "hunk."

As soon as she entered the car, the man's demeanor changed. He locked the doors electrically from controls in his door and took off without even asking her where she lived. Five minutes later, with Shelly crying and begging to be let out, he pulled into a dark street, pulled out a knife, and ordered her to take her panties off and to unzip his pants. Terrified of the knife and his threats to "cut her throat" Shelly obeyed, and in less than ten minutes she had been forced to fellate the man and then submit to being both raped and sodomized. He then threw her out of the car, naked and bleeding. To this day, the man has not been found.

Vance came home the next day and was greeted by an angry and crying Andrea, who screamed at him that it was his fault that Shelly had been raped. His guilt and shame were immediate and long-lasting, and he still sees a therapist to deal with his resulting depression.

In his upper-middle-class neighborhood, Vance had never heard of any serious crime and certainly could not even imagine that an abduction and rape could occur where he lived. He had allowed his daughters to go out evenings alone and to walk to their friends' homes or to take a bus to a neighborhood mall by themselves. He never worried about them being hurt or sexually molested until now.

There was no way that Vance could have predicted what happened to Shelly. That is why *safety thinking* has to become a way of life both for parents and for their children. Dangerous possibilities need to be discussed but in a manner that will not produce a paranoidal atmosphere for the family. Weighing the possibility of a tragedy against the possibility of producing fear in family members, there is really no choice. Even if there is only one chance in a million that something might occur, it is not worth taking that chance.

Shelly will never be the same. She is now involved in long-term treatment and doing fairly well, but her fears, nightmares, shame, and embarrassment have produced social isolation, staying home almost all of the time, refusing invitations, and serious anxiety about facing teachers and schoolmates daily.

Trusting Mates Too Much in Troubled Relationships

This error is especially relevant to cases of incest and to cases of pedophilia and hebophilia perpetrated by a live-in "friend," a stepparent, or a foster parent. The offenders can be males or females.

Surprisingly, a large percentage of the convicted rapists (sexual assault cases) that I have either tested or treated, or both, were victims of sexual abuse by mothers, aunts, foster mothers, stepmothers, and female baby-sitters. None of those that I treated ever reported nor would they allow me to discuss the abuse with the offending person. Unfortunately, later in life, their hatred and reactive anger at the female offender were generalized onto innocent female victims in a compulsive manner with some of them accumulating as many as sixty victims.

Some of the same rape group were sexually assaulted by males, including fathers, uncles, grandfathers, foster fathers, and stepfathers, but they still blamed their mothers since "she should have protected me and should have known what was going on." It is difficult, where these molestations or assaults took place on a long-term basis, for the surviving males to believe that their mothers did not know what was happening and, if they did, then they passively condoned it. This feeling results in the anger and revenge projected onto innocent females, often in the same age-bracket or with the same general appearance of their mothers.

In chapter 5, where incest was discussed and five incestuous fathers were presented in case form, all of the abused children felt that their mothers either definitely knew what was going on or, at the least, suspected it. None of these child and adolescent victims was able to go to his or her mother for help. That, in itself, is strong evidence that these children believed that their mothers knew about the sexual abuse.

Of the mothers that I have been able to interview once the incest was exposed, either legally or privately, two categories emerged.

1. In the first category, denial was rampant. The mother knew something was going on but did nothing to find out what or to stop it. This group was composed of grossly inadequate women who were terrified of their spouses and who had extremely low self-esteem. None of them felt that she could survive without her husband. Their inadequate personalities were definite factors in their denial.

2. In the second category, the mothers knew what was going on (either consciously or unconsciously) but either felt helpless to do anything about it or, secretly, were glad that their mate was going to the children and leaving them alone. As unbelievable as it seems that a mother would behave in this manner, these mothers admitted it to me with intense feelings of guilt and shame. This group tended to be less inadequate and was composed of women who were either professionals or business women with careers of their own. Until confronted in later life by their children with the effects that the unresolved, untreated incest had on them (attempted suicides, alcoholism, drug addictions, bulimia and anorexia, chronic depression, compulsive spending resulting in constant debt, job failures, lack of drive or ambition, and so on), these mothers, for the most part, remained consciously unaware of their mate's sexual assaults or chronic seductions of their children but did nothing about it. Once the incest or sexual molestation was revealed, this group suffered more breakdowns and psychological problems than the first group.

Allowing Communication Problems to Fester

As stated earlier, in all of the cases of sexual molestation, abuse, assault that I have worked with, the one common factor was a partial or total lack of communication between parents and children, especially where adolescents or teens were involved.

All parents should have daily, constant, close communication with their children or adolescents (commonly referred to as "quality time"). This appears to be the best solution to the problem of sexual abuse. Parents need to remain available to their children for discussions whenever the child has a need to talk, not when it is convenient for them. One can never know how important the topic the child or adolescent wants to discuss may be. Also, as a general rule, since it takes a great deal of courage for a child to discuss being or having been sexually abused, it may be the only time that the child will make an attempt to communicate that fact with anyone. This caveat applies to teachers, counselors, police personnel, relatives, neighbors, and so on. Too often, that one attempt on the part of an abused child is thwarted, and only in adult life are the effects fully discovered. The mothers in both groups discussed above did not follow these guidelines.

In fact, many of the women in the second group had abdicated their parental role to their mates, even with young children, in order to prosper in their professions or in their business or political careers. Several were politicians, several were M.D.'s or Ph.D.'s, several ran businesses in the community; and others had businesses that required constant travel out of town. Always, the mate cheerfully accepted the dual role of mother and father and tragedy resulted.

It is more than obvious that these mates, male or female, can have their professions and their businesses or careers without abdicating total responsibility for their children. Their families should always come first, and even a phone call from an out-of-town hotel can maintain communication and alert the parent, who certainly should be able to tell by a child's voice or pleading for that parent to return, that something is wrong. All of the children in the cases of parental, relative, or sibling incest that I have treated made some attempt to alert the parent that something was wrong. The most frequent methods young children use is to whine and cry when it is time to go somewhere for an overnight or weekend visit or to make an unusual or unnatural fuss when the mother is leaving them with someone (even their own father) to go on a trip. Ignoring these warning signs is tantamount to condoning the misbehavior of the mate or other predator. Here again, when a parent suspects that a mate may be physically, emotionally, or sexually abusing his or her children, arranging for another adult to be present during the absence will usually help prevent any abuse from occurring. Grandparents are excellent in this role.

The second suggestion for this group of parents is that, upon returning home from a day at the office or from a business trip, they should spend time with the children to discuss what went on in their absence. Evasions such as "I forgot" or "I don't remember" are obvious warning signs. Other warning signs include:

- looking at their father, brother, sister, aunt, uncle, or anyone else before answering a question;

- becoming nervous and upset at questions about what went on while the parent was away;

- exaggerated answers to any questions, usually being too positive; and

- any other unusual behavioral reaction to being asked these questions.

With really young children, clinging behaviors, obvious physical discomfort, and unusual shyness about having diapers changed or undressing are typical warning signs as well. For all ages, regressive behaviors and nightmares should be considered warning signs, especially when they follow a parent's absence. More on this subject in chapter 12.

PREVENTING RECURRENCE IN CASES WHERE SEXUAL ABUSE HAS ALREADY OCCURRED

Survivors of sexual abuse are extremely vulnerable to a recurrence of the event. This is partly due to their perceived guilt that they continue to experience for their part in the sexual abuse. This is especially true when the survivor cooperated (did what he or she was told to do) in order to prevent being seriously harmed or even killed by the molester. **JAY** in chapter 1 is a good example of this type of self-protective cooperation.

Some survivors unconsciously set themselves up for a recurrence due to this perceived guilt. This is true primarily in cases where the abuse was not reported and the survivor was not treated. Reporting the abuse as soon as possible and then seeking and accepting treatment with a specially trained therapist in the area of sexual abuse and survivor treatment is the only method that I know that can definitely help to prevent such recurrences.

All of the above-mentioned actions require support from everyone involved in any way with the survivor: the family, especially parents; siblings; friends; the authorities (especially the first officer or detective to speak to the survivor); the courts; school or employment personnel; and so on. When this support is not available to the survivor, the results can be disastrous. The worst result is suicide, when the survivor can no longer live with himself or herself. Prostitution, becoming a recurring victim, and even reversing the process by becoming a sexual predator all are negative consequences when the survivor is not supported.

Everyone in society has to become involved in preventing child and adolescent sexual abuse and, where it has already occurred, has to become involved either directly or indirectly through supporting treatment programs for survivors, demanding better legislation for the prevention of sexual abuse, and so on. In New Jersey and New York, Megan's Law is a good example of community support on a legislative basis.[1]

---

1. Megan's Law is a New Jersey statute that requires (1) all sex offenders to register with the local police where they reside; (2) an interview with an appointed person from the prosecutor's office to determine the degree of danger that the offender presents to the community; and (3) a subsequent placement into one of three categories ([a] not a threat; [b] a moderate threat; [c] a severe threat) that determines what notification will be made to the community of the offender's presence there. The offender has the right to a hearing if he or she disagrees with the category that he or she is placed in. There are still constitutional challenges to the statute, and there will be for years to come. While I support the concept of Megan's Law, there also must be equitable considerations for the treated and released sex offenders who have proven, through successful community reintegration and continued positive behavior, that they have profited from treatment and are ready to return to society as productive citizens. This law should be firmly imposed upon recalcitrant sex offenders who did not become actively or cooperatively involved in treatment and who still pose a threat to children, adolescents, and adults as well. This determination should be made by trained therapists who know the individual.

8

PARENTAL TEACHINGS

Beside the parents' behaviors that contribute to the danger of their child or teen being sexually abused, there are the values that parents teach that potentially contribute equally to this ever-present danger. I will discuss the most important ones and solutions to some of them.

PARENTAL MISTAKES AND SOLUTIONS

Overemphasis on Obeying Authority Figures

Of all the possible dangerous values to teach a child, this is the primary one. Blind obedience accounts for literally thousands of sexual molestations every month. It should be obvious that if a predator wants children or teenagers to sexually abuse or molest, then he or she must necessarily be where the potential victims are and also be in a position to exert some influence or control over them. As a result, sex offender facilities are full of teachers, religious leaders of all denominations, scoutmasters, Big Brothers, YMCA staff, childcare institution staff, crossing guards, school bus drivers, school maintenance men, public park personnel, amusement park staff (including individuals from traveling carnivals and circuses), baby-sitters, daycare staff, and personnel from any and all other areas where children congregate or are in mandatory attendance.

Most sex offenders in the above professions with whom I have worked have eventually admitted (mostly during treatment) that their preoccupation and/or obsession with a specific sex or age group played a major role in their choice of education and training as well as in their employment or volunteer work. Again, preventing these people from having easy access to children is possible with proper, mandatory screening by trained personnel of all potential staff, including upper-level supervisors, who will have any direct contact with children or adolescents. In addition, as stated in chapter 7, parents can greatly help in prevention here by learning about these leaders before giving permission for their child or teen to be in their trust and care.

Suggested Solutions

From as early an age as possible (I suggest eight months to two years old), children should be taught that, where authority figures are concerned (including relatives), they should obey only rules that make them feel comfortable, or that do not feel wrong, or that do not contradict values that they were taught in their homes.

Not Distinguishing Types of Touching and Privacy

Sex offenders, once they have chosen a potential victim for seduction, often begin with touching to see how far they can go without the child protesting. This often begins with a seemingly innocent arm around the shoulders, progresses to touching further down the back, then to patting the buttocks on the child's leaving the situation, and on and on until an actual sexual touch occurs. Predators can "feel" resistance in the child to being touched in a certain way or at a certain place and will "pace" themselves to these responses. A firm "No!" or "Don't do that!" or "Leave me alone!" does wonders to frighten the seductive offender into retreat and into rethinking his or her choice of victim.

Besides touching, invasion of the child's or adolescent's privacy also must be discussed. Predators, under the guise of supervision, often invade locker rooms, shower facilities, bedrooms, or bathrooms to either "be sure that everything is OK" or "to be sure that you have washed or cleaned yourself properly."

Two cases already cited in detail (see **MR. DON** [pp. 31–32] and **MR. HOWIE** [pp. 130–132]) offer graphic examples of these predatory behaviors, and the reader is encouraged to go back and consult those cases. An additional case will further dramatize the point.

CHAD was a twenty-six-year-old graduate student who worked at the local YMCA evenings to supplement his scholastic scholarship. At first, he was assigned to the Boys' Department Games Room where he supervised a large number of boys playing pool, Ping-Pong, chess, cards, and other indoor games. Part of his assignment was to check out equipment, and in this way he became familiar with all of the boys and soon knew them by their first names.

After a week or two, Chad asked to be reassigned to the swimming pool area as a supervisor. Because Chad had done exemplary work in the games room, the Boys' Department Secretary (a YMCA designation for department head) happily gave Chad the assignment with carte blanche to reorganize the swimming pool procedures.

At first, Chad appeared to concentrate on safety and boosting the membership in the swim teams. However, he quickly shifted to an emphasis on health concerns and imposed the following procedures:

1. the locker room had to be supervised by an adult while even one boy was changing clothes;

2. swimming would be in the nude for health reasons and in order to prevent clogging of the pool's filters;

3. showering before swimming was mandatory, and the showers were to be supervised by an adult to prevent any accidents from occurring; and

4. a body check was mandatory upon leaving the showers and entering the pool to be sure there were no contagious rashes or diseases; this included each boy bending over and spreading the cheeks of his buttocks and also pulling back his foreskin, if he were uncircumcised.

Naturally, Chad supervised all four activities, taking any opportunity to touch a boy that he could arrange. "Did I see a boil on your butt?" "Do you have a rash in your groin?" "Did you pull back your foreskin to clean your penis?" were only a few of the questions he would ask, then touching the boys in areas that interested him.

Amazingly, his supervisors not only agreed with these new procedures but presented Chad with an award for his excellent interest and achievements for youth.

Within a month, Chad molested his first boy in the locker room, feigning a "medical check" and examining the boy's genitals for a problem ("Your testicles look swollen; let me check them for you"). The boy became erect, and Chad masturbated him to orgasm. This began a series of some fifty molestations before one of the boys, a minister's son, left the locker room, went home, and told his father. All hell broke loose, and a major investigation resulted. Chad was arrested and sent to a sex-offender treatment unit where he spent some ten years.

I have dealt with literally hundreds of sex offenders who molested boys and girls using this same initial "touchy-feely" approach to test a potential victim's reactions. Naturally, this does not occur as frequently in the sexually assaultive personalities, who use force or a weapon to abduct and then molest their victims, although even here it might be initially used to lure the child or adolescent away from a crowded area to an isolated place where the abduction could occur more easily and more safely.

Suggested Solutions

Children and adolescents should be taught to allow themselves to be touched only by individuals they know and fully trust and, even then, only on parts of their bodies where they feel comfortable being touched. Children and adolescents must be taught to vehemently object to being touched in any way that makes them feel uncomfortable or that produces feelings that their personal safety or rights are being violated. Each parent must choose appropriate words to use to teach this value to his or her child. Specific examples should always be included such as those suggested in the "good touch/bad touch" model as wonderfully depicted in the play *Touch!*[1] and in a resource titled *Red Flag, Green Flag People.*[2]

For parents who are not familiar with these models, there are books on the subject, and there are also miniplays or skits that are provided regularly by child abuse prevention groups around the country. Basically, the concept revolves around being touched in a too-familiar manner or on parts of the body that the child is not used to having touched by strangers or even by relatives. The reason touch is so important should be obvious. The following section helps explain this.

Overemphasis on Self-Reliance and Independence

Another damaging value that parents teach their children and adolescents is total independence, regardless of the readiness of the child or adolescent to assume that responsibility. This defective value, more than any other, destroys the communication between parents and their children that is so necessary for family cohesion and happiness. Many parents regret teaching this value in any form, but this regret usually only occurs after a tragedy or loss.

This value is even more destructive in homes where there is either a parent missing or little time or concern for the children, who are forced to grow up on their own or to look outside of the home for adults who can serve as substitute parents. These parents do not want to take responsibility for their children and force them to assume responsibilities that they are not ready for in order to gain freedom for themselves to do as they please — that is, to live as if they were either single or did not have children.

---

1. For information on *Touch!* contact the Illusion Theater, 528 Hennepin Avenue, Suite 704, Minneapolis, MN 55403.

2. For information on *Red Flag, Green Flag People*, for which both a skit and a coloring book are available, contact Red Flag, Green Flag Resources, The Rape and Assault Crisis Center, PO Box 2984, Fargo, ND 58108–2984.

Sex offenders are primed and waiting for these children and adolescents and know all of the right moves, as well as the right things to do and say to ingratiate themselves with these "lost" children. They readily offer their services as a substitute father or mother and provide these children and adolescents with all of the material and emotional needs that do not exist in their own homes and that they so desperately crave.

Suggested Solutions

The solutions to this and the following two problems are covered in the "suggested solutions" already given in this chapter.

Overemphasis on Trusting Neighbors

Neighbor predators look for children or adolescents who are overly trusting. Sex offenders live in the same community as all of us and are unrecognizable to the average person. They tend to know everyone on their block and know a great deal about everyone's business. Also, they are constantly and persistently looking for victims to seduce or molest. It may seem surprising that a large percentage of predators seduce or molest in their own neighborhoods, but statistics support this hypothesis as do my personal experiences. Naturally, there are those who will drive to another town or as far away from their area as possible for safety reasons. An example of neighbor-predator molestation will clarify.

VINNY, a thirty-six-year-old, single male, lived with his mother in a middle-class neighborhood of a small suburban community. Vinny's mother worked in a local community hospital in the gift shop and was both well known and well respected in her community. She often worried about Vinny and his lack of social contact, especially dating. She sincerely wanted grandchildren.

Unknown to anyone, Vinny feared all adults. As a growing child, he had been a "sissy" and was the victim of every bully that came along. He isolated himself and had no close friends. He lied about all of this to his mother, and when he came home bruised or with torn clothing, he manufactured an accident in sports (which he never participated in) or on the playgrounds.

Vinny lived in a fantasy world and envied the neighborhood children who appeared happy and "normal" to him. He would sit on his front porch and watch them playing in the streets or in their driveways and wish that he could be like them. This was especially true when he saw other boys talking with and touching girls their own age. Vinny had never had a real girlfriend, only the one he manufactured in his fantasies, which always resulted in masturbation.

Living next door to him was a happy-go-lucky family with a teenage girl. **MARTHA** was thirteen and had only recently entered adolescence and "blossomed" (Vinny's term). She was usually a happy girl and seemed to be popular with all of the boys in the neighborhood. Martha liked a particular boy, who usually paid her a great deal of attention. Lately, however, Vinny had not seen that boy around, and Martha seemed to always be alone. Martha was one of Vinny's favorites, and he often fantasized about her being his girl. These fantasies always ended with a sexual encounter between them, and Vinny masturbated almost daily to this fantasy about Martha.

One day, as Vinny came out onto his front porch, he noticed Martha sitting on the steps of her front porch crying. He was both surprised and moved by the sight. He walked over and asked her what was wrong and discovered that she had finally allowed her boyfriend to have sex with her and that he then turned on her and told all of the boys at school that she was a "slut." He also told her that because she had given in to his sexual pressures ("If you really loved me you do it!"), he no longer trusted her and no longer respected her. Their relationship was finished. Martha was crushed.

Vinny immediately took advantage of the situation. He told her that he would always be her friend "even if they had sex" and that he would always love her. He invited her to his home and gave her some cookies and milk, telling her that whenever she was upset or lonely she would always be welcome.

On Martha's third visit, Vinny seduced her, first getting her to masturbate him, then to having oral sex, and finally to intercourse (his first). The relationship lasted for over a year until Martha met another boy at school who liked her, and one day she told him about Vinny. He insisted that Vinny was a pervert and that Martha had to report this to her parents. She did but changed the seduction to a forced, one-time rape. Vinny was arrested and refused to defend himself. He was given a twenty-year sentence and sent for treatment.

I have treated a large number of cases of neighbor-predator molestation involving both boys and girls. Offenders ranged from ministers, to scoutmasters, to carpenters with toy shops in their garage, to retired businessmen, to teachers. The offender can be an individual of any background or profession. Women also were included, but a minimal number, since reporting of women has really only recently begun.

Teaching "Do as I Say, Not as I Do"

As discussed earlier in some detail, too many parents "preach" one thing to their children and then behave in a completely opposite way. Smoking and drinking are two good examples of this hypocritical behavior. While "preaching" that these are destructive and dangerous behaviors and forbidding both to their offspring, parents go on their merry way, drinking and smoking as much as they please.

Religious and moral hypocrisy is even more confusing and damaging. Parents who insist that their child or teen believe in a specific religion and attend services at a church or synagogue of that denomination and who then, in their daily lives, exhibit contradictory behaviors to what the child is being taught damage their children, sometimes for life. An example will help clarify.

MATT, a sixteen-year-old male, until recently had been the "perfect kid" (his mother's comment). He has now been referred to me for evaluation and therapy for a careless breaking and entering of a local store in a shopping district of his hometown. He loudly forced the door open, and as soon as he walked in the alarm went off. He calmly gathered his tools, walked out, and strolled along a main street that he knew the police car would be coming down. Naturally, he was caught and readily confessed his crime.

After several sessions of lies and rationalizations, Matt finally decided to tell the truth as time drew near to appear in court and the strong possibility of several years in a reformatory loomed before him. The following story is in his own words.

"About a year ago, after attending religious schools for over nine years and after trying to be the best kid I possibly could, my parents stopped going to church. One night, I asked why, and they told me, over the dinner table, that they didn't believe in the faith that I was being forced to adopt. I felt I had been lied to. It didn't do much for my morality, and it made it easier to do things that were wrong. My conscience was blown away to dust."

Matt began shoplifting and didn't get caught. The challenge he first felt diminished, and he needed to do something bigger so that he could feel "powerful." In any way he could, Matt was trying to do things that were the opposite of what he had been taught in religious education since he now felt that these values and beliefs were hypocritical and provided him no satisfaction.

Therapy for Matt will be a long process since, at this point, he is so grossly confused, angry, and depressed. He is also quite vulnerable to being a victim of a sexual molester, and there are indications that this may have already occurred. To date, Matt has never discussed his reactions to his parents' revelation with them, and they remain in the dark about this abrupt, radical shift in behavior.

Teaching That Sex Equals Love

The notion that sex equals love is one of the most destructive values parents can teach their children; it is a value that contributes mightily to the ease with which predators are able to molest children and adolescents.

As I discussed earlier, it is primarily in the puritanical United States that sexual intercourse is referred to as "making love." In most European countries sex is sex, and in most Asian countries, specific words and phrases are used to indicate sexual behavior. American uneasiness and discomfort in talking about sex in private, in mixed company, or in the presence of children result in this confusing, distorted, and misleading description of sex. **PHILIP**, whose story was presented in chapter 5, is an excellent example of the type of damage that results from the use of this phrase as a substitute for calling sex what it is: sex!

Suggested Solutions

1. Preparation. In teaching sex education, parents should first either take a night course on the subject or read a professional book on the subject written explicitly for parents. Next, during any and all discussions with children or teenagers on the subject of sex, parents must use specific, acceptable terms for each and every sex act and affix honest and moral values to these discussions.

Parents need adequate preparation if they are to have thorough and beneficial discussions with children and adolescents about sex, for there is no way to know what questions will be asked.

2. Language. It is essential to permit and accept, without embarrassment, the language that children and adolescents bring to these discussions. They are simply repeating slang that they have heard from peers, and when parents react with shock or punitive threats, it will definitely be the last time that a particular child or adolescent will come to them with sexual questions and doubts. In response to "street terms," parents should insert the correct terms in their response to any and all questions. Parents should also explain that this technique is not meant to put the children or teens down or to imply that they are either "stupid" or "dirty" but to help them to learn correct sexual terminology for the future. An example of the need for parents to be prepared for such discussions follows.

When a new, mandatory, sex-education law was proposed and was being discussed around New Jersey, I was invited to a PTA meeting in an upper-middle-class county. I was a proponent of the law, and there was a small faction that was vehemently opposing the law on the grounds that it was a parent's right and obligation to sexually educate his or her children.

Knowing that logic and common sense would not work, I invited the most vehement proponent of parents' rights to control sex education, **MRS. COFFEE**, to join me on the stage and to aid me in proving her point. The lady in question proudly accepted my challenge.

I asked Mrs. Coffee to role-play with me being her teenage son (we were at a junior high school), and she happily agreed. I walked off stage and in a minute returned with a "Hi, mom!" entrance. As her son, I then asked her if I could ask her a question about sex that was bothering me, and she replied that she would be happy to help in any way she could. I waited a second and then blurted out: "Hey, mom, what's a blow job and how do you do it?" Mrs. Coffee fluttered and flitted and gasped. She then stood up and said to me: "How dare you use that language with me!" She then huffed off the stage.

I turned to the audience and said: "I rest my case." For the next forty-five minutes I had their undivided attention. My "mom" had left the auditorium with a following of about six to eight parents.

Fortunately for the children, the law passed although it was watered down, and it prohibited values from being included in the courses.

How would you, as either a parent or an adolescent, have acted in the role-playing scenario I sketched above? If you were playing the mother, what would have been your answer to the boy's question?

3. Additional Materials. Many library books cover the subject of how to deal with children's and adolescent's questions on sex. Many are included in the reading list at the end of this book. In addition, articles, editorials, and discussions constantly appear in monthly magazines such as *Ladies Home Journal, Family Circle,* and *Parent's Magazine.*

For example, the May 1995 issue of *Ladies Home Journal* contains an excellent, short article discussing errors parents make with their teenagers.[3] The author, Andrea Warren, lists the following five errors:

1. talking down to teens;

2. refusing to give up control;

3. being too critical;

4. shutting out your teen's friends; and

5. not supporting your teen's activities.

Each error is then briefly discussed with some suggestions for changes. The article takes up only one page, can be read in five minutes or less, but is incredibly accurate and important for all parents to understand and follow. All of the teenagers whom I have treated have complained about at least four of these issues. These five errors by themselves hamper, if not destroy, any true communication between parents and their children or teenagers and make parents undesirable individuals with whom to discuss serious concerns or problems.

---

3. Andrea Warren, "Five Mistakes Parents Make with Teens," *Ladies Home Journal*, May 1995.

I should have added at least a sixth error: not believing your teen. Too many sexually abused children and teenagers did go to their parents and were disbelieved and even punished for "lying" about the molester, especially if the molester was an authority figure. **Hans** in chapters 3 and **Kyle** in chapter 2 are excellent examples of this lack of belief.

9

PEER TEACHINGS, SUGGESTIONS, AND INFLUENCE

A main characteristic of adolescents is the need to be equal to and accepted by peers. Adolescents feel alienated from all adults to a degree, and adults are sometimes perceived as "the enemy."

Secrets abound, especially about body changes, self-image problems, and, most of all, sexuality. No teen wants to appear inadequate or "stupid" to his or her peers, and this becomes a serious problem for the naive individual. If that individual cannot ask questions of adults and, at the same time, cannot ask peers, where does he or she get answers? The answer is simple. Adolescents either imitate their peers or listen intensely to "locker room conversations" (my term). These discussions can take place almost anywhere that the teens feel they are secure or have some form of privacy from adults and especially from authority figures. These places include gym locker rooms; streets and sidewalks between home and school; shopping malls; tents on camping trips, especially Boy Scout and Girl Scout overnights; teens' bedrooms with doors closed and often locked; "hang-out" spots in parks, playgrounds, and so on, especially at night; and anyplace where teens congregate and feel they are not being listened to.

What follows is a discussion of a number of the damaging values that teens pass on to one another in these places.

DAMAGING VALUES TEENS TEACH TO EACH OTHER

Sex Proves Manhood/Womanhood

The typical bragging that teens do, especially males, is often believed by the more innocent and naive teens and can lead to disastrous results. Being a "virgin" becomes a reason for ridicule and is to be avoided at all costs. Hints of homosexuality are attached to virgins as well as to passive and nonaggressive youngsters. Proving their manhood then becomes a major focus of their lives, dimming all other goals and endeavors. An example will clarify.

> **DAREN** is an eighteen-year-old, good-looking, well-built young man who is attending a local community college while working to support himself and his education. He is extremely well liked and popular but has a great deal of self-doubt, especially about his masculinity.
>
> Daren constantly compares himself to his peers and always comes up lacking (in his own perception). He is ultrasensitive to any challenge to his strength or manliness, and one result is that he is constantly involved in fights, especially in bars. Socially and sexually, he is in and out of relationships in only a few months but never really knows why. While he denies it, he obviously needs a large number of female conquests to feel that he is a man. Daren is now miserable, and all of his achievements, whether athletic or scholastic, no longer boost his now deflated self-image. He just does not see himself as a "real man" like all of his peers, and he does not know what to do about it.
>
> One evening, as he was waiting for his girlfriend to get dressed at her home, he spent the time with her brother, age fourteen, and her sister, aged twelve. Daren coaxed them into a game of "truth or dare." He lost and was "dared" to expose himself, and he did. When they lost, he got them to strip and expose themselves for him He then felt both ashamed but still "manly" and "in control." He could not explain his behavior since

he was having sex with their older sister at the time. When the incident was reported, he admitted his involvement with no excuse

Fortunately he received probation with treatment. He remains in college and is doing well there and at work. doing quite well in both. With proper treatment and value reformation he now has found a new girlfriend, and they have chosen abstinence for their relationship until they are more mature and are sure that the relationship will last.

Daren still continues to prove his manhood at every possible opportunity and will need continued treatment for a lengthy period.

If It Feels Good, Do It

The value "If it feels good, do it" reflects the sensual nature of the emerging adolescent and also his or her rebellious and independence-oriented attitude. On the grounds of emancipation and self-determination, this value flaunts the moral values and standards taught in many homes. This value and some others (for example, "I'm my own boss and person") give individuals permission to do whatever they want with little or no thought of the consequences. Thus drinking, drug experimentation, sexual freedom and permissiveness, daring feats to prove masculinity or femininity, and moral, religious, and social rebellion all become routine and standard practices among teenage populations, especially in teenage "gangs."

These values and a sense of invulnerability actually begin in pre-pubertal (junior high school) years. This belief in invulnerability is most visible in the absence of fear of AIDS, as seen in the refusal of a majority of teenagers to use condoms. Most teenagers I have dealt with who are sexually active laugh and offer ridicule when the suggestion for the need for condoms is made. "Nothin's gonna happen to me!" is a common response, coupled with the dislike (in those who have tried condoms) of the lessening of sensitivity. Even when the newer and much more sensitive condoms are offered, the same refusal continues based on the ever-present invulnerability. The results are disastrous and include unwanted teenage pregnancies, an epidemic of sexually transmitted diseases among teens, and teenage abortions.

This belief in invulnerability plays a role in problems regarding drinking and driving, speeding and "chicken races," and the combining of drugs, all of which result in so many teenage deaths. It also plays a role in gang shootings, lack of concern over killing or being killed, and the pessimistic, fatalistic attitude of an ever-growing number of adolescents.

Finally, this value results in an increasing number of child and teenage sexual assaults (kids raping and molesting other kids), including rapes of both females and males, sexual seductions of teenagers by predatory adults, and finally sexual-assault deaths that frequently include torture and mutilations. Hedonism and absolute freedom of choice have their prices.

Suggested Solutions

The only sure solution to this problem is parents teaching moral and ethical values, beginning almost from the cradle. Infants can and do learn right and wrong and acceptable and unacceptable behaviors. As discussed earlier, parents can demonstrate, through motions and sounds, approval or disapproval of what a baby does. Right and Wrong are dramatically imprinted even in infancy. This parental approval/disapproval behavior continues throughout childhood and into adolescence but too often without any explanation, discussion, or rationale for the physical and verbal reactions of approval or disapproval.

To truly teach values, a parent must always answer a child's or adolescent's questions with facts and explanations. Essential to this teaching is proof of the parent's belief in a particular value or principle by example in his or her own behavior and lifestyle on a consistent basis. If parents assume a "Do as I say, not as I do!" lifestyle, then the children or adolescents will not internalize any value or principle that the parents are trying to impress on them because the parents behaviorally are proving that they do not believe in or practice that particular value or principle. **MATT** in chapter 8 is an excellent example of this problem.

A large percentage of the children and adolescents whom I have treated over the last thirty-three years have made some form of complaint regarding this factor. Some, for example, were criticized for having had beer at a party by parents who often came home intoxicated from parties they had attended; others were expressly forbidden to even consider having sex (especially girls), but the mother and father refused to answer questions about their own first sexual experience; others complained that a parent refused to discuss contraception on the basis that the child or adolescent was too young, even when the child knew that the parent had had a baby while an adolescent or had had a sexually transmitted disease as a teenager.

This double standard prevents both belief and further attempts to communicate with parents or to seek advice from them. This, in turn, forces the children or adolescents to go elsewhere, either to their peers or to other adults, which can be both dangerous and disastrous. An obvious danger, besides potential sexual seduction or molestation, is that the outside source will offer a value or principle that is contrary to the parents' personal, moral, or religious beliefs. Conflicts at home result, and distancing between the parents and the child or adolescent is inevitable.

Very few of the children or adolescents that I have treated for having been sexually molested or for having sexually molested someone else were able to talk about sex or anything personal or important to them with their parents. **CHESTER**, discussed in chapter 4, and **JARED**, whom we met in chapter 5, are excellent examples of this factor.

In my years of work with both convicted and nonconvicted adult sex offenders, there has never been one who had discussed sexual issues or problems with either of his or her parents, and those who tried were either rejected, punished, or put off for some lame excuse or other. All of them went either to their peers or to other adults (teachers, coaches, neighbors, priests, ministers, scoutmasters, and so on), with the result being misinformation, sexual molestation, or both.

A sizeable percentage who went to older peers were taken under their wing and initiated into sex in a traumatic or demeaning way or learned dangerous false values that led to eventual disaster (sexually transmitted diseases or unwanted pregnancies).

Idealization of Certain Body Types and Images

Of the many damaging values that children and adolescents learn from their peers, distorted body-image values rank among the most damaging. The Adonis and Barbie Doll complexes (my designations) dominate and control the self-image and self-esteem of a majority of our youth today who are not adequately prepared by their parents to understand the differences among bodies. Usually this traumatic realization occurs in prepubertal years when a child moves from the relative protection of grammar school to the all-new world of junior high school. A main reason for junior high school being the setting for this trauma is the fact that, for most children and adolescents, junior high is the first time that they are involved in gymnastic activities with locker rooms and group undressing and showering.

Comparison is automatic and natural, and due to the large variety of different ages at which puberty and growth occur, without adequate preparation, these comparisons can be disastrous.

Boys. For boys, this comparison primarily involves penis size and muscular development. Height may also be a primary comparison factor (as in **JARED's** case). Adolescent boys who are not prepared by parents or the school system for this event can glean distorted and defective values ("rulers") regarding their manhood and their normalcy. Although these "rulers" are not formally written or stated, comments, criticisms, ridicule, and jokes relay the message quite clearly. The effect of these messages and comparisons is always dependent on the ego-strength and self-image with which a boy enters this new and frightening developmental stage.

In addition, the effect may be magnified due to another major trait of all emerging adolescents. Prior to adolescence, boys and girls want the approval of adults and authority figures rather than peer approval. Now, at adolescence, this need dramatically changes to the exact opposite. Adolescents want and need the approval of their peers and not the approval of parents and other authority figures. This is one of the reasons that the emergence of adolescence is so traumatic for both unprepared parents and their children. Were parents aware of this impending change, they could adapt more readily and also prepare their children for the event.

Some of the major defective and distorted values that boys will learn from peers are the following:

1. Penis size determines manhood and sexual prowess.

2. Physical strength determines manhood.

3. Sports ability determines manhood.

4. Virginity indicates inadequacy, abnormality, and/or homosexuality.

5. Homosexuality is bad and makes you bad, a "fag."

6. "Looks" determine popularity, leadership, and peer-praise.

7. Intelligence and scholastic achievement do not compensate for lack of the above traits.

8. Peer acceptance and belonging are dependent on the above factors.

Finally, for boys, the "Adonis complex" plays a major role in peer and opposite sex acceptance during adolescence. Short, obese, acned, awkward, tall and thin, slight, shy, or intellectual boys are rejected and considered abnormal by their teenage peers. Only the handsome, muscular, aggressive "hunks" are admired by both their male and female peers. The rest of the boys are "losers" and will do anything to be accepted. They become easy prey to be used by the more aggressive and sophisticated male and female peers as their desperation for acceptance becomes known. (**BRUCE** and **RUSTY**, in chapter 2, **HANS**, in chapter 3, **BIF**, in chapter 4, **JARED**, in chapter 5, and others throughout this work are excellent examples of this problem.)

Girls. The comparison of bodies can be equally disastrous for girls who are not given adequate preparation prior to the move to junior high school. Breast development is the main "ruler" for female adequacy. Television makes sure that this "ruler" is deeply imprinted in all girls and in boys as well (women with small breasts are berated, and women with large breasts show them off). Besides television, this "value" is emphasized by swimsuit calendars, *Playboy,* discussion of breast implants and augmentation, and so on. The constant audible comments of boys in school and in malls or clubs remain focused on breast size and appearance.

Next comes attractiveness. The Barbie Doll preoccupation with physical and external beauty, the image of the beautiful but dumb blonde in movies and on television, the lack of emphasis on internal beauty, intelligence, and accomplishment — all form the "rulers" of the teenage girl.

Sexual attractiveness, openness, and experience follow naturally. Being a "virgin" today is just as dumb and unnatural for girls as it has always been for boys. Being sexually active is a norm, not an exception, as is persistently discussed on talk shows like *Geraldo.* By glorifying gangs and promiscuous and/or prostituting teenagers and women, these shows make emerging, rebellious adolescents envious of them. By publicizing these deviant behaviors, television is providing defective and dangerous role models for today's rebellious youth. The few shows that discuss positive values and that handle controversial issues in a moral and healthy way are relegated to the PBS stations and last only a season or two (for example, the Canadian productions *DeGrassi Junior High* and *DeGrassi High).*

Some of the defective and distorted values that girls learn from peers are the following:

1. Breast size determines womanhood and sexual prowess.

2. Seductiveness determines success in relationships.

3. Competitiveness with males determines success.

4. Being sexually active wins the man you want and the admiration of female and male peers.

5. "Looks" and clothing determine popularity, leadership, and peer-praise and envy.

6. Intelligence and scholastic achievement are not what boys want and do not compensate for the lack of the above traits.

7. Peer acceptance (especially by males) is dependent on the above factors.

Mothers fail with teenage daughters as fathers fail with teenage sons when adequate preparation for the emerging adolescent daughter is not made and proper values about physical appearance and sexual behavior are not taught early in the child's development. As with the boys, girls learn defective and distorted values from their peers as well as from the examples of their parents and other adults.

Suggested Solutions for Boys

The primary responsibility for preparing boys for puberty, a potentially traumatic event, belongs to the parents, especially the father. The prerequisite to teaching correct values on the changes to come is knowing at what stage a boy is developmentally. Several excellent books on the subject have been written and are available for parents to give their sons in preparation for the onset of puberty. One of my favorites is *The What's Happening to My Body? Book for Boys*, by Linda Madaras (complete listing in the reading list). A book like this can be an eleven- or twelve-year-old's birthday gift or, for parents who are uncomfortable in discussing subjects of this type, can be left on a coffee table, on the boy's bed, and so on, with a note suggesting that he read it and write down any questions he may have. These questions can then be discussed at a later time. In my experience, when the correct book (or books) is chosen, there are usually no questions.

Suggested Solutions for Girls

The primary responsibility for preventing trauma and problems during the puberty of a girl belongs to the parents, and to the mother in particular. While it is true that most girls and mothers discuss body changes (due to the onset of menstruation) more than boys ever do with their fathers, it is also true that questions of sexuality are too often avoided due to parental embarrassment. Even when these discussions do take place, the concentration is on avoiding pregnancy or sexually transmitted diseases. Most of the other sexual matters and acts are not discussed, and the girls, like the boys, gain answers to their questions from peers. As we all know, that information is distorted, biased in favor of the prevailing teen position, and not based on morality but rather on popularity, pleasure, rebellion, and peer acceptance.

Parents need to be actively involved in their daughter's physical developmental and pubertal changes (which come earlier in girls than in boys). When these changes are discussed, moral, ethical, and religious values where relevant to a particular family's belief system need to be included and emphasized. Embarrassment cannot be used as an excuse to avoid this responsibility. The book titled *The What's Happening to My Body Book? for Girls*, by Linda Madaras, can be a help to both parents and girls going through these changes.

THE SEXUAL-ABUSE TIE-IN

What happens to those emerging adolescents (both boys and girls) who do not fall into their peers' ideal group as measured by the above-listed values? When they have an inadequate personality and a poor self-image prior to entering puberty and prior to entering junior high school, the following dangers exist:

1. They are easy prey to more clever, manipulative peers and can easily be sexually exploited by them.

2. They are vulnerable to sexual assault and seduction from adult sexual predators who are always looking for the rejected, inadequate preteen and teen as potential victims (for example, **MR. JOHNSON** in chapter 7, **MR. DON** in chapter 4, **VINNY** in chapter 8, and many others throughout this work).

3. They can become sexual molesters of younger children themselves in order to be able to "brag" to their peers that they are experienced and nonvirgins (for example, **HANS** in chapter 3 or **JARED** in chapter 5).

4. They can brood privately and masturbate with fantasies of sexual acting out or become either female or male prostitutes.

5. They can overcompensate in intellectual or other ways for their own perceived sexual inadequacy (**JARED**'s excellence in wrestling).

6. They can smolder in anger and hatred until later years and then become sexually assaultive persons.

7. They can associate with younger children (often from their former grammar school) so they are bigger, more knowledgeable, and in control. In the latter case, a false sense of pride in leadership often develops until they are forced to compete with age-peers and fail.

8. They can accept their being inadequate and remain in that role throughout life.

9. They can find many other nonadaptive, nondesirable solutions.

The solutions having to do with sexual molestation and prostitution are the major concerns in this discussion. An example will clarify.

DORIS was always a rather plain and somewhat overweight girl. She came from a family where both parents worked, and she was left in the care of her two older brothers, **BOYD**, thirteen, and **ERNIE**, fifteen. Doris's household was not one where open communication existed, and her parents always seemed "too busy" to pay any serious attention to their children. In effect, they were left to raise themselves as best they could.

At school, the "locker room talk" that Boyd and Ernie heard was mostly about girls and sex, and their peers were bragging about no longer being "virgins" and about the girls with whom they had had sex. The boys would look at each other and become instantly embarrassed since neither of them had even been on a simple date with a girl. Also, neither of them had ever seen a girl naked.

As Boyd and Ernie entered junior high school and simultaneously entered adolescence, Doris celebrated her eleventh birthday. The boys gave her a party with her friends in the afternoon. At night they decided to have a private party of their own. Both boys drank several bottles of their father's beer and were "feeling no pain" (their phrase).

High and giddy, they coaxed Doris into playing strip poker and set her up to consistently lose. Piece by piece, Doris lost articles of clothing until she was down to her panties. The boys, both sexually excited, quickly played out the next hand and, when she lost, insisted on their reward. Reluctantly and with a great deal of embarrassment but trusting her brothers, Doris removed her panties and stood naked before the two horny boys.

Without thought, they also stripped naked "to make Doris feel more comfortable" and stood there with erect penises. Doris had never seen a penis before except on her baby cousin and stared in disbelief. What followed occurred so quickly that none of the children realized what was happening. Ernie suggested a games of "I'll let you touch mine if you let me touch yours." Next, Boyd suggested "Let's play doctor," and before ten minutes had passed, he had Doris masturbate him to orgasm. Ernie demanded his turn, and Doris masturbated him next.

When they were finished, both boys swore Doris to secrecy and told her that if she told their parents, they both would say that it was all her idea. Frightened, she agreed.

From that day on, whenever the boys pleased, Doris became their "sex toy" and brought them to orgasm, initially through masturbation, then by oral sex. The boys in turn tried to stimulate Doris manually and orally, but while she did feel "something," she knew that there was something wrong in these games with her brothers. Sensing her discomfort, the boys began giving her presents and money after each sexual encounter, and this made Doris feel somewhat better.

On one occasion, Doris refused to satisfy her brothers, and they hit her, refused to play with her, and wouldn't talk to her until she complied. Being alone and wanting her brothers to like her, Doris agreed after several days to resume their nighttime rituals.

Entering high school, Doris, still rather "plain and plump" (her description), found she was not attractive to the popular boys. She also found out that the popular "jocks" preferred girls "who put out." When time for the first dance of the year came around and Doris had no date, she went to her brothers and asked them what to do. Both boys instantly suggested that she hint to the boy she was attracted to that she would make him feel better than he had ever felt before. The meaning was obvious. They told her she had become "terrific" at their sex games and that any boy would appreciate her skills.

In desperation, Doris finally relented and made her chosen beau "an offer he couldn't refuse." She finally had her first date, and the dance was "cool." Afterward, she kept her word and performed oral sex on her date. Word spread quickly, and Doris suddenly had more "dates" than she could handle. She was suddenly one of the most popular girls in the school.

At age eighteen, in college, continuing her "dating offers" Doris was caught, expelled, and referred to the authorities. Fortunately, she was refereed for therapy.

Questions for Discussion

1. What responsibility do Doris's parents have in her eventual prostitution?

2. How might sex education have played a role in this case?

3. How did the school fail Doris and the other "plain and plump" female or male students?

4. What responsibility do Boyd and Ernie have for Doris's problem?

5. How could what happened to Doris have been prevented?

Doris is by no means an unusual or isolated case, nor is Jared or any of the other survivors described in this work. Adolescence is a difficult time for both the child and the parents. It is made much easier and progresses more smoothly when communication and a close relationship of trust begin as early as possible in a child's life. When this relationship is consistent and regularly reinforced in a family, there are fewer adolescent adjustment problems, and everyone is happier.

Schools also are failing our children and teens. The three children in the Doris case never had any contact with school counselors or psychologists. While they had a short sex education course, it was purely mechanical and did not discuss values, sex practices, ages for initiating sex, moral considerations, and so on. In none of their course or school experiences was the problem of the Adonis complex or the Barbie Doll complex ever mentioned or discussed in a mature and realistic manner.

As stated many times in this work, the safety and welfare of all of our children and teenagers are not just the parent's responsibility, but are everyone's.

A word of additional caution. The "perfect" child or adolescent who never gives his or her parents any problems or grief may also, in my opinion, be a distressed and disturbed individual. Parents who are close to their children and teens will be able to distinguish between a problem and maturity in these cases.

When parents are unsure in cases of this type, the easiest solution is to initiate discussions that will expose the teen's values, feelings, and position on any issue. This can easily be accomplished using a television talk show, an article on the front page of the newspaper, an article in a book or magazine, and so on. Teenagers are opinionated and easily involved in arguments regarding moral and ethical issues. By initiating these arguments, the parent will know what areas to be concerned about and what areas need to be discussed in more depth.

If all else fails and parents have a concern over their teen's development, professional help is always available. It doesn't hurt to be sure, and this can be done easily and quickly by a trained counselor or therapist.

10

THE ROLE AND PRESSURES
OF SOCIETY

Society contributes to many problems in developing children and adolescents. In this chapter our major concern will be those societal pressures that directly or indirectly aid in developing either sexual predators or sexual victims.

Developing children and adolescents are constantly looking for role models. The majority of children and adolescents want to be either equal to or superior to their peers, and this becomes a source of fear and anxiety throughout their formative years. Few, if any, children or adolescents consciously desire to be inferior to their peers.

Conforming to the standards of one's peers assures being accepted by them. Children's and adolescents' normalcy is defined by doing what their peers do, using words that their peers use, wearing clothes that their peers wear, and even eating what their peers eat. The more insecure and sensitive a child or adolescent is, the more vulnerable he or she will be to peer influences. Several major areas should be of concern to all parents, educators, religious groups, and other adults with influence over children or adolescents. They are (1) body-image values; (2) behavioral norms coupled with age norms; (3) learned values and religious beliefs; (4) the choice between celibacy and contraception; (5) and pronounced inhibitions and abnormal fantasies. I have listed these five areas in what I consider the order of their importance as it relates to the topic of sexual abuse.

BODY-IMAGE VALUES

Of all of the destructive comparisons that an emerging child or adolescent can make, those involving the Adonis complex and the Barbie Doll complex are probably the worst. Everywhere the child or adolescent looks, there are body-image comparisons to make: at home, in the neighborhood, at school (especially in gym classes), at the malls, on television, and in the movies.

Television constantly presents images of either the ideal male body (Adonis complex) or the ideal female body (Barbie Doll complex) emphasizing size, facial appearance, muscle development, breast development for girls, and genital bulge and size for males. Talk shows directly discuss these factors and emphasize their importance in exaggerated ways. Ironically, even in weight-loss programs, mostly ideal male and female bodies are presented as normal. Overweight and physically underdeveloped bodies are used in the "before" pictures and presented as undesirable and unacceptable images. Regardless of the format (advertisement, drama, soap opera, talk show, and so on), the same macho males and buxom, svelte females are presented as ideal and desirable.

Children and adolescents who do not live up to these ideals are either motivated to attempt to conform to them or accept themselves as inferior and undesirable. Whether fat, skinny, small, tall, weak, or underdeveloped, these children and adolescents have no role model they can associate themselves with and rarely discuss their feelings on the subject unless directly asked. Even then they often lie (denial). According to television, if a male is a "stud" or an "Adonis," then he will have girls and women groveling at his feet. Isn't this a wonderful image for both males and females to see as their ideal? The perfect body, male or female, is equated with success in all fields of endeavor. One of the only honest and real exceptions to this disastrous trend is Richard Simmons and his weight-loss program that utilizes videotapes of men and women of all sizes and shapes and offers help to all of them. Unfortunately, most children and adolescents do not watch these programs, though parents, teachers, and others should encourage them to do so.

As in most other areas that result in either rejection by adults or peers or situations wherein a child or adolescent is given the sense that he or she is "different" (in a negative and unacceptable way), two possible negative outcomes may occur when children or adolescents measure themselves harshly against others. (1) The child or adolescent uses some desperate means to make up for the perceived deficiency in order to feel "equal" and/or "peer-accepted." (**Jared** in chapter 5, **Jane** in chapter 3, and **Doris** in chapter 9 adopted this solution with disastrous results.) (2) The child or adolescent becomes an easy and available prey to the sexual predators who are constantly looking for victims who are loners, who are isolated from their peer group, and whose needs of the moment the predator can fulfill. These needs might be "love," physical contact and affection, or companionship, and they always involve the acceptance that the child or adolescent is not receiving either at home or from his or her peer group. (Again, **Jane** in chapter 3 and **Martha** in chapter 8 are good examples of sexual predators taking advantage of this type of situation.)

Suggested Solutions

Parents have to be aware of their child's or adolescent's physical build and development. Discussions about body image, the individual's feelings about his or her body, the need for acceptance of that body for the present, and the possibilities for change in the future should all be held on a regular basis and especially in connection with a television comparison or an incident at school, such as the use of names like Fatso, Bones, No-Chest, Shorty, and other degrading or insulting names that children in their cruelty often call each other.

Television specials such as the *After School Specials* series, or the HBO *Lifestories: Families in Crisis* series, or the Canadian *DeGrassi Junior High* or *DeGrassi High* series (both of the latter shows provide free guides for each episode), or the *Discovering Women* series on PBS can help children and adolescents in dealing with a variety of critical issues including body-image problems.

Children and adolescents who do not look like Adonis or Barbie need to be helped to understand that these are only external qualities and in no way account for the true value of a person. Parents, teachers, and other adults involved with children and adolescents cannot wait for the child to bring the topic up. This needs to be a continuing educational endeavor from the earliest age at which children begin comparisons (as soon as they begin interacting with peers). Both boys and girls are affected, and thus both parents need to be involved in this issue. When parents are uncomfortable with either their own body image or their child's body image, outside help will be necessary. This is especially true where obesity is the issue.

Children and adolescents need to be encouraged to be themselves not only physically but intellectually. When a child prefers reading to playing sports and parents are sure that this is not an avoidance behavior, then reading should be encouraged. In these cases, family physical activity often can be a method of balancing the physical with the intellectual in order to assure a "healthy mind in a healthy body." Balance is the goal to be sought rather than obsession with one type of activity over another.

BEHAVIORAL NORMS COUPLED WITH AGE NORMS

In addition to size, weight, and physical development, conformity to peer behaviors is of equal importance to the developing child or adolescent. This is especially true when the child enters puberty, usually in junior high school. Comparisons and the need to be equal or superior are at an all-time high during this period.

Sex also now becomes a major issue and, too often, determines normalcy as well as peer acceptance and respect. As discussed earlier, "virgins" are ridiculed (both boys and girls), especially in high school. Tragically, I have heard the same value promoted in a middle-class junior high school by twelve- and thirteen-year-olds.

The story of **JARED** (see pp. 158–159) clearly exemplifies this point. Although meeting the Adonis standard as captain of the wrestling team and state champion, his mentioning his virginity to his teammates in the locker room nearly destroyed his life and his career. Fortunately, he was placed in therapy and is now attending college in another state, where he won't be so open and sharing about his private life.

Girls appear somewhat luckier in this regard. Many girls can remain virgins without calling rejection or ridicule upon themselves, but for others the anxiety about the matter can have disastrous results. **JANE** (see pp. 80–82) is an excellent example of the latter type of girl. Like **JARED** and so many others, her need for acceptance and love became her major priority and overshadowed her self-respect and self-image. Unfortunately, there are literally thousands of Jareds and Janes in today's world, and the sexual predators are ready and constantly searching for them.

Questions for Discussion

1. In both Jared's and Jane's cases, why did no one notice their inadequacy and lack of self-esteem early in their development?

2. Why do you feel that their parents didn't prepare them for puberty and their awakening sexuality?

3. Where were other responsible adults in their lives, such as teachers and relatives?

4. What defective values were involved in both cases?

5. How can adolescents like Jared and Jane be helped early enough to prevent tragedies such as theirs?

LEARNED VALUES AND RELIGIOUS BELIEFS

Future sex predators and victims begin learning values — like all people — from birth. Any value that contributes to feelings of either being "different" or being in any way "inferior" to one's peer group will have a profound bearing on personality development and self-image. Negative values too often lead to the development of the inadequate personality found in both sex offenders and a large percentage of seductively molested victims.

The Never-Satisfied Parent

As we have seen in previous discussions, the never-satisfied parent is a major contributor in the development of both the sexual molester and the sexual victim. Beside developing the need to be perfect, children and adolescents of these parents are never satisfied with anything they do when they become adults. They cannot accept praise for any accomplishment and develop a need to be seen as inadequate and/or inferior. Little by little, they adopt the attitude of the never-satisfied parent and become "comfortable" being inadequate. From this point on, they make no attempt to change. **GLEN**, discussed in chapters 1 and 4, is a perfect example of this reaction.

Major problems result in persons with inadequate personalities. Beside being unable to accept praise for any accomplishment, their motivation to progress and to take risks in any area (educational, professional, or social) is diminished and often nonexistent. At the same time, they are sad, lonely, and depressed and verbalize the need to change but do little or nothing to effect that change. Even if a new change is made, they take no credit for it and perceive it as a fluke, not a real change. They then rarely take the risk of attempting that behavior again.

This group of inadequate, perfectionist individuals includes the child or adolescent who scores 98 percent on a test and then insists that it should have been 100 percent; if the score is 100 percent, he or she will rationalize that the test was "too easy." These individuals' perception becomes "selective," and they see only what they want to see, only what fits their now-imprinted need to be inferior and/or inadequate. Reality no longer matters, and the harder a teacher or friend attempts to show them who they really are, the more they deny it. Some go so far as to "prove" how inferior or bad they are by deliberately misbehaving or failing tests.

Any child or adolescent in this group is vulnerable to either becoming a sexual predator as **JARED** (see above) did, or becoming a repetitive victim, as **JANE** (see above) did. Most of the cases presented to this point involved inadequate personalities who ended up as either molesters or victims.

For this disastrous result to occur, parents, teachers, other authority figures, or peers need only persistently judge a child or adolescent negatively or consistently suggest she or he will never succeed or be anything. They need only stress how little the child accomplished and how he or she has failed. These failings can be physical, emotional, educational, athletic, social, or behavioral. It doesn't really matter; the results will be the same.

In Jared's case, his virginity was persistently emphasized by his peers, but his wrestling prowess and success, even his championships, were overlooked and never stressed. In Jane's case, there were never any positives discussed, only her "being different" (physically, socially, and so on). Her scholastic achievements were totally ignored or overlooked. All she was good for was to be a sex-object to please men. Eventually, she believed this, and it has become a major treatment barrier.

Negative Sexual Values

In addition to perfectionist values imposed early in a child's development, negative sexual values come next in importance. It is my sincere belief, reinforced by many years of dealing with sexual predators and their victims, that the first sexual behavior of a child or adolescent with another human being *imprints for life*. This first sexual behavior could be as innocent as a young boy "playing doctor" with a little girl. If discovered by a parent or older child or sibling who displays a negative reaction of any kind (name calling, physical punishment, banishment to his room, being told he can never again be trusted, and so on), the imprint will be that his body and the body of his playmate are bad, dirty, not to be touched.

If this behavior involves being caught masturbating and the intruding parent, older peer, teacher, or other authority figure reacts negatively, a negative imprint regarding masturbation will occur and last throughout life. The masturbation will not stop, but it will engender shame, guilt, and feelings of being abnormal. I have treated adult males who still cannot masturbate without feelings of incredible shame and guilt, although intellectually they realize that this behavior is normal and will not produce any of the proffered dire results that they heard screamed at them when they were first caught. **MITCH**, in chapter 4, is an excellent example of this problem.

The Role of Religion

Religions are also guilty of producing these negative reactions. I have treated Catholic males with severe masturbation guilt who were told in confession that their penises and the hand they used to masturbate would burn in hell for eternity. Even though this attitude has changed somewhat in the Catholic church, adult males from forty upward are still traumatized by what they were taught when only nine, ten, or eleven.

The extended problem here is that even though they were caught masturbating, these children or adolescents (especially boys since masturbation is still more common in males than in females) project these negative feelings on all sex acts and often become sexually dysfunctional as adults. This is especially true if as children or adolescents they were in the inadequate personality groups. After more adequate and assertive children and adolescents are caught masturbating, they simply become more cautious of where and when they do it, and there are no negative imprints on their sexuality. Fortunately for society, this group is in the majority.

When mutual genital exploration by two children (gender does not matter here) occurs and they are caught by someone who displays a negative reaction, the imprint will be that sexual curiosity or sexual pleasure is bad and to be avoided. This second situation has consistently been at the root of adult sexual dysfunctions for both males and females and manifests itself primarily in impotence and frigidity. **PHILIP**, in chapter 5, is a good example of this factor.

Another value that is too frequently taught to children and adolescents (more to boys than to girls) is that sexual performance proves manhood or womanhood. Where does this value come from?

Invariably, it can be traced to a child's or adolescent's home and either the direct or indirect (by personal behavior) teaching of one or both parents. Direct teaching in sex-education courses that this is not true and not a value to be adopted does little or no good in the inadequate personality group. Boys, especially, are overly concerned during their prepubertal and pubertal years about their "manhood" as perceived by their peers or by society. The desire to be "normal" or "equal" to their peers overrides parental, religious, or educational teaching, and this area must be carefully monitored by everyone involved with these children and adolescents.

Suggested Solutions

Open discussion of sex and of all sexual issues and values as early as possible in a child's life will develop an atmosphere where questions that are of concern to children can be safely asked of parents, teachers, and others. This process should begin with preschool children, both boys and girls, at home on an appropriate level by a sexually well-adjusted parent or parents. The reason for beginning this early is that as soon as the child is sent to preschool or even some nursery school settings, where interaction with peers is inevitable, exposure to the values of others (both peers and staff) occurs. When children are totally naive sexually, they, being impressionable, are more likely to be affected by what they hear and see. When children are even minimally prepared, this effect is diminished, and they are usually able to "hold their own" and express what they have been taught at home or to bring the matter up with their mother or father when they arrive home.

Terminology for Body Parts and Bodily Functions

Forbidding or avoiding discussion of sex, body parts, and body functions can do irreparable damage in the home and society. This damage can result from a number of factors.

Using Slang and "Cute" Terms for the Genitals. A simple example involves terms used for body parts and bodily functions such as urinating and having a bowel movement. It is amazing what slang children learn in these circumstances from peers who know no more than they do or from staff, including teachers, who have their own "cute" terminology.

It is important for parents to use correct terminology with their children as early as possible to avoid confusion when the first non-domestic discussion of these functions occurs. Little boys should know that they have a penis, not a "pee-pee," "peter," "tinkler," "peanut," "birdie," "fire-hose," "ding-a-ling," "monkey," "worm"...; little girls should know that they have a vulva, not a "pee-pee," "flower," "saltfish," "slit," "cunny," "baby-door," and so on.

The terms above are a small percentage of terms for the genitals that I have heard from young children whom I have interviewed or treated. There were over one hundred terms for the male genital organs and upwards of fifty for female genital organs. A very small percentage of the children I interviewed had any acquaintance with correct terminology.

Excessive Modesty. The major problem with excessive modesty is that it communicates the message that something is wrong or "dirty" about the body. Small children go through a stage where running around naked ("streaking") is normal, and it should be treated as such. As the child grows older, this is the perfect opportunity for parents to discuss modesty in realistic terms. How can children who are seen naked by their mother or father while being dressed or bathed understand that when they run out of their room naked that this is different and wrong? Children can learn to grasp this only if parents carefully and sensitively make a distinction between those who should and those who should not see them naked.

When parents in a family setting practice nudity as a norm, children have to be taught from the earliest age that this is a normal behavior only "for their family" and that other parents may hold different values and beliefs on the subject. In one very sad case that I was called in to handle, the child told his schoolmates about the family's nude behaviors, and the school reported it to the authorities, resulting in the removal of the child from his parents for two weeks while an investigation was completed. All of this could have been prevented with proper value training and guidance.

Inadequate or Improper Preparation for Sexual Development. It is amazing and at times astounding how many adolescents today in the United States have had absolutely no preparation for puberty. This is particularly true for boys. As discussed earlier, girls are more fortunate since at least they are prepared by most mothers for their menses. Also, girls generally tend to talk more freely with mothers, teachers, and peers about sexual matters than do boys.

Parents need to prepare their child, male or female, for (*a*) pubic and body hair growth and development; (*b*) genital growth and the emphasis on size, especially for boys, including the large amount of differences in the time when puberty will occur; (*c*) wet dreams for boys and menstruation for girls; (*d*) sexual facts including contraceptive methods to prevent not only pregnancy but also sexually transmitted diseases.

As I will state over and over again, if parents feel uncomfortable in teaching sex education to their children fully, they may choose a professional (a certified sex educator or sex therapist would be my primary choice), a close relative whom the parents and the child trust and relate to, school or group sex-education courses and discussions, self-teaching manuals, and so on.

THE CHOICE BETWEEN CELIBACY AND CONTRACEPTION

Teenage pregnancy is a major problem. Most of these pregnancies result from incest, sexual molestation, sexual assault, sexual promiscuity, or carelessness. A small amount of teen pregnancies are deliberate and preplanned. In this later category, males either are proving their manhood in an extreme way or are simply narcissistic, placing all responsibility on the girl, whereas girls often simply want a child to care for and, in many cases, where they themselves were abused, are attempting *to undo* the treatment they received as children with more positive replacement behaviors with their child.

Except for the cases of sexual assault (rape), all of these pregnancies are preventable. Someone has to accept the responsibility of sex-educating all of our maturing adolescents from as early an age as possible. *Value-formation* in children and adolescents is critical to this endeavor. Earlier and at considerable length I discussed some false or distorted values that can result in ill-timed sexual activity and pregnancy. Some of these are the following:

- Sex equals love.

- Sex is only for pleasure and fun.

- Love needs to be bought with sexual submission.

- Sexual acting out proves manhood/womanhood.

- Virgins are nerds, sissies, queers, and so on.

- Contraception is for weirdos.

- "Real men don't wear raincoats!"

Because the source of these distorted values is either parents or peers, it might be helpful to give a very brief sketch of a case in which a parent's distorted values were assumed directly by a child.

HARVEY, during my initial questioning, shared vivid memories of his father taking him on business trips and bragging to him about having many female friends and sex partners. Wanting to emulate the father he loved, Harvey became confused: on the one hand, this man was his hero and idol; on the other hand, he loved his mother and felt his father was wrong in cheating on her and betraying her trust. Harvey never said a word about his feelings to his father but acted out promiscuously with five or six girls. Each time it came to having intercourse, Harvey was impotent. This embarrassed him and continues to occur even in his marriage today (the reason for his self-referral).

Harvey picked up the "value" of promiscuity from his father. At the opposite end of the spectrum lie conservative parents and educators who feel that discussing sex or contraception encourages sexual acting out in youths who would not normally be sexually active. This is nonsense. The topics of delaying the onset of sexual behavior, celibacy, contraception, and the dangers of promiscuity can and should be included in discussions between parents and adolescents. The risk of an unwanted pregnancy or of sexually transmitted diseases that are life-threatening or that may result in sterility or other genetic damage overshadows the concern that inactive youngsters will become active simply from discussing these matters.

Suggested Solutions

As stated over and over in this work, proper and complete sex education, including the teaching of values, is the only logical solution to these problems. If parents feel they are prepared and comfortable in sex-educating their children, so be it, but this should not mean that these children should not participate in sex-education courses at school. To forbid their participation would be a disastrous error and increase feelings of being different or alienated from their peers. It also will mean very little since they will discuss what went on in the course with their peers anyway and possibly be given erroneous information. When parents are secure in their communication and their relationship with their children, permitting their children to participate in sex education with their peers does not pose a threat but rather presents an opportunity for the parents to know what their children are being exposed to in school and what their peers think and feel. With an open line of communication regarding sex (and other topics important to the child), when a conflict exists between values being taught in school and the values being taught at home, the child can broach this conflict with his or her parents rather than remaining confused or ambivalent or being put in a position to choose between the two. Too often this is the position a child is put into when there is no open communication at home regarding all subjects. Had **JARED** (see above, pp. 158–159) been able to go home and discuss his concerns over his virginity with his mother and stepfather rather than finding his own defective solution to his problem, he would not now be on probation with a sex offender history in his record.

Of the many, many teens that I have discussed contraception and related matters with, I have been alarmed, as stated earlier, at their attitudes of "invulnerability." For sexually active adolescent males, not using condoms is much too frequent as are attitudes like "Nothing can happen to me" and "If she gets pregnant, that's her problem, not mine." The second statement clearly indicates another serious attitude or value problem: the large number of adolescent males with a complete lack of responsibility or concern for anyone but themselves, a form of total narcissistic selfishness.

In today's age of AIDS, celibacy for prepubertal and adolescent boys and girls is the only truly safe sexual behavior. How to teach this value to our youth is the problem. All avenues of a child's or adolescent's life must be in agreement on the issue, and the forum, in my opinion, must be a peer-group setting rather than an individual one. This is the "peer stage" where, unfortunately, the opinions and judgments of peers often override the opinions and beliefs of parents and other adults.

Thus, in addition to the carefully prepared and delivered sex-education courses mentioned above, it is imperative to provide supervised rap sessions and/or discussions in which all adolescents participate and which are conducted by other adolescents who have already made serious and even tragic value decisions regarding sexual invulnerability. These sessions should include adolescents who are pregnant and the fathers; where possible, adolescents with sexually transmitted diseases, especially AIDS; and adolescents who have acted out sexually in an illegal manner and are now either incarcerated or on probation. Appearing at and conducting these supervised rap sessions could easily be made a part of the sentences (community service) for the latter group. A trained and responsible adult counselor or therapist should attend these sessions as an observer or facilitator but not as a member. The group should approve the choice of adult if the process is to work since trust is an essential issue, and only the group knows whom they will trust.

These supervised rap sessions can be especially important for those preadolescent and adolescent males and females who have already begun antisocial sexual acting out on a minor scale. This might include, for instance, voyeurs and exhibitionists who are too young or too inadequate to commit more serious sexual crimes such as sexual assault but who are already having fantasies of committing these crimes.

PRONOUNCED INHIBITIONS AND ABNORMAL FANTASIES

In my experience, too many of these "minor" offenses are considered petty or nuisance behaviors simply because untrained juvenile officers and investigators never focus on the fantasies that accompany these behaviors. An example will clarify.

DERRICK is a twenty-nine-year-old male who is now serving a twenty-year sentence for the aggravated sexual assault of four college students on their own campus. During treatment, Derrick revealed that his sexual acting out had begun where he was about ten or eleven years old. His older brothers were sexually active and physically more developed than he was (he was very ashamed and embarrassed by his perceived small penis). The three brothers all shared the same bedroom, undressed in front of each other, and the two older brothers openly discussed their "sexual conquests." They also slept in the nude. Derrick would wait until they were asleep and then openly stare at their bodies, especially their genitals, fantasizing that he was as well endowed and as experienced as they were.

Derrick's family spent one month at the New Jersey shore each summer, and he was left pretty much on his own since his older brothers did not want him around. In the evenings, after dark, Derrick would wander around the many other cottages and "peep" into bedroom windows. When he found a teenage girl or an adult woman undressing, he would masturbate with fantasies of entering the room and having sex with them but with his brothers' bodies, not his. Once he climaxed, he returned immediately to reality and would run home ashamed and disgusted with himself.

As Derrick grew older, his fantasies became more aggressive and assaultive. While "peeping," he would fantasize entering the window and forcing the girl or woman to submit to his wishes and tell him how great he was. These fantasies occurred whenever he was able to "peep" on a couple engaged in sexual behavior (which was surprisingly quite often). Afterwards the results were always the same: depression and disgust over his inadequate body and his inadequate personality.

On one or two of his more than fifty peeping episodes, Derrick was caught by either a husband or a boyfriend and threatened or slapped around. Neither individual told Derrick's parents or reported the "peeping" to the police.

By his early twenties, Derrick had physically developed. He attended a gym regularly and worked out for hours and hours. Standing in front of a mirror in the nude, he admired his body but still felt his penis was small and that women would either reject him when they saw it or laugh and ridicule him. This made him angry. Masturbation was now fired by rape fantasies, but it no longer satisfied him. One night, while "peeping" in the window of a young female who he knew was alone, he acted out his fantasy by entering the window and raping her. When he was finished (he prematurely ejaculated), he threatened her life, and the woman never reported the incident. This made Derrick feel masculine and powerful, and that fall when the family returned from the shore and Derrick moved into a college dormitory, he began his career as a rapist.

Derrick's case is typical of many men who end up in a prison or treatment facility. He never had any formal sex education, had poor communication with both of his parents, and never discussed his feelings with his two older brothers out of fear that they would only reject and ridicule him more. He had very few friends in grammar school or high school and, while he did excel in sports, never hung out with the "jocks." Since he was well behaved both at home and at school and was always polite and gentlemanly to all adults, no one ever suspected a problem, and he slipped through the cracks. Five young women had to pay the price for this obvious neglect, and Derrick himself lost all chances for his desired career in law.

Questions for Discussion

1. How could this tragedy have been prevented?

2. Where did Derrick's parents go wrong?

3. Why didn't the two adult men who caught Derrick report his behavior to anyone?

4. How often is good behavior mistaken for good adjustment?

5. Can this same situation happen to girls?

While Derrick became a sexual predator, he could have just as easily become a sexual victim. His vulnerability, his need for acceptance and approval, his need to be seen as equal to his brothers and to his peers, and his negative feelings about himself all fit the requirements that the sexual predator seeks in a potential victim. There are just as many cases of victims in this type of adolescent (both boys and girls) as there are cases of sexual predators.

Suggested Solutions

In Derrick's case as in the cases of other adolescents like Derrick, early communication in the family is a must. It would have been less likely for Derrick's sexual pathology to develop had he been able to talk to at least one of his parents or at least one of his brothers about his feelings of inadequacy and inferiority.

Derrick's good behavior became equated with positive growth and adjustment. Too often this mistake ends up in some form of tragedy. A second mistake his parents made was assuming that nothing was bothering Derrick simply because he did not complain. Why didn't anyone notice that he was a loner and that he was not associating with peers? Why didn't his sexually superior brothers ask Derrick about his sexual experiences? Why didn't they notice that their brother was not dating or having sexual experiences at the age that they had begun? Why did Derrick simply exist in his family rather than being a part of it?

Derrick enthusiastically gave me permission to use his story. He wanted it published in the hope that other adolescent boys like him would not end up in the same predicament. When asked what would have helped him, he gave me the following list:

1. Time to sit down and talk to either his mother or his father or both about his concerns about his physical smallness.

2. Recognition by his brothers of his physical and sexual smallness compared to them and an open discussion about this with him so he could ask them questions.

3. Sex education in his junior high school and also in his high school; there was none in either, and no class environment or group discussion opportunities for him to ask important questions about body and genital size.

4. Being caught "peeping" so he could finally tell someone what he was going through and get help, especially when the violent fantasies began.

5. Someone to tell him that regardless of his physical and genital size he was all right (normal) and girls could and would accept him as he was.

Many societal norms, values, and pressures contribute to the formation and sustaining of the inadequate personality. Among these are values regarding money, success, homophobia, early and active sexual behavior, and manhood. The positive values of family, self-respect and respect for others, honesty, satisfaction with one's body and one's intellectual capacity, ethics, and morality are conspicuously missing.

TELEVISION'S ROLE

Television, which has an immense responsibility, contributes to these damaging values with soap operas that project all of the distorted and damaging values possible including the glorification of murder, infidelity, and sex outside of a meaningful relationship. The vast amount of violence and unsolved crime emphasized daily adds to the negative model that television portrays. Talk shows, which could do a world of good, often are just as guilty of glorifying everything negative, from incest to rape, to murder, to violence as a solution to problems, to drug use.... Talk shows rarely include positive role modes for children and teenagers. Shows on individuals who have done something positive in society are rare and, for some talk show hosts, nonexistent.

Public television struggles along as one of the only broadcast media through which these positive role models can be found, but how many parents watch these positive shows with their children and teenagers and later have a discussion on what was just seen? — a relatively small minority, I assure you.

11

SELF-IMPOSED RULERS

DANGEROUS COMPARISONS

As discussed earlier, a "ruler" is a measurement used by all human beings to compare or evaluate themselves on a single trait or on many norms. "Rulers" are first learned from parents during the child's earliest formative years. Because an understanding of rulers is tied to a grasp of the stages of human development, it would be helpful here for readers to refer back to pp. 114–117 on the five stages of value formation.

Most of the children and adolescents whom I treat as sexual-abuse survivors fit into either stage 1 or stage 4. **JARED** is a perfect example of a stage 4 type who when rejected by his peers is subject to a regression to stage 1 and is thus vulnerable to an adult sexual predator. Instead of falling into this trap, Jared, like so many others, attempted to become equal to his peers by molesting his younger cousins.

LEW, discussed in chapter 2, fell into the trap, and when he felt that he could not compete with or be like his adolescent peers, he submitted to the sexual molestations of his scoutmaster over a lengthy period of time. Later in life he identified with the scoutmaster and ritualistically repeated what was done to him by role reversal.

Suggested Solutions

All of the cases of this type that have been presented in this work were preventable. When parents of children who were in treatment for having been a sexual victim or for having perpetrated a sexual abuse were questioned about developmental problems, every parent that I interviewed recalled having been aware of developmental lags, especially on the social and interpersonal levels. The most common rationalization to do nothing about these lags was: "He [or she] is just slow in maturing and will eventually catch up with his peers." This fatal error resulted in a new victim or in the development of a new sexual abuser.

Parents first and then relatives, neighbors, teachers, ministers, priests, and even friends of the family all have an obligation to observe and comment on a child's or adolescent's obvious problems in interpersonal relationships or peer-social involvement. Loners stand out, and someone needs to take notice and confront the situation in a positive manner.

How is this accomplished? To begin, there must be an established line of communication between the child or adolescent and his or her parents, some other adult, or an older peer. Without this communication link there will be little, if any, change accomplished. For any change to occur, the problem must first be accurately identified.

In Jared's case, if his size and shyness were wrongfully identified as the problems, then the suggested solutions would also be wrong and no change would have occurred in the sexual problem area. For Jared to have told anyone of his "small-penis concerns" would have required a great deal of trust. His fears of ridicule and rejection because of his perceived small penis would have precluded him trusting most of his peers since he changed and showered with them and selectively perceived that they were all much more developed than he was.

For the first month of his treatment, Jared insisted that the sexual abuse of his cousins resulted from his being a virgin and his shame about having told this secret to his teammates, who subsequently ridiculed him. There was no mention of his concerns about his small penis. It was only after I told him that I felt that there was more to his motivation than his virginity that he reacted so uncomfortably and was so insistent that there was no other reason. Being inferior to his peers due to his virginity and his small penis was Jared's self-imposed ruler. Jared's treatment must necessarily include the development of a new self-image, and this is the present goal of his treatment.

Girls are just as likely to suffer from self-imposed rulers as are boys. **JANE**, discussed in chapter 3, is a good example of this factor. Comparing her body size and appearance to her peers, Jane decided that she did not compare and therefore that she was inferior to them; this, then, became her self-imposed ruler. Once this judgment was made, her isolation behavior and depression quickly and almost automatically followed. Her value on external appearance completely overshadowed her intelligence and her personality. The result was her vulnerability to anyone who would like and accept her. Uncle Jack, her neighbor, quickly perceived the problem and, just as quickly, took advantage of it for his own perverted needs. Where were her parents, relatives, friends, teachers, and so on, while all of this was happening? Certainly, her isolation was obvious; her not associating with peers was just as obvious, and her being a loner at school had to be noticed by someone. Yet no one did anything about it. Her parents never talked to her about it; her teachers never referred her for counseling; and her "best friend" actually reinforced her feelings by leaving her to associate with other peers.

SELF-IMAGE DEVELOPMENT

While I do feel that some children and adolescents have an inherited tendency to a poor self-image and shyness, I also firmly believe that this value and perception can be altered by the earliest possible recognition and concerted effort by parents and others.

In families where persistent negative criticism is the norm, the children have no chance of improving their self-image. **GLEN**, in chapter 1, clearly demonstrates this situation. The "never-satisfied parent," discussed in chapter 10, destroys any attempt on the part of the child to improve his or her self-perception, and eventually the child succumbs to this parent's negative perceptions and "joins the enemy."

In families with two or more siblings, parental comparisons can be disastrous. Statements such as "Why can't you get As like your sister?" are reprehensible, especially when the parents have not taken into account the differences in intelligence, motivation, teachers, and so on. A child with a poor to negative self-image can succeed in school as an overcompensatory mechanism but can just as easily project the negative body image onto their entire personality including intelligence factors and achievement desires.

A very low percentage of parents attend parent-teacher conferences. Yet here is a perfect opportunity to receive an outside, professional opinion about a child and suggestions for improvement, but parents are "too busy" or "too tired" or afraid of being perceived as "bad parents." Even those who do attend are often embarrassed when they are told that their child is deficient in a subject or in behavior. When they leave, threats, punishments, or restrictions are all that they can think of rather than discussing the problem and finding positive changes to help their offspring. Many parents also simply assume that one child is dumber than the other and let it go at that. The old "You can't get blood out of a rock" is used to justify their negligence.

Next in line of responsibility come the teachers, especially those who are suffering from burn out. Teachers, more than any other individuals in the child's life, should be sufficiently trained to observe a child in trouble. This might be a child who isolates, a child who shows potential every now and then but is not working up to that potential, a child obviously not up to social demands related to classroom work, and so on. It should then be the teacher's responsibility to notify someone about the situation or to attempt to help the child in some individual way. I believe there is always a way to accomplish this goal. If the teacher truly is overloaded and too busy, there are certainly one or more children in the class who are above class levels and who are bored when they have to wait for the class to catch up. These brighter children can be assigned as tutors for the slower children and can be given the time and place to tutor them without making them feel different or inferior. I have seen this system work with positive self-image results for both the tutors and those whom they tutor. I have also seen social relationships form in these small groups that last throughout the years and outside of school as well.

Both parents and schools need to teach positive body-image values as well as positive and realistic scholastic and achievement values. The smaller/taller, fatter/thinner, beautiful/plain, handsome/nonattractive, and athletic/studious dichotomies need to be addressed and self-acceptance or change promoted. Self-acceptance for the present must precede any attempt to change. Placing the negative trait in perspective is also essential. An obese child may also be an intelligent child with a positive and healthy personality. However, if this child or adolescent sees only the "fatness" and perceives it as making his or her whole person negative and undesirable, no motivation to change will develop. While working on the weight problem a great deal of support is needed as well as an emphasis on all of the other qualities that the child possesses.

This is especially true when the negatively perceived trait is unchangeable, such as height, physical defects (missing or distorted limbs, severe acne, asthma, and so on), facial appearance, or breast or genital size. Acceptance in all of these cases is a must, and the value that acceptance does not mean like or approval needs to be taught from the earliest possible time.

Recently I saw a talk show the topic of which was "mothers rejecting daughters due to the daughter's weight." Obese girls were presented who were either depressed, runaways, on drugs, or acting promiscuously (buying acceptance with sex), all due to these girls' nonacceptance of their weight, which was constantly being reinforced by their rejecting mothers. Can you imagine the effect this program had on other overweight girls (and boys!) watching it? Fortunately, Richard Simmons participated and offered the girls acceptance, love, and hope that they could change, but, most importantly, he stressed that their weight said nothing about the type of person they were or could be. Why couldn't the parents have either taught the same positive value or referred their daughters for help when the problem began (by program time they were all older adolescents or young adults)? All of the girls on the show were so desperate for acceptance and love that they stated that they were willing to do anything to find it, including becoming sexual slaves.

As I have emphasized throughout this work, sexual predators are well aware of these children and adolescents, both girls and boys, and are out there willing and able to provide the acceptance and "love" these kids want, but that acceptance and "love" have a price. Unfortunately, when rejected at home, school, and by their peers, these vulnerable kids will pay that price and end up damaged, some for life.

SELF-IDENTITY PROBLEMS

Next, it is important to discuss the issues surrounding self-identity. While a large percentage of children struggle to find an idol or model early in life, others appear to know who they are at a surprisingly early age. These assertive, self-confident, strong-willed, and independent children develop happily and normally with one crucial exception, the child who is positive that he or she is homosexual.

There has been a great deal of controversy recently regarding homosexual development and whether there is a hereditary gene involved or whether it is strictly a learned or acquired trait. For those children who know they are gay, the origin of their identity is not a pressing problem. The problem centers around the need to conform, to be like their peers (that is, heterosexual), to please their parents and then their friends and associates, and, in general, to fit into society's molds and models.

Children like **HANS**, introduced in chapter 3, who from an early age feel "different" from those around them, face conflicts at all developmental ages until they reach stage 5 (see the outline of stages, pp. 114–117), if they ever reach that stage. Hans, when in treatment as an adult sexual molester, insisted over and over again that he knew at age four that he was not like other boys. He knew that he was attracted to boys and that being with them or having any form of physical contact with them excited him (nonsexually). At age five when he was approached by and sexually seduced by his older cousins, Jeremy, who was ten, and Kurt, who was eleven, he knew that this was what he wanted and that he was homosexual (although, at that time, he did not know the word).

Had Hans not been sexually molested at age five, he would not have known that he was homosexual until possibly puberty or until he was exposed to sexual knowledge and practices. He would still have felt "different," would still have preferred to associate primarily with boys, and would still have enjoyed any and all physical contact with them.

When Hans was twelve or thirteen — when he became pubertal — his grandmother caught him and another cousin, **TOMMY**, age sixteen, in bed having oral sex. Amazingly, she blamed Hans, called him "dirty," "nasty," and so on, and told him that he was "gonna go to hell!" Hans felt "like scum" (his words), and he stopped all sexual activity for two full years. Sex, for Hans, from then on was something that was "dirty" or "nasty." This value came from being put down by his grandmother and from the fact that his father had sex with his mother only when he was drunk and his mother didn't want to.

After the two-year hiatus, Hans went on a camping trip with another friend, whom he really liked. That night, the friend undressed and sat naked on his blanket, and the old feelings returned. Within a few minutes, they were touching, feeling, and ended up having oral sex. This time Hans rationalized: "If we both like each other and have sex, then it must be OK." Using this new but distorted value based on the camping episode, Hans began molesting boys much younger than himself toward whom he felt strong attraction and something akin to love. As stated in chapter 3, he ended up molesting some thirty boys before being apprehended and sent away for treatment.

Questions for Discussion

1. Who could Hans have gone to at age four or five to discuss his feelings of being "different" and being attracted only to other

boys? Certainly not his parents or his friends since he "knew" that it was wrong to be this way.

2. After Hans was molested at age five by his older cousins and new feelings began that this was the way he always wanted to be, who could he have discussed this with?

3. What effects did being caught by his grandmother in a homosexual situation have on Hans's self-image and his homosexual identity?

4. Why do you think that following this traumatic incident, Hans began molesting younger boys when prior to the trauma he had always been with older boys?

5. Can you think of a parental factor that could have prevented these traumatic and later illegal acts from occurring?

SELF-JUDGMENT

In addition to the identity issues, those next in importance concern and revolve around self-worth. These issues involve moral and ethical judgments, learned from the earliest years from parents and other caretakers. Religion and then peer judgments come next and, for those individuals who never reach stage 5 (The "I stage") of emotional development, the judgment of all of these other groups is an essential determinant to all self-worth issues.

The first and primary problem area is that of self-judgment. All human beings are in a continual process of self-judging in all areas of their lives: physical, emotional, scholastic, social, moral and religious, and, of course, sexual. These self-judgments affect all areas of human endeavor, including motivation, and result in socialization or isolation, happiness or depression, self-satisfaction or self-hatred and self-rejection. A pervasive sense of "I'm just no good!" can be found in most children, teenagers, and adults who have been victimized and are referred for treatment. Why couldn't they have been referred before they were victimized? Could the reason be the belief that taking a child or teenager to a "shrink" makes the statement that the parents have somehow failed or are inadequate?

As we have seen in the section on the "never-satisfied parent" (chapter 10), a learned pattern of perfectionism develops in some individuals, and this need to be perfect is then equated with "acceptance." An obsessive need to find and obtain acceptance at any price may, and often does, develop. These individuals are then extremely vulnerable to the seductions of the sexual molesters. As I have said over and over in this book, the sexual predator watches for and expertly observes this need in the potential victims that he or she is pursuing. Most adults who work with children can recognize these children or adolescents but don't take advantage of them; only the sexual predators and other antisocial manipulators will.

Of the sex offenders I have worked with, this ability to spot vulnerable victims is universal. When they find a child or adolescent with this desperate need for acceptance, sex offenders are thrilled and excited. They know that the potential for a successful seduction of this type of individual is very high.

Suggested Solutions

As in most of my other suggested solutions, the primary prevention occurs when parents really know their children. Where this issue is concerned, since parents are the ones who usually have caused the problem, a reevaluation of their child-rearing techniques is definitely in order. The more abused and damaged children I see, the more I feel that potential parents should *all* be required to takes courses on child rearing during or even before the pregnancy. This should include both parents since consistency in rearing is essential. It takes only one parent to do the damage where perfectionism is concerned.

Too often, parents commit this terrible error with the best of intentions, especially wanting their sons or daughters to have a better life than they did. Children and teens, however, need to make mistakes — that is how they learn. These mistakes have to be accepted by parents as part of the growth and learning process. When they are not accepted and are constantly nagged about, a negative self-judgment process is born and flourishes.

When a behavior is too strongly objected to and punished, it is fairly simple for a needy and insecure child or teen to expand the behavior rejection onto the total self. Where some form of punishment is necessary, it should always "fit the crime," and when it is over, parents have to say and do things to assure the child or teen that he or she is still loved. If this caveat is not followed and the child feels a deep sense of rejection from the parents, he or she will go elsewhere to find that acceptance and love that, following any form of punishment, are needed even more intensely. Remember, the sexual predator is ready, willing, and able to replace the rejecting parent and supply all of the love and acceptance that these children and teenagers need. **JANE,** in chapter 3, is a perfect example of this type of sexual molestation.

"What Am I?" issues are integrally tied in with "Who am I?" issues, and, for the most part, they cannot be separated. Both questions play a major role in the formation of the adult personality and also a strong role in motivation for success in later life. There are countless inadequate adults who are lost where these two issues are concerned. Several negative factors result.

1. Their identity comes from other people rather than from themselves.

2. They cannot make decisions and suffer over the smallest ones for days at a time, asking all of their friends and associates for advice. What they really want is for someone else to make the decision.

3. Socially, they isolate, since they anticipate rejection, and it is better to be alone than face that rejection. The reason for this is that any rejection confirms their negative self-image and adds more reasons to feel badly about themselves.

4. Failure is dreaded since they have had so many in their lives. The result is that they are unwilling to take even the smallest

risks. They rarely apply for promotions in their workplace or for scholarships, if they are students. They anticipate that they will not be chosen and so fear the pain of such a rejection. It is easier to simply not try. Rationalizations abound. If asked why they are not applying in either instance, the answer will be that they are simply not interested.

These inadequate individuals, more than any others, need to be found as early as possible in their development and referred for professional help. They are persistently vulnerable to every form of abuse, especially being used by psychopaths and sexual predators. Their incredible need for acceptance knows no bounds, and they are willing to pay any price to be accepted.

Everyone involved in a child's life should feel responsible for this type of child or adolescent. If parents are unconcerned, then relatives, teachers, and any other adult who has contact with them must make every effort to correct this misperception as early as possible. The longer it exists, the harder it is to change, and, at some point, it may be impossible to change. An example will clarify.

DENNIS, a thirty-year-old, is a seriously inadequate individual and has a defective self-image that effects all of his interpersonal relationships and all other aspects of his life, including his employment. He sees himself as a "nerd" or "dweeb" (his terms), and, unfortunately, these are both realistic and appropriate descriptions.

Dennis also is a virgin; he has had no total sexual involvement with anyone. He is a compulsive masturbator with fantasies of young boys, around age seven, whom he watches in parks, in school yards, in his neighborhood, and so on. His greatest fear is that he will eventually molest one of them.

All of Dennis's fantasies and sexual desires are male-oriented. He has never been sexually interested in or excited by women. He has several gay friends and frequents several gay bars. In the last year or so, his fourth year in therapy, he has had several sexual encounters with a gay friend who cares for Dennis and is willing to do anything to help him. In all of their attempts, Dennis will go so far as to give pleasure to his friend but will never permit his friend to give pleasure to him.

Dennis has many, many rationalizations. The most blatantly absurd one is that his masturbating to fantasies of having sex with one of the boys he has just been watching is not homosexual "because he is a little boy and not a man." The second bizarre rationalization (a form of denial) is that his sexual acts with his gay friend, although they result in a climax for the friend and he masturbates himself at the end, are not homosexual acts "because I didn't let him get me off." The ultimate denial and rationalization is that neither of these behaviors makes him homosexual. When asked what his sexual orientation is, he replies, "I haven't decided yet."

All of Dennis's childhood memories repeat the theme of his being inferior and inadequate in comparison to his peers. Although one of his brothers insists that this was not true, Dennis says he never communicated any of his feelings to his parents or to his brothers and allowed them to assume whatever they chose to assume about him.

At work, where he is a supervisor in the financial section of a major corporation (surprise!), he associates with no one and cannot maintain eye contact with his staff or with his supervisors for more than a few seconds. He brings a bag lunch and eats on a park bench, rather than in the cafeteria with the rest of the staff.

Recently a promotion was posted on the bulletin board that could lead to advancement. After brooding and being indecisive over applying, Dennis missed the deadline and then rationalized, "Well, I wanted to apply but I kept forgetting until it was too late."

Concurrently, Dennis wanted to move closer to his employment and actually did go and see one apartment. He told the landlord that he would take the flat and then, as anticipated, brooded over the decision, vacillating pro and con and calling everyone he could think of to ask their advice. He ended up canceling the deal by telephone with a ridiculous reason that he didn't like the color of the paint in the kitchen. He had discussed this factor with everyone he called, and several of his friends offered to help him repaint the kitchen, and the landlord offered to pay for the paint. It didn't matter. The *risk* of change was too great. Now, a month after this incident, Dennis still brings it up, asking if he made the right decision.

While Dennis may seem an extreme case, he is not. I have treated over a hundred similar convicted sex offenders with the same frightened, indecisive, inadequate personalities. All of them, were they discovered at an early age (seven to twelve), could have been helped and, as adults, would have been able to cope with life's rejections and necessary risks. None of them was ever happy.

SUMMARY

In chapters 7 through 11 I discussed the major factors that I have found contribute to our children and teenagers being sexually abused. I have also made suggestions as to how these victimizations could have been prevented and who I feel was primarily responsible in each type. Each subject covered could have become a book unto itself since these areas are so complicated and so individualized. Of the hundreds of offenders and victims I have seen, no two were identical. Each had his or her own special traits and characteristics. However, there were commonalities, and these are the ones I have tried to present.

In the next and final part I will cover my experiences with recognition and treatment both for the sexual offenders and for the survivors of their offenses.

Part 3

Recognition and Treatment

12

RECOGNITION AND WARNING SIGNS

FACTORS THAT AFFECT THE DEGREE OF TRAUMA

It has been my consistent experience that each person reacts differently and individually to any form of trauma. There are, however, several consistent factors that affect the degree of the trauma and thus the degree of visible signs that a trauma has occurred or is occurring. They are the following:

- the individual's personality, ego-strengths, and weaknesses;

- the stage of physical and emotional development that he or she is in;

- the value base of the individual at the time of the trauma;

- the specific circumstances of the traumatic occurrence;

- the actual words used by the sexual predator;

- whether or not the trauma was witnessed and by whom;

- how the sexual abuse was perceived by the survivor;

- how the sexual abuse was uncovered or exposed and by whom; and

- the reactions of parents, other authority figures, and friends to knowing of the abuse.

WHEN DOES SEXUAL ABUSE BECOME TRAUMATIC?

Not all sexual abuse is perceived by survivors as traumatic at the time of the occurrence, especially when all of the elements of the abuse are pleasant and perceived as positive. Several examples have already been presented. **HANS**, in chapter 3, for example, perceived all of his molestations as pleasurable and desirable and looked forward to his next encounters with his older cousins. **RUSTY**, in chapter 2, also perceived his molestations by **KARL** to be pleasurable and not only would look forward to the next occurrence but would initiate it himself.

JAMIE, in chapter 5, was incestuously molested by his father, **GENE**, over a period of years and never complained. In treatment, he admitted that he enjoyed having sex with his father. None of the thirty boys who were molested by **KEIF**, discussed in chapter 2, ever complained or reported him, although the molestations occurred in front of their peers. They also consistently volunteered for his future science-oriented camping trips. Finally, **LEW**, in chapter 2, who was raped by his scoutmaster, continued to volunteer to go alone with him to open the camp, knowing what was going to occur and actually looking forward to it.

The trauma in all of these cases occurred in later life either when the sexual behaviors were exposed or when these survivors learned what their parents (stage 1), other authority figures (police, detectives, judges, teachers, priests, ministers, and so on) (stage 3), or peers (stage 4) felt about kids having sex with adults, especially when the behaviors involved homosexuality. The attitude or reaction of the all of these groups when discussing the sexual abuse with the survivor is a paramount determining factor as to the degree of trauma that the survivor will experience. Parents' anger and judgmentalism, insensitivity from detectives who are not properly trained in dealing with survivors of sexual abuse, negative reactions from peers, put downs, and so on, all may become much more traumatic than the sexual acts themselves.

This is not to say that children, adolescents, or adults enjoy being sexually molested, but they may enjoy the physical feelings and the emotional ambiance of the act or incident. As I have stated repeatedly above, sexual predators who seduce and molest children or adolescents (not assault them) take great pains to create a pleasant, accepting atmosphere. Male molesters seducing and molesting boys are experts at making the sexual molestation as pleasant, physically stimulating, and emotionally satisfying as possible. Emotional bribes — "love," acceptance, concern, attention, physical contact, appreciation — are used to lure the victim into a false sense of acceptance, safety, and security. When the molester is positive that the "hook is set," then the first, cautious, sexual touch begins and progresses from there to an actual sexual molestation. Once the needs of the survivor are fulfilled by the molester, the survivor will almost always agree to further contacts with the molester and may even initiate at least one of the sexual encounters.

Haven't you ever wondered how these long-term relationships can continue undiscovered and unreported for three, five, or even seven years? It is because the vulnerable child or adolescent is more than willing to pay with his or her body for the "benefits" offered by the molester. It is only when they realize that they were being used that the real damage and trauma set in.

REPORTING CONSIDERATIONS

What determines whether or not the child, adolescent, or adult will report the attempted or actual abuse? In my experience, the most important determinant revolves around the values that the individual has learned very early, primarily from his or her parents or primary caretakers. The three key determinants are as the following.

1. If children or adolescents fear that they will not be believed, they will not report. This decision is based on their own past experiences with their parents or guardians when having reported other issues. If they were not believed in the past, why should they think that they will be believed now, especially about such an important issue as sexual molestation? Both KYLE, in chapter 2,

and the children of **Art**, in chapter 5, are excellent examples of this situation.

2. If children or adolescents fear scolding, punishment, and rebuke, they will not report. This decision is also based on their prior experiences with parents, teachers, and so on. **Hans**, in chapter 3, is a good example of this factor and the next one as well.

3. If children or adolescents fear that they will be blamed or judged for the approach or seduction, they will not report. Questions such as the following can suggest to them that they are at fault:

"What were you doing that made him choose you?"

"Did you smile or talk to her?"

"Why did you let him see you in a public rest room?"

"Why were you there alone?"

"Why did it take so long for you to tell me?"

"Did you have an orgasm?"

"Why didn't you fight him off?"

All of the above questions place blame directly on the survivor whether or not that was the intent.

WARNING SIGNS

The one consistent warning sign that I have observed that parents, relatives, teachers, and other adults too often overlook is that of a sudden and unexpected change in behavior, usually for the worse. This change might include one or a combination of the following.

Regression to an Earlier Stage of Development

In younger children regression may include bed-wetting, soiling during the day, thumb-sucking, nightmares, clinging behaviors, fear of going with other people or going to school, fear of a baby-sitter, and so on. In adolescents, the regression may take the form of sliding backward to a former level of achievement or competency. Coaches, for example, have commented to me (once a molestation or assault was exposed) that a "star" player abruptly began playing as if it were his first game, forgetting rules, game plans, and so on.

Regression occurs even in adults. A bank president I knew referred one of his tellers to me whom he was planning to promote to an assistant. The problem was that she had abruptly begun making serious errors in the nightly close-out routine and, when working alone at the night window, began making serious errors in customers' transactions, resulting in a bevy of complaints. After two or three sessions, this young woman related to me that she had been sexually assaulted in a subway station the previous week and, being threatened ("I know who you are, where you work, and where you live!"), did not report the incident, nor did she go to a hospital emergency room. She also, during the next week, refused to see her fiancé or to have a conversation with him on the telephone. No one who observed these abrupt changes could get her to explain them.

Isolation Behaviors

Isolation behavior affects survivors of all ages. Children, adolescents, and adults who were previously gregarious and highly social may abruptly quit all clubs, sports, and other organizations and spend inordinate amounts of time in their room, lying on the bed, listening to loud music, or looking out the window with an almost blank stare.

Adolescents often abruptly stop seeing their friends, quit sports or other after-school activities, or break off a relationship with a boyfriend or girlfriend. Adults often abruptly become workaholics as a means of avoiding social activities at the workplace such as coffee breaks, stopping for a drink after work, and attending parties or dances.

It is important to note here that for this factor to be a warning sign, the behavioral changes must be both abrupt and out of character for the individual.

Problems with Hygiene and Unkempt Appearance

One easy way to lose friends and associates is to develop body odors and wear dirty and smelly clothing. I have often seen this behavior used by survivors to keep people away from them and to avoid any social interaction. When a previously neat and hygienic individual (especially adolescents) abruptly becomes unhygienic and unkempt, it is a warning sign that something may have occurred.

Daydreaming and Loss of Concentration

Teachers, more than parents, first notice these two symptoms in children and adolescents while work supervisors or co-workers notice them in adults. From a bright, energetic, and consistently involved student, the survivor of sexual abuse abruptly becomes a daydreamer, looking out the window and unable to concentrate on his or her work or on what the teacher or the class is involved in. Individuals in this situation begin to make "stupid mistakes" and if asked about them do not seem to know why. While apparently studying at home (sitting at a table or desk with a book open), their minds are constantly replaying the details of the molestation, trying to find a way that it could have been prevented and then loading themselves down with recriminations and guilt.[1]

The adult, at work, also abruptly begins to make "stupid mistakes" and cannot concentrate on anything. He or she asks the same questions over and over in an interview, cannot concentrate on what a client or co-worker is saying, and seems "lost in another world." Naturally, this person's work suffers, and, since this change is abrupt, supervisors and friends take immediate notice. Unfortu-

---

1. This warning sign should not be considered as by itself indicating that abuse has taken place. It may also indicate Attention Deficit Disorder (ADD) in children and adolescents.

nately, in most cases the wrong approach is used: scolding or threat by supervisors or persistent questions by friends suggesting possible problems and solutions.

At these times, neither the child/adolescent group nor the adult group is usually ready to discuss what is really bothering them, so they make up excuses or alibis for their slump or having an "off-day." The more parents, friends, supervisors, and teachers try to force the issue, at this time, the worse it will become. Patience is the only course of action. Giving survivors "time off" to straighten themselves out only increases the probabilities of deeper isolation and worse. The more they are treated normally, the quicker they will regain former levels of performance.

Decline of School Grades or Work Performance

An immediate consequence of the above factor for school-age children and adolescents is an often dramatic deterioration in school performance that begins abruptly and for no apparent reason, and grades plummet.[2] When asked, the child or adolescent is unable to explain this change and becomes extremely upset at being confronted with the problem.

For adults who are employed, co-workers and supervisors notice the dramatic change in work performance as well as in the individual's demeanor. I have treated cases where work performance dropped so dramatically that the survivor was warned that he or she was close to being fired, and some actually were. Supervisors also complain of hygiene and clothing problems, with the survivor coming to work in a disheveled state: hair uncombed and clothing rumpled or soiled, often with a noticeable body odor. These behaviors had never been noticed before.

---

2. One exception to this pattern is when all but one grade lowers or deteriorates. This often happens when the child or adolescent is being molested by a teacher and has developed an idolization or "love" for that teacher. In these cases, the child or adolescent may excel in that teacher's class while doing minimal work in all other classes.

Hyper-Modesty

Another warning sign is abrupt changes in habits having to do with dressing and undressing, bathroom functions, showering, changing clothes in a locker room for gym classes, showering with other students in school, and so on.

The survivor of sexual abuse feels soiled and tainted, and some actually believe that if they are seen partially undressed or in the nude that an observer (be it parent, peer, teacher, or someone else) will be able to tell that he or she was sexually abused or is sexually active (in cases where the molestation is ongoing).

I have had several cases that were discovered when the child or adolescent refused to go to school because of mandatory gym classes that involved changing clothes and also showering after the gym class was over. When children or adolescents like this are referred to me for truancy and this excuse is used, I tend to become suspicious either of a perceived difference between the child or adolescent and his or her peers (such as not having begun the pubertal changes when most or all peers have) or of possible physical or sexual abuse. In these instances, I slowly but carefully explore these areas at a pace comfortable to the child or adolescent. One cannot suggest sexual abuse to a potential survivor but must give that individual every opportunity to become sufficiently comfortable with the interviewer and to feel safe enough to trust him or her with the facts.

PROBLEMS REGARDING TOUCH

I learned a very long time ago that touch is also a key to discovering survivors of sexual or physical abuse. Survivors of sexual abuse are extremely sensitive to being touched following a molestation or assault. This even includes being touched by parents or friends who have touched them many times before. While this is an excellent clue to physical trauma, determining the true nature of the trauma necessitates further probing and evidence. If the sensitivity to touch is coupled with hyper-modesty, locker-room changing problems, or showering problems, the likelihood increases that the abuse was sexual, but this is still not sufficient evidence to jump to that conclusion. Only the direct testimony of the child or adolescent will clarify the matter, and, therefore, developing a relationship of trust, over time, is essential. (See also the section on readiness in chapter 13).

Changed or Bizarre Sexual Behavior

Exhibitionism. Some young children who have been molested or abused are preoccupied with touching or exposing their genitals, and this behavior is performed anywhere, with no concern for being observed. This can lead to a sexual dysfunction of its own, and many of these individuals, as adults, become compulsive exhibitionists ("flashers").

Masturbation. Adolescents who have been abused or molested may be persistently sexually preoccupied and may engage in compulsive masturbation almost anywhere and everywhere including school, public rest rooms, theaters, even in church. They lose all control over their sexual impulses.

Undoing. This is the time period when adolescents may attempt to undo their own sexual molestation. **HANS**, in chapter 3, when caught and castigated by his grandmother, almost immediately began molesting younger children. This undoing does not work. These survivors try over and over again to undo what happened to them and often end up becoming classic compulsive sex offenders as adolescents and adults.

Exaggerated Privacy Needs. Where more shy and inhibited children and adolescents are concerned, they suddenly spend an inordinate time in the bathroom or shower and often close or lock the door to their bedrooms. If a parent walks in unannounced, they are often found fondling themselves or outright masturbating.

Inserting Objects. Little girls (if raped or digitally penetrated) often insert objects in their vaginas while boys (if they have been sodomized) insert objects in their anuses. Unfortunately, these behaviors are often also performed on younger siblings or friends with whom they are playing as another "undoing" and "equalizing" behavior.

School Behaviors. Teachers observe sexual play in school (mostly fondling and masturbating themselves through their clothing or pockets) and often find sexual drawings in these students' school notebooks or lists of "four-letter words." Schoolmates, often from a lower class, may complain of being touched, stared at in the bathrooms, or actually touched or propositioned. Many of these school problems result in panic by the staff and legal involvements.

Explicit Sexual Drawings. In my experience with hundreds of survivors of sexual abuse and/or assault, explicit sexual drawings play an important role in ventilating feelings and reality-testing following the molestation or attack. There are periods of time when denial mechanisms are active to an extent that the child or adolescent or even adult is not totally sure that his or her memories are real. Explicit sexual drawings of the molestation or assault, in these cases, help survivors both to recall specific facts in the abuse or assault and also to anchor the facts in reality. Thus, for me, these drawings are positive and therapeutic and not a symptom of mental problems or psychotic behavior, as some psychiatrists and psychologists believe and publicly profess.

When survivors hear statements from a therapist judging them to be severely "sick" (for example, regarding their explicit drawings), this makes it even more difficult for them to disclose anything about their molestation. All therapists should be aware of the dangers of making generic statements of this type on radio and television or in the newspapers and magazines.

Survivors who were abused as children or adolescents and who were sexually affected by their abuse take one of two dramatically different courses in adulthood: (1) they develop a sexual dysfunction such as loss of all sexual interest ("Desire-Phase Dysfunction" [DPD]), impotency (males), or frigidity (females); or (2) they become sexually overactive, promiscuous, and/or preoccupied. Men often become satyrs to regain their perceived lost manhood (especially when they were molested by an adult male and sodomized), and women often become prostitutes because that is what they believe they are or that is what they were told either by the sexual predator or by family, relatives, or friends who found out about their abuse. Either of these choices of handling the sexual molestation or assault is damaging and can have far-reaching consequences, including many sexually transmitted diseases and/or AIDS.

Loss of Self-Respect and Development of a Negative Self-Image

One of the most devastating effects of sexual abuse is the development of a negative self-image and loss of self-respect. Both of these negative changes result in problems in all aspects of the survivor's life: loss of motivation to succeed, diminished self-worth, loss of the feeling of being worthy of others' friendship and love, self-hate to a dangerous degree, and strong needs to deny the occurrence or to undo it by molesting others. The exception to this scenario occurs when, as stated elsewhere in this work, the survivor correctly places all blame and responsibility on the molester.

Young children, depending on their ego-strength and emotional development at the time of the assault or molestation, can quickly go into denial and this denial can last until adolescence. Once in adolescence, they can become preoccupied with sexuality and either openly discuss sex with their peers or avoid such discussion due to fears that their involvement in the molestation will be discovered. Often, the memories become repressed, and, years later, a word, picture, movie, discussion, or any other stimulus can "trigger flashbacks." The memories usually return in fragmented pieces and produce fear, confusion, nightmares, and other forms of post-traumatic stress disorder (PTSD).

Adolescents, already sexually active and preoccupied with sex, are even more vulnerable to serious damage (trauma) from sexual molestation. Girls face the danger of pregnancy from a self-centered, careless adult predator with whom they are involved and then must face judgment and ridicule from parents, peers, and society. Too often they try to hide the pregnancy, deliver the baby themselves, and then dispose of it, often killing the newborn rather than having to face the shame. When pregnancy does not occur, the dangers of sexually transmitted diseases, depression, suicide attempts (too often successful), and negative self-image and self-worth problems are ever present. Boys, regardless of whether they are molested by an adult woman or man, cannot share their involvement with their peers or with their parents. Secrecy is paramount and insisted on by the adult predator. The longer the relationship exists, the harder it is for the boy to come forward since he knows he will be asked: "Why did you wait so long to tell us?" Some police investigators, social workers, and many parents still fall into the trap of asking this question. When the boy is involved with an adult male, a "double trauma" occurs. It is practically impossible for him to tell anyone since he anticipates the rejection of peers, teachers, parents, the law, and so on, for being homosexual. Homophobia is always a friend and ally of the male sexual predator involved with teenage boys.

Adult males develop an even more terrifying fear of exposure for their homosexual involvement with either teenage boys, college-age males, or another adult. This is especially true if they are married and have children of their own. Adult males who have been sexually assaulted (sodomized or forced to perform oral sex) are especially vulnerable to self-image damage. They feel dirty, used, and, when sodomized, feel "used like a woman." All areas of their lives are affected, and their relationships with parents, wives, children, friends, and associates are all severely damaged. Adult females who have been abused, especially mothers who have been sexually assaulted (raped and often worse), suffer severe self-image and self-esteem damage. Whether they have reported the assault or not, returning to their husbands and children and resuming a normal life with them becomes an impossible task. If any form of oral sex was involved, they often will not allow themselves to be kissed or shown any affection since their shame is too great. As with men, if they experienced an orgasm during the sexual assault or molestation, they often perceive this as cooperating or are told so by the sexual predator.

Pervasive Guilt

Even young children who have been abused or molested know that what happened to them was wrong and too often feel that somehow they should have prevented it. Sexual predators are experts at instilling guilt into their victims (in order not to feel too guilty themselves). Too often in the cases that I have treated, the words of the sexual predator did more damage than the sexual assault or molestation itself. I have listed some of their typical remarks earlier (for example, "If you weren't so cute, I wouldn't have gotten sexually turned on and molested you"; or "You had an orgasm, and that means that you enjoyed what we did, and so you're just as guilty as I am").

Even when sexual offenders do not instill guilt, others upon finding out about the abuse often will. Survivors themselves also often do a good job of second-guessing their behavior. They will often give me a lengthy list of things that they should have done or could have done to prevent their own molestation or assault. Dealing with this guilt is one of the most difficult tasks in therapy (see chapter 13 on treatment issues).

Depression and Suicide Attempts

Visible depression that is debilitating is too often seen following sexual abuse. All of the above self-judgments, guilts, and so on, weigh on the survivor, and somatic (physical) symptoms begin including headaches, gastrointestinal problems, heart palpitations and increase in blood pressure (or higher blood pressure where it already exists), and eating disorders, both bulimia and anorexia. Psychological symptoms also occur including impotence and frigidity, loss of sexual desire, memory problems, concentration problems, and many others that I have already discussed.

All of these disorders are forms of self-punishment resulting from the guilt and self-recriminations either that others, beginning with the sexual predator, have heaped upon the victims or that they have heaped upon themselves. Getting survivors to see that this is the cause of their physical and/or psychological problems is a long and sometimes impossible task. This problem can be so serious that many survivors are in need of intense medical and/or psychological treatment for many years, especially those survivors who have never divulged to anyone that they were sexually assaulted or molested.

For many untreated survivors, this depression can increase to the point where it and the guilt become unbearable, and then suicidal thoughts and behaviors result. While these suicidal gestures may also be a "cry for help," the danger is that the victim can take too many pills, cut too deeply, miscalculate someone's finding them in time, and so on, and death then results.

REACTING TO THOSE WHO HAVE BEEN SEXUALLY ABUSED

Several careful steps are necessary once exposure of a sexual abuse has taken place to assure that the survivor's rights are honored and that help rather than further trauma results. Some of the most important steps that I have learned over the years follow.

Caution

Extreme sensitivity and concern for the privacy and feelings of the survivor are paramount considerations. It is impossible to predict either the readiness of survivors to discuss their sexual molestation or assault or their choice of individuals with whom to share the details of this shame- and guilt-producing trauma.

Most people might be surprised to discover that family and friends are not usually the survivor's first choice. This is due to the dread of potential or anticipated rejection if individuals close to the survivor knew what had occurred. A stranger with whom the survivor is not emotionality involved, such as a counselor or therapist, is often an easier choice for the survivor to confide in since there is no fear of personal rejection or judgment, and the survivor can always walk out of the office or not return for further appointments.

Readiness

One of the worst possible choices, too often made by parents of molested children and adolescents, is to pressure or try to force them to "tell all" to police, investigators, social workers, and so on, in the parents' presence. This approach will always either fail outright or result in a sketchy and legally useless tale in which all of the truly important and traumatizing details are avoided or denied. A case at this point will help clarify.

> DIANA, a health club instructor, was brutally and viciously sexually assaulted while providing private instruction in a client's home. Her original story to the police, to her husband, and to me was as follows.
>
> After a ten-hour day of working at the spa, Diana went to dinner with friends and then taxied to her client's hotel room. While preparing for the planned workout, the client started touching Diana in a personal and intimate manner. When she protested, he became extremely angry and revealed a side of himself that Diana had never seen at the spa. She asked him why he was acting this way and what he wanted, and he gave her a convincing, long, and convoluted story about being rejected by his wife and sex-starved for almost a year. Diana immediately became afraid and tried to leave. Her client blocked the door and told her he was going to get all that he wanted, or she would not walk out of the hotel room alive.
>
> His whole demeanor changed from the friendly and innocent-looking young man she knew at the spa to a threatening, vicious, and dangerous person. He shoved Diana on the bed, called her a litany of filthy names, and accused her of sexually satisfying her "special clients" but always rejecting him. When she tried to get up and resist him, he punched her in the jaw and knocked her out.
>
> When Diana regained consciousness, she was naked and tied "spread-eagle" to the bed. The attacker was naked and raping her viciously. Unsatisfied that he was producing sufficient pain and

humiliation, he then sodomized her as forcibly and as viciously as he could. Unable or unwilling to be satisfied with the rape and sodomy, he then forced her to perform oral sex on him, continuing his verbal onslaught and threats of impending physical damage and death.

When he was finished, he knocked Diana out once again, and when she awoke, it was daylight of the next morning. She was bleeding rectally; she was bruised all over her body; and her clothes had been ripped to shreds. She laid there for a time, in shock, wondering what to do. She feared that she would be blamed for coming to this man's room of her own free will and wondered if her purpose, of helping him with his gym exercises, would be believed. Finally, she called the front desk and told them what happened. They immediately called the police. When the police arrived, Diana told them only of the beatings, the threats, and the rape and the sodomy. She never mentioned the oral sex.

After being treated at the emergency room of a nearby hospital, Diana went home. She related the same story to her husband and family that she had given to the police, and eventually she told that same story to me.

Almost a year later, still having nightmares and unable to enter a hotel or motel, even with her husband and children, Diana called and asked if I would see her.

The immediate impression I received on her first visit was that of a survivor who was still in serious shock and turmoil. Her personal guilt was incredible, and she stated that she could not stop blaming herself for agreeing to instruct that client in his hotel room. She insisted that this was the only cause of her intense guilt. The problem, for me, was that this reason for the guilt did not explain why she refused to kiss her husband or children or be kissed by them. Why was this particular symptom present, and why was there no respite from the severe guilt she was experiencing?

Deciding on a direct, confrontational technique, I strongly suggested that Diana was hiding something that was the true cause of the guilt and accompanying strange behavior. While at first resisting and denying that there was anything else, Diana finally broke down and after a hysterical, drenching, crying session of over twenty minutes, she related the additional information of the forced oral sex.

After painfully and viciously raping and sodomizing her but not reaching his climax, the attacker had sat on her chest and gave her the following choice: "Either get me off by oral sex or I'll slit your throat!" He then showed her a large steak knife and forced his soiled penis into her mouth. Diana believed his threats and reluctantly did as she was told to save her life, so that she could see her husband and children again.

It took Diana over thirty minutes to get these facts out between hysterical sobbing and hiding her face in her hands as well as gagging throughout. When she recovered sufficiently, she then angrily stated: "I should have let him kill me rather than doing that filthy, putrid, and disgusting act."

Now the core of the trauma was exposed and treatment could begin. Surprisingly, Diana did most of her own therapy with her husband (to whom she told the secret, on my advice), and within a six-month period, she was ready to take the next big step: traveling with her family and staying in a hotel that was similar to the one in which the sexual assault occurred. While this was difficult to do, the support and love of her family made it both possible and much easier to face.

Within a few more months, all of the symptoms began to disappear, and the guilt greatly subsided, although there were residual elements that would continue to surface for several years. Individual therapy, while appropriate in the beginning of Diana's treatment, no longer sufficed at the six-month stage.

She and her husband continued in marital therapy, and he willingly gave Diana the control of their sex life, being patient regarding oral sex for almost a year. Today they are living again normally, and Diana has returned to her career at the spa.

Preparation

Imagine that Diana had decided to confide the hidden details of her sexual assault to you? If you reacted with shock or horror or disgust, imagine the effect on Diana's already damaged self-image and the huge amount of guilt that she was experiencing. I have had cases where less occurred than in Diana's case, and yet the guilt and shame were as great because of the responses of those closest to the victims. For example, a husband upon learning that his wife had been forced to perform oral sex on a sexual predator and that he completed the act would no longer kiss his wife or have any intimate contact with her. All sex stopped as did former everyday affection such as a kiss upon arriving home from the work. The wife's already high level of depression and guilt increased further, and she was hospitalized after a near-death experience from a suicidal overdose of sleeping pills and alcohol. The marriage ended in a nasty and damaging divorce less than a year later. The husband simply was not prepared to accept what had happened, secretly blamed his wife, and fantasized her enjoying what she did. To this day, he has never remarried; he is now a womanizer ("user"); and oral sex has become an obsession with him. Therapy, to this point, has not helped.

Most nonprofessionals and even some untrained professionals are unable to remain objective and nonemotionally reactive to this sort of disclosure. For some therapists, only many years of treating survivors and listening to many horrible cases eventually numbs them to the point where they can remain nonreactive and therefore are able to help these survivors.

One of my controversial practices is to advise survivors not to disclose highly traumatic details to anyone except their therapist. Why? First, it does not add to the legal case against the sexual predator already charged with aggravated sexual assault, as in Diana's case; second, it imposes an additional burden on parents, spouses, siblings, children, and so on, that too many of them are unable to deal with. Helping the survivor to return to his or her preassault level of life must be the primary goal of any treatment.

Nonjudgmentalism

When survivors disclose the incident, they have already judged themselves, usually in a harsh manner. What they now need, when the assault or molestation is exposed, is understanding, acceptance, and belief. If the chosen confidant expresses judgmental questions, implied doubt, anger, or blame, then this guarantees that this will be the one and only attempt to communicate with anyone about the details of the assault or molestation. Once this opportunity is lost, there may never be another one, and the trauma will remain unresolved for life. This is why everyone associated with survivors of sexual abuse must be completely trained and desensitized by an expert in this field.

SUMMARY

Recognition is an essential and normal process in dealing with the survivors of sexual assault and molestation. Observant parents, siblings, relatives, teachers, co-workers, and friends all become the first step in the chain of recovery for these individuals.

It is an awesome responsibility to be the first person to whom a survivor chooses to disclose all of the details of his or her sexual trauma. Learning to listen is an important skill in this regard, as is having the common sense to realize that these traumatized individuals are in need of specially trained professional help. The chosen person's support, understanding, continued acceptance, and love all are essential to as full a recovery as possible for these innocent victims of the sexual predator.

13

TREATMENT ISSUES

My purpose in this chapter is not to discuss specific treatment techniques but rather treatment problems revolving around survivor's support persons (parents, siblings, relatives, teachers and school personnel, religious authority figures, friends, co-workers, and associates). For a complete discussion of specific techniques utilized to treat the survivor of sexual abuse, please refer to my second book, *The Merry-Go-Round of Sexual Abuse.*[1]

Several issues must be discussed in this chapter that are essential to the rehabilitation of the survivor of sexual abuse. These are treating the survivor normally; readiness; confidentiality; getting all the nitty-gritty details; acceptance versus "Forget about it!"; and helping the survivor develop a new self-image.

TREATING THE SURVIVOR NORMALLY

The first and most important of these issues is that of treating survivors normally, that is, as they had always been treated prior to their abuse; this means not treating them as strange individuals around whom everyone must "walk on eggshells."

Parents and other authority figures or friends who were closely associated with a survivor prior to the sexual abuse often feel personal guilt, sensing that they should have or could have done something to prevent the abuse from happening. This is especially true when young children are concerned. The parents, friends, or others then make one of the worst mistakes that can be made with a

1. William E. Prendergast, *The Merry-Go-Round of Sexual Abuse: Identifying and Treating Survivors* (New York: Haworth Press, 1993).

survivor, although their intentions and thinking are natural and understandable. That mistake is to treat the survivor in a protected and special way, making too many allowances for misbehavior as well as for behaviors that increase and encourage negative adjustment choices. An example will clarify.

RANDY, at age fourteen, was sexually molested by three seniors at his high school who were on the football team and who were his idols. One Friday afternoon, they invited Randy "to join their secret club in the woods," and Randy, desperate for their acceptance, gladly accepted.

Once the four boys arrived at their secret clubhouse, they offered Randy some marijuana, and although he had never smoked or used drugs, Randy accepted, fearing they might revoke their offer of friendship. After thirty minutes or so, the leader of the group announced that it was time for Randy's "initiation." Randy was ordered to strip naked, and while he was undressing, so did the other boys, "to make him feel more comfortable." Once they all were naked, Randy was instructed to perform oral sex on the three other teens, being assured that they all went through the same initiation and that it would remain totally secret. Randy reluctantly obeyed, and within an hour or so was a full-fledged member of the "Alligators" (their secret club's name).

Over the rest of the school year, Randy was continuously invited to the club, and each time was coaxed and coerced into performing either manual or oral sex on the other club members. They, however, never reciprocated. Toward the end of June, the week of the other boys' graduation, a celebration was held at the clubhouse with marijuana and beer as well as shots of whisky. Within an hour all four boys were "higher than they had ever been before," and when time for sex came, they decided on a "special session" with Randy. While three of the boys held the naked boy on his knees, the leader forcibly sodomized him with little concern for the pain and damage he was doing. When he finished, the other two boys did likewise.

By the time they were finished, Randy was sore and bleeding rectally. He limped home in a great deal of pain and, after showering, went straight to bed. He awoke some time later in severe pain, and the bed was soaked in blood. He screamed, and his mother ran to his room, took one look, and drove him to the emergency room of their local hospital.

After several questioning sessions, Randy invented the story of having been abducted and raped by an older man whom he had never seen before. He was believed, but after several sessions at the police station looking at mug shots of convicted sex offenders, he was unable to identify his assailant.

Randy refused to return to school, although the doctor felt he was physically able to do so. His parents allowed him to stay home and hired a tutor. (Mistake number 1.) Randy also became arrogant and demanded a new television and stereo for his room. His parents went out and purchased them for him. (Mistake number 2.) Randy then angrily, and with vile language, ordered his mother to serve his meals in his room, she did. (Mistake number 3.)

These behaviors continued and increased in absurdity. Each time a new demand was issued, his parents agreed to it. Randy was becoming uncontrollable and yet remained in complete control of his parents and the entire household. The tutor quit since he couldn't stand Randy's arrogance and his refusal to pay attention, or to do any of his assignments.

Finally, the school authorities demanded that Randy receive treatment or he would be expelled and an order of incorrigibility would be signed with the potential for juvenile detention. Randy finally agreed and was referred to me for possible treatment. There will be more about Randy as this chapter develops.

READINESS

The next important treatment consideration is readiness. One of the most insane factors in cases of sexual abuse is forced therapy for either the sexual predator or his or her survivors. It is impossible to force people to participate in treatment when they are either not ready or unwilling, and attempts to do so will invariably fail. Yet parents, judges, school administrators, and so on, do just that on a regular basis.

In my practice, the primary condition under which I will accept any patient for treatment is that he or she wants treatment and is willing to face the hardships and pain that it will present, especially the exposure of all of the "nitty-gritty" details of his or her behaviors, motives, reactions, emotional feelings, and self-judgments.

I make it a general principle not to agree to accept all referrals of either sexual predators or sexual survivors. I inform the referring source that my first interview with the proposed client will be structured in such a way that both the proposed patient and I will be able to determine whether or not we can work together.

During this first interview I begin with one simple question: "Why are you here?" When the reply makes it clear that the individual's presence is not his or her choice but is the result of the demands of either parents or judges (via court orders), is a condition to avoid punishment (restrictions for children and teenagers, prison for adult predators, and so on), or is due to pressures from friends or associates, I then make it quite clear that I am only interested in treating patients who

- realize and accept the reality that they have a problem,

- realize that they cannot solve the problem by themselves, and

- realize that they require professional help.

Potential patients who are in denial and are not ready to begin professional treatment are informed that when they do reach readiness, I will then and only then be interested in accepting them as patients.

In my private practice, I have refused to treat survivors and predators due to their lack of readiness, and I explained the reasons to them. A majority left and then returned as long as two to three months later, stating in their appointment calls that they had reached the readiness level and were ready to begin. (Of course, this could be a ploy due to continued threats from authorities, and it needs to be tested.) I feel that I save a great deal of time and frustration using this method. Unfortunately, too many therapists who have large financial burdens (rents, clerical help, insurance, and so on) accept anyone and everyone who calls them regardless of their readiness.

Survivors who are referred and are still in shock are exceptions to this rule. While making my position clear, I do provide supportive therapy through this time period and especially if there is a trial of their molester pending at which they will have to testify.

At the correctional institution where I was employed for some thirty years, all of the individuals were sentenced there "for treatment" whether or not they admitted to their offense(s) and whether or not they accepted the fact that they had a serious problem and needed professional help. The frustration that I and the other therapists felt was tremendous since the entire program was designed for repetitive-compulsive sex offenders, not for innocent citizens who claimed to have been wrongly convicted (the usual denial statement).

CONFIDENTIALITY

Confidentiality is a serious and controversial issue in treating survivors of sexual abuse and the predators who perpetrate the abuse. One of the primary reasons for this controversy is that many states have specific laws requiring anyone who suspects or is aware of a child or teenager being physically, emotionally, or sexually abused to report this abuse to a child protection agency. In New Jersey that agency is the Division of Youth and Family Services, commonly referred to as DYFS. The normal client-therapist confidentiality rules are suspended in these cases, and there have been indictments of psychologists who did not report instances of child or adolescent abuse as soon as they became aware of them. The overall result is ambivalence on the part of the therapists who treat these cases (I have discussed this subject with literally hundreds of them during my training presentations) since the majority of them believe, as I do, that reporting should be the choice of the survivor.

Where child or adolescent survivors are concerned, one method to deal with this dilemma that has worked successfully for me is to thoroughly discuss the issue of confidentiality in the first session before the new patient reveals any facts about his or her abuse. The specific laws involved must be discussed and thoroughly explained with examples. Time for questions that the survivor may have should also be provided. In this manner, the patient has until the next session (usually one week) to consider what choices lie open to him or her. Use of this method usually prevents further trauma for the child, adolescent, or adult.

Where adult survivors are concerned, this reporting law is not an issue. Confidentiality in these cases is the same as in any other treatment case; however, it still must be discussed since survivors need to know that they are in control and that nothing they share or reveal will be divulged to anyone, including marital partners, parents, siblings, and so on, without their specific permission (always in writing).

Where adult abusers, referred by the courts for treatment, are concerned, the same discussion takes place with the caveat that if any new and relevant facts emerge during the course of treatment that were not part of the original case, then these facts will have to be reported. For adult offenders, other crimes, other than child physical or sexual abuse, are covered by confidentiality if the commission of those crimes does not indicate that the offender still poses an imminent threat to the community. This fact of law must also be explained.

Where really young children are concerned (my youngest to date was three years old), this issue of confidentiality must be discussed with the primary parent or guardian (the one bringing the child to therapy who has legal custody and who is most involved in the primary care of the child). This is especially important and essential when the case involves incest.

If, following this clarification of confidentiality laws, new facts are offered either by the survivor identifying his or her abuser or by the abuser revealing additional victims, then it appears obvious to me that the client wants these facts to be reported to the appropriate authorities. I then contact DYFS, usually in their presence.

A majority of the survivors I have treated handled the confidentiality situation appropriately. Most of them chose to disclose the abuse but remained general or vague about the abuser, making it impossible to report the occurrence. For example, they gave statements such as: "I didn't get a good look at his face, but he was an adult who hangs around the school." (I informed the local Police of the danger.) or "I think he lives in the neighborhood, but I'm not sure and I don't know his name." (The police were already observing the area.) A few months after making these statements both survivors, as therapy progressed, identified the abuser and confessed that they had known who it was all along. They simply were not ready to report or were experiencing guilt feelings as a co-offender (both were cases of long-term abuse).

Abusers, on the other hand, are especially self-defensive and protective of facing any further legal charges or penalties. When they admit to additional molestations, they are just as vague as the survivors.

A teacher who was convicted of molesting two boys in his class by fondling them through their clothes stated: "There were thirty or forty other students that I molested as well but I simply don't recall any of their names, and I'm no longer at that school." Therapy revealed that he had been sexually involved with his young students for over ten years. A compulsive rapist who was charged with only one count of aggravated sexual assault and who plea-bargained to attempted sexual assault (there was no evidence of penetration or ejaculation since the victim showered and didn't report for two weeks) stated: "It didn't matter who they were; I raped anyone I could find in the park. I never even paid attention to their faces and never asked their names. Yes, there must have been fifty or sixty others but it's all a blur." Neither of these two sexual predators (who were convicted but given probation with the condition of outpatient therapy) ever acknowledged the identity of any of their other victims.

Shockingly, since none of the other victims ever reported, both predators were able to get away with all of the additional molestations and assaults to which they admitted. Both, after completing their probation, quit therapy (although they were by no means ready to leave), and both have committed the same or other offenses. This is the reason that reporting is so terribly important. If for no other reason, reporting gets these predators off the street and hopefully into treatment to resolve the causes of their behavior and to prevent further victimization of innocent children, teenagers, and adults.

GETTING ALL THE NITTY-GRITTY DETAILS

It is essential for recovery that all of the nitty-gritty details of the abuse be uncovered. In the beginning of therapy, the core of the abuse may not be what appears obvious to the authorities or even to the therapist.

For example, in sexual assault cases, the forced sexual assault that is reported may not have been the most traumatic part of the abuse. The most dramatic aspect may have been the words of the predator; some other act that the predator made the victim perform that made the survivor feel humiliated, disgusted, degraded, and even more embarrassed or guilt-ridden; or the fact of experiencing a pleasurable orgasm during the assault. Any of these can be at the hidden core of the present problem.

In sexual molestation cases, enjoying the sexual pleasure (orgasm), having strong emotional feelings for the molester, wanting to see the molester again, or wanting sex with the molester again may be at the core of the present problem. Also in long-term sexual molestation, having initiated the sex, even on one occasion, may be more guilt-provoking than anything else and will often be hidden, especially by male survivors where homosexual acts are concerned.

Many survivors spend much too much time in therapy, even several years, simply because they are hiding a specifically gruesome or guilt- and shame-producing detail of their sexual abuse. Diana in chapter 12 is a good example of this type of hiding. The disclosure of all of the nitty-gritty details should occur whenever the survivor is ready and willing to discuss the details of the sexual abuse. This rarely occurs at the first session.

It is quite normal and common for children, adolescents, and even adults to try to get away with revealing as little as possible since in order to tell the therapist all of the nitty-gritty details, they must hear them again themselves and therefore relive the abuse, to some degree. While this is therapeutic, the survivor needs a great deal of trust in the therapist (especially not to reject him or her or to be judgmental) in order to reveal these hidden facts. Survivors often prefer to use vague statements such as: "He made me have sex with him"; "She made me do dirty things"; "He made me touch him"; "She, you know, did it to me"; and hundreds of other similar evasions of the true and terrible facts. These vague and evasive statements are only signs of underlying matters, but they may be all that the survivor is able to share on the first telling of the incident. Slowly but surely, the therapist, using encouragement and support, must elicit the remainder of the story in a gentle and reassuring way until nothing is left unexposed.

In my experience, each time the events of the abuse are retold, at least one new element is added. Eventually the "core" of the abuse is revealed. Finding and exploring this core are the ultimate goals of this stage of the survivor's treatment. An example of a male with a hiding problem (similar to that of Diana, discussed above) will help to clarify this issue.

RANDY, introduced above, is a good example of a hiding problem in therapy. From the first session, Randy stuck to his story about being sexually assaulted in the park by an older man whom he did not know and whom he could not identify. When asked for further details, Randy insisted that the man had a knife and that all he did was sodomize him.

Part of sex therapy is to use part of one session to take a sex history. Randy acted uncomfortable about doing his history but reluctantly agreed. He admitted to masturbation at age thirteen but insisted that he had had no sexual relationships with either males or females prior to the sexual assault. He denied any unusual sexual fantasies and said that he used *Playboy* centerfolds as masturbation stimuli. I did not believe what Randy was saying, but following "readiness" principles did not confront him on these issues.

A separate session was held with Randy's parents. I insisted that they stop coddling him and that he be treated normally. The first step was to get him back to school. He was to follow his parents' rules around the house and was not to receive any special privileges unless they were earned.

My next session with Randy was filled with his anger and rage at the "new rules" that his parents had imposed on my suggestion, especially the rule that he had to return to school. He threatened to run away. I responded that he could do anything he wanted to do as long as he was willing to pay the price for his behavior. He was silent for quite a long time and then tearfully asked me how he was to face the kids at school (his first error). I asked why this would be a problem since his sexual assault had been kept secret by the police and everyone else involved. Also, his parents had obtained a doctor's note stating that he had had mononucleosis and consequently had needed a month or more at home with private tutoring.

Embarrassed, blushing, and flustered, Randy cried and cried. He said that there were problems at school with some of the older boys, but he would not elaborate on them. I told him that when he was ready to discuss these problems, I would help him with them.

Some three months of supportive but surface therapy ensued with no further revelations. Randy attended school but came home immediately after his last class and participated in no school activities, nor did he attend any social functions with his friends. He continued to isolate, but his behavior gradually improved, as did his grades.

In his fourth month of therapy, Randy asked if we could confidentially discuss what really happened to him, as he was having nightmares and unwanted sexual fantasies to a point where he couldn't handle them anymore. He then related the true story (see above) and added that he had been masturbating to fantasies of the sexual acts he had performed on the older boys and was inserting bananas and other phallic objects into his rectum to achieve a greater orgasm. Randy felt terribly ashamed of all of these behaviors and perceived himself as both "weird" and "queer."

Now therapy really began. The first and most important discussion we had was about sexual preference: the ability to choose types of sexual behavior and of sexual partners. Randy had been convinced that the old saying "Once a homo, always a homo," which he had heard so often at school, applied to him. His relief at the concept of sexual preference was immediate. He excitedly asked if that meant he could have a girlfriend and maybe someday get married and have children. My answer in the affirmative gave him immense pleasure and new hope. I then explained that, due to imprinting, he probably would still have fantasies of the sex with the boys, would still want anal stimulation, and would possibly become aroused in the locker rooms or showers with his other classmates after gym. But I emphasized these things were all right and were the result of the long-term abuse, and I further emphasized that he didn't have to act out the fantasies unless he wanted to. As I was finishing this explanation, he excitedly broke in and related that these things had already happened: that he had started to become erect in the showers when he caught himself staring at the other boys' genitals and panicked. He quickly dressed and went home sick. His relief that these reactions were the results of the positive imprinting that had occurred with the club members prior to his being sodomized was both visible and satisfying.

Randy then suddenly looked ashamed and hung his head. I asked what the problem was, and he then painfully admitted that after the initial pain and, by the third boy, he began to enjoy the sodomy as well. I again explained that sexual preference played a role here and that a heterosexual partner could also stimulate him rectally during their sexual encounters. Again he was relieved and stated: "I guess I have a lot to learn about sex, right Doc?"

By his sixth month of therapy, Randy was 95 percent back to his normal self. He had quit the "club," found new and compatible friends at school, was again socially active, and had a "steady" girlfriend. He was promoted to monthly therapy status (he had previously been promoted to biweekly status) and was on his way to call-in-when-necessary status.

ACCEPTANCE VERSUS "FORGET ABOUT IT!"

As discussed earlier, one of the most important therapeutic considerations in treating survivors of sexual abuse, regardless of their age, is that of acceptance of what has occurred. Acceptance does not mean that one has to like the behavior or that the behavior or trait will remain permanently. It simply means that something happened, and there is nothing to do to change it.

I often use the analogy of a time machine or the movie *Back to the Future* to illustrate this point. I ask the survivor if he or she has a time machine or has mastered time travel. Obviously, the answer is always "no." I then go on to say that when and if such a machine or process is invented, then maybe we can return to just before the molestation and attempt to prevent what is about to occur. Otherwise, our only choice is to accept that it happened and go on with our lives. Naturally, this is not as simple or easy to do as it is to say.

Part of the process of acceptance and moving forward is to remember all of the nitty-gritty details of what happened and to ventilate the associated emotions and feelings that have attached to the incident as well as the judgmental self-recriminations that became attached to behaviors that are perceived as negative, shameful, sinful, or antisocial. Advising the survivor to "Forget about it!" is the worst possible advice that anyone can give. Parents who do this are simply so uncomfortable with the molestation, especially the details, that they give this advice to protect themselves, not the survivor, from further emotional pain and self-blame. In the process, they seriously damage the survivor.

Where young children and inadequate adolescents are concerned, this bad advice facilitates repression of the molestation for the present, but be assured it will rear its ugly head at some future time and will also continuously effect the survivor's self-image, self-esteem, motivation, and interpersonal behaviors.

Outside Support during Therapy

During this long process of getting to the nitty-gritty details, family, friends, teachers, and anyone else involved with the survivor are crucial to his or her treatment. Support is essential, as are encouragement and constant reaffirmation that the survivor is not to blame and that he or she is still loved and cherished. This parental and other outside support is especially essential in cases where survivors have turned to prostitution following a sexual assault or molestation. Only if these survivors feel acceptance and love from family, friends, and others in society will they have a chance of ending this pattern and returning to their former personalities.

All those involved with survivors need to be aware of the "readiness" principle so that they will not attempt to force the survivors to discuss their abuse or assault. Only the survivor should initiate such a discussion and should choose the party or parties to do this with.

Returning Control to the Survivor. It is essential that survivors regain control of their lives. Parents, siblings, relatives, and friends should not impose their advice on survivors regarding what they should do, how they should react, what they should feel or think, and so on. This does not mean that survivors should be allowed to act out or isolate or harm themselves. They should be treated as normally as possible, as the best means of aiding their recovery.

HELPING THE SURVIVOR DEVELOP
A NEW SELF-IMAGE

The bottom line of all treatment of survivors of sexual abuse must include the formation of a new self-image since how survivors feel about themselves will determine treatment success or failure and any possibility of future happiness. Nothing anyone else can say or do will alter their self-image. Only the resolution of guilt will permit a new self-image to develop. As long as survivors harbor negative, deprecatory feelings toward themselves, no real change can or will occur. This is a major reason that professional therapy, with specially trained therapists, is essential in cases of sexual assault and molestation.

An effective technique that I call "self-confrontation" works wonders in survivors where self-image problems exist. For readers who are interested in the lengthy details of this technique, I again refer them to my second book, *The Merry-Go-Round of Sexual Abuse.*

THE RELATIONSHIP BETWEEN THE THERAPIST AND
SIGNIFICANT OTHERS IN THE SURVIVOR'S LIFE

One of the touchy and misunderstood concepts in therapy is that the confidentiality between therapist and survivor excludes passing along certain information even to parents and family members. Even the youngest survivor has a right to confidentiality, and parents must both understand and accept this principle.

There must be a relationship of trust between the therapist and the survivor if therapy is to succeed. There is no way that survivors who do not trust their therapist will disclose "all the nitty-gritty details" of their abuse, especially those elements that they feel could bring judgment, guilt, shame, and even punishment upon them should their parents, relatives, siblings, or friends ever find out. Factors such as experiencing pleasure (orgasm), initiating the sexual behavior on at least one occasion, feeling love and affection for the molester, having been forced to perform an act that the survivor feels is "filthy," "disgusting," "perverted," and so on, are the most difficult to relate to anyone.

If survivors fear or suspect that the therapist will disclose these "terrible secrets" to their parents and others, how can we expect those children and adolescents to disclose them? We can't. Therefore, confidentiality is essential to foster the necessary trust to elicit these essential facts.

I make it a practice to inform parents or other guardians of my confidentiality rules before I accept the case. I do this in the presence of the survivor so that there are no secret arrangements made between myself and the parents. Randy's parents, for example, were never told the story above, at Randy's request.

The same guarantee of confidentiality must also exist in adult-survivor and adult-predator cases. I inform spouses, parents, probation officers, and survivors that this is the rule and that I cannot and will not release any information without the explicit written consent of the patient. If there is any disagreement with these conditions, I do not accept the case. All of these situations are handled in the first, exploratory session.

IMPRINTING

A Definition

A word or two on imprinting is necessary so that the reader will fully understand the next section and the case examples in it. The *American Heritage Dictionary* (1982) defines "imprinting" as: "A learning process occurring early in the life of a social animal in which a behavioral pattern is established through association with a parent or other role model." *Sexual imprinting* occurs when an individual experiences his or her first orgasm with another human being. If the result is pleasant, enjoyable, and with a person who is liked or loved, the imprinting will be positive; if the result is painful, frightening, and with a person who uses force, threat, or intimidation, even though an orgasm may occur, the imprinting will be negative.

By extension, I use *positive sexual imprinting* in sexual abuse cases to mean that when a child (male or female), who is prepubertal and anorgasmic, is sexually molested and that molestation results in the child's first orgasm (with or without ejaculation), and the child perceives both the sexual experience and the relationship with the abuser as positive, a lifelong imprint will occur. Even when the abuse later becomes traumatic and is totally repressed (due to negative reactions of parents, authority figures, peers, and so on), the imprint remains and will surface at some future time when triggered by an event that, in some way, is associated with the elements of the original abuse. In these resurfacing events, the content of the abuse may (and often does) remain repressed while the effects (physical, sexual, emotional) are experienced vividly and to a disturbing degree. These are the positive sexual imprints. **RANDY**, discussed above, experienced positive imprinting.

Imprinting may also be negative, especially when a sexual assault occurs with accompanying fear, pain, threat, humiliation, degradation, and so on. These assaults may also produce lifelong imprints resulting in sexual dysfunctions, characterized by aversions, frigidity, panic reactions, impotence, punishing behaviors, and so on. In the last thirty-three years of treating individuals with sexual dysfunctions, I have had literally hundreds of clients who have reported instances of unwanted, disturbing, and guilt-provoking thoughts, fantasies, or behaviors that either could not be explained by the client's present values or attitudes or could not be logically seen as the result of consciously remembered sexual traumas.

Four Indicators of Imprinted Sexual Behaviors

There are several different ways in which these imprinting phenomena can become manifest. I suspect the presence of an imprint when the client reports one of four situations or a combination of them: (1) unwanted sexual reactions or turn-ons; (2) self-punishing behaviors; (3) negative self-esteem reactions; and (4) unwanted and unexplained isolation behaviors. In my experience, the first of these effects is the most important. The other three factors appear to result from the first. Therefore, we will look in greater detail at that first factor and how to deal with it.

Unwanted Sexual Reactions or Turn-Ons. This category includes all unexpected and unplanned sexual thoughts, fantasies, and overt behaviors that have never occurred before nor been part of the individual's lifestyle. In fact, when these phenomena first occur, they are so unanticipated that a type of shock results that most individuals are unable to deal with. A type of reaction-formation follows and everyone, including the involved person, is able to see the abrupt, contradictory, or inverse behavior patterns that result. An example, at this point, may prove helpful.

> **AMOS** was sexually molested by his father from age eight to age fifteen. His father used the "sex-education" ploy and told Amos that it was a father's duty to prepare him for the sexual changes that soon would be occurring. He began by teaching Amos how to masturbate and concurrently how to masturbate him, "so that you can see what sperm is and will know how babies are made." After several months of mutual masturbation, Amos's father felt it was time for the next lesson, oral sex. He taught Amos to fellate him, and he fellated Amos in return. It was during one of these oral sex sessions that Amos experienced his first minimal ejaculation, and he was thrilled.
>
> Following each of their sex-education sessions, Amos's father would take him out for some type of treat: McDonald's, bowling, baseball in the park, and so on. Amos began looking forward to his sex-education sessions and would rush home after school, refusing to participate in after-school activities with his friends, in the hope that his father would be there.
>
> When Amos was thirteen, on his birthday, his father decided to expand Amos's sex-education knowledge and experiences to anal sex. He carefully prepared Amos, telling him that this was how men and women made babies and that he had to practice. Again Amos's father went first, and although the pain was intense to begin with, Amos "got used to it." He also enjoyed sodomizing his father and experienced intense orgasms that way.

At eighteen, Amos began using his younger brothers and sisters for sex when his father was not home or available (with his father's permission and encouragement). He repeated his father's original ploy and insisted that it was time for his younger siblings to learn sex education. Within a short period of time, his sister (then ten) developed an infection and when asked by the school medical personnel what had happened, she explained Amos's sex-education sessions to them. An investigation by DYFS uncovered Amos's molestations of his siblings, and he was arrested by the police. When asked, Amos told them all about his father and their relationship, and the father also was arrested.

Both Amos and his father were sent to the same treatment facility. Needless to say, Amos's anger was intense, and he would not initially even talk to his father. Later they were both in the same therapy group and resolved their problems. JIMMY, in chapter 5, was in Amos's group.

Imprinting in Amos had occurred, and, less than a week after his being admitted to the treatment facility, he was actively engaged in homosexual behavior with an older inmate whom he perceived as a protective, father figure. The behavior became compulsive, and Amos informed his therapist that he was ashamed and guilt-ridden over his homosexual acting out and was terrified of contracting AIDS (no condoms were available in the facility, a serious mistake in my opinion) but that he could not control himself.

Amos, through his homosexual prostitution, was looking for that early father-son love and affection that he felt when his father had first begun sex education with him. He always chose older men and, following each incident, experienced severe guilt, humiliation (he was caught in the act several times and punished), and shame. These reactions reached suicidal proportions, and he finally made a feeble suicidal attempt that was really a call for help. Fortunately he was in a treatment facility, and intensive therapy relieved the suicidal threat.

By the time of his release some seven years later, Amos had decided to accept his homosexuality and also chose to live in the community with one of his "lovers" from the treatment unit. He now is an adult homosexual and no longer has pedophilic fantasies or desires. Only time will tell if he will remain committed to older men or whether he will return to children.

While the above discussion focused on positive sexual imprinting, *negative sexual imprinting* may also occur. In these cases, some facet of painful, negatively perceived sexual behavior occurs over a long period of time and is eventually repressed. Years later, often in adulthood, these survivors experience unwanted negative reactions to normal sexual stimuli. Feelings of abnormality result, and even thoughts of being "insane" occur. Suicidal thoughts and attempts are common in this group and need to be elicited and handled on a priority basis.

The major difference between negative sexual imprinting and positive sexual imprinting is that the former is not necessarily permanent and can be resolved and changed to a large extent through therapeutic intervention. The main difference in treatment technique is that of desensitizing the client to the trigger stimulus that produces the negative or phobic reaction. A case will clarify.

MARY, now thirty-one, was seduced by an aunt when she began menstruating. The aunt performed clitoral stimulation to the point of pain on a regular basis until a horrifying day when her mother saw them naked in bed.

All of these factors slowly emerged in the course of Mary's therapy. The last one — being caught by her mother — resulted in a plethora of curses, slurs, put-downs, and name calling that ended in Mary being blamed for what the aunt (the mother's sister) had initiated.

Sex for Mary was labeled as sinful, dirty, evil, the invention of Satan, and so on, and Mary was forbidden to ever touch herself "there" again. As time passed, Mary repressed this incident but not the admonitions about sex. Although she did not remember it (her memories returned periodically in small segments), there must have also been a warning about men and sex with men.

Mary initially was unable to respond sexually to a man or even to masturbate. Sexual thoughts, themselves, caused a great deal of guilt, and she avoided them at all costs. Nothing in her therapy or in her exposed repressions accounted for this aversion or for her anorgasmia. Therapy concentrated on desensitizing her to sexual thoughts, fantasies, and eventually to masturbation. To date, many of these barriers no longer exist, and Mary has begun masturbating and has finally achieved her first orgasm. She enjoys her body and wants to continue to destroy the old prohibitions that have prevented her from becoming "a complete woman" (her phrase). As the remaining barriers are broken, desensitization to the male body and sexual anatomy has also begun, utilizing nude pictures. Prognosis for change in this case is positive, and the long-term goal will be to completely extinguish Mary's phobic aversion to sex. Were this a positive imprint, this goal would be impossible.

The above cases reveal not only the dynamics of imprinting, positive and negative, but also the differences when trauma results. The devastating effects each type of imprinting can produce when they remain unrecognized and untreated should be obvious.

Self-Punishing Behaviors; Negative Self-Esteem Reactions; Unwanted and Unexplained Isolation Behaviors. These three reactions are grouped together since they all occur almost simultaneously and frequently converge. All are based on or result from the extreme guilt that survivors experience, even when the facts of the assault or molestation should place all responsibility and guilt on the predator of the abuse. This pervasive guilt becomes one of the most difficult issues to resolve in treatment. **DENNIS**, in chapter 11, is a perfect example of these three results and the difficulty in resolving them in therapy. It has been almost five years and residual guilt still remains.

As discussed earlier, one of the most frequently seen and most common factors in a majority of survivors of sexual assault or molestation is the "I'm the only one!" phenomenon. This is especially common and consistent in long-term sexual abuse or molestation and in long-term incest. Both during and after the abuse, child survivors do not perceive their peers, friends, and even their siblings (in incest) as ever having been sexually molested, nor do their peers and other friends commonly discuss this issue in their daily lives. When they are chosen by a sexual predator and are abused, they feel that they are the only ones who have ever had this type of an experience or were involved in these types of sexual behaviors and, therefore, are negatively unique. Quite often, the predator projects this idea as well as the blame and responsibility for the sexual behavior onto the victim. Some typical predator rationalizations and projections are difficult to believe. The following are a number of examples from actual cases of sexual offenders whom I have treated or from the survivors of their abuse:

- "If you weren't so cute, this wouldn't have happened."

- "You know you wanted me to do this to you."

- "You came back for more, didn't you?"

- "If you weren't such a bad little boy/girl, I wouldn't be doing this."

- "If you weren't dressed like that, I wouldn't have raped you."

- "You smiled and gave me the come-on and then refused, so it was all your fault."

- "I know you had an orgasm, and that means you wanted and enjoyed what happened."

Unfortunately, the survivors — children, adolescents, and adults as well — too often believe these rationalizations. Already traumatized, these survivors tend to easily assume the guilt for the offender's behavior, and this becomes a major resistance factor to reporting. When in therapy, this guilt becomes a major barrier to any therapeutic progress. The real danger lies in the survivors who do not report and are consequently not treated. They then may use the process of "undoing" to deal with the abuse, as **HANS** in chapter 3 did.

Another serious treatment consideration is that of the need for the survivor to personally confront his or her abuser, where this is possible. I have attempted to arrange this confrontation with all of the survivors I have treated, and approximately 75 percent have actually taken place. Of the remainder, the abuser was either dead, nowhere to be found, or, when contacted, unwilling to cooperate.

One particularly interesting case that taught me a second element that was needed during this confrontation was that of **ELLA**, in chapter 5, who was molested over a long period of time by her police-chief father, **GENE**. Ella was in private treatment with a female therapist whom she trusted and liked a great deal. Gene was in treatment with me at a correctional treatment center for sex offenders.

In Ella's ninth month of therapy, her therapist contacted me and told me that she had reached a plateau in Ella's treatment and did not know where to go next. She felt that Ella had not completely released all of the anger she felt toward her father, but she did not know how to elicit the remainder. I suggested the possibility that facing her father might be just the "trigger" that was needed, and the therapist said that she would discuss it with Ella. I also decided to discuss it with Gene. He readily agreed to do anything he could to help his daughter.

Ella agreed as well, and a meeting was arranged that would take place in my office with Ella, her therapist, Gene, and I present. Gene was sent for after Ella, her therapist, and I had some time to discuss the "rules" of the meeting. In general, the only prohibition was physical violence.

Gene arrived, entered the office, and closed the door. He stood at the door and said nothing. Ella, at first, would not or could not look at her father but eventually did. She then suddenly ran over to him and began hitting him on the chest while screaming: "I hate you! I hate you!" There was then a pause when we did not know what would happen next. Ella then hugged her father and, while crying profusely, stated: "But I still love you!" This last statement took us all by surprise, and Gene broke down, weeping in his daughter's grip.

I then realized that there were no dangers in this confrontation and that the two therapists did not have to remain. We left them alone for some twenty minutes so Ella could ask questions of her father that were no one else's business. The most frequently asked question in these face-to-face confrontations is "Why me?" This is especially true in multiple-child families when only one child is molested. Surprisingly, the answer by the incestuous parent (either father or mother) is always the same: "Because I loved you the most." What may be surprising to those not involved with sex offenders is the fact that the offender's answer is probably the truth according to his or her distorted values and perceptions, especially the "love equals sex" value. **OLIVER**, in chapter 5, was told consistently by his mother, after she sexually molested him, how much she loved him and how special he was to her.

SUMMARY

The subject of the treatment of the survivors of sexual assault or molestation is lengthy and complicated. It is also, in general, the responsibility of specially trained and qualified professionals in this field. In this chapter, I have attempted to give parents, older children, and teenage survivors some basic ideas on the subject.

If the reader is interested in delving more completely into this area, my second book, *The Merry-Go-Round of Sexual Abuse,* contains a full and complete coverage of the subject including specific treatment techniques for each type of sexual abuse. These techniques are intended for the training of counselors and therapists who are interested in treating survivors but may also be of interest to parents and relatives of survivors as well as to survivors themselves.

14

FINAL THOUGHTS

Our husbands and wives, sons and daughters, children and adolescents are our most precious treasures. Physical, emotional, and especially sexual abuse tarnishes these treasures, and too often for life. Anything that we can do to prevent these abuses from occurring is a gift of love but is also our obligation. Prevention is much, much easier than dealing with the physical damage and pain, the guilt, shame, and humiliation that the survivors of sexual abuse experience, even with professional and specialized treatment, which is a long-term process.

KEYS TO PREVENTING SEXUAL ABUSE

In my opinion, the majority of child and adolescent sexual molestations are preventable. I include many instances of forced sexual assault in this belief — cases in which extremely poor judgment (for example, jogging in Central Park alone after dark) was used and cases in which parents or other supervisors were too trusting where children and adolescents were concerned (for example, dropping children or young teens off at the malls or in the parks with no adult supervision and especially when these children or adolescents are alone).

As we have seen throughout this work, most of the survivors of sexual molestation, especially long-term molestation, have many traits in common, including the following.

1. They are naive individuals with a poor self-image and low self-esteem who really don't like themselves and who don't see

themselves as equal to their peers. (Why wasn't anything done about this factor during their formative years by parents, teachers, and other involved adults?)

2. Open communication is not part of their lives. This is especially true where parents, other authority figures, siblings, and friends are concerned. (Where did this trait develop, except in the home?)

3. They have strong feelings that they are not loved and not accepted as themselves. Consequently, they are constantly imitating others, their ego-ideals (the persons they would most like to be). (How did they learn this belief? Who taught them that they were unlovable? Why didn't anyone notice or do something about it?)

4. From parents, they have learned to be self-judgmental, while at the same time they are accepting and nonjudgmental of everyone else. For the most part, they are unhappy with any accomplishment and find it difficult to accept praise (since they feel undeserving). As a consequence they tend to be perfectionist, which always bodes failure. (Who taught them to be judgmental, and who taught them that no matter what they did it was never good enough?)

5. They never live up to their extremely high and demanding expectations. (Where did they learn to set goals so high and so unrealistically? Again, this trait begins with demanding parents who are never satisfied with anything the child does. It does not matter if the parents' motivation is well-meaning. "I wanted my children to have a better life than I did!" is probably the most often used rationalization when tragedy hits.)

6. They are unsure of who they are or who they want to be. (Why didn't anyone help them to find themselves when they were little children, searching for identity? Where were their parents, teachers, priests, ministers, and all of the other authority figures with whom they were involved?)

7. The lack of acceptance and love they feel makes them desperate for feelings of acceptance and love from anyone (and the predators know it). Consequently they are willing to pay any price to obtain acceptance and love. (Why weren't they accepted in their own homes, in the neighborhood, in their schools, in society? Was

it that no one paid attention or observed this need in them, or was it that no one cared?)

Finding Potential Victims

Potential victims can be found as early as the first grade. They are the loners who do not mix socially, who constantly look at the floor when spoken to (no positive eye contact), and who are obviously desperate for attention and approval. I have never met a grammar school teacher who, when I presented this concept, was unable to instantly name one to three children in his or her class who fit this description. Why didn't they do something about it? Most answer that they feared parental ire and lawsuits.

The Seven A's and One C Test

A simple test for all parents is to imagine a scenario in which their child brings them a report card with seven A's and one C. Most parents, upon reading such a report card, would immediately ask, "Why is this C here?" I suggest that parents imagine not reacting in any way to what's on this report card and imagine returning the card to the child or adolescent and asking them how they feel about it.

The normal child or adolescent would emphasize the A's with statements such as: "Hey, how about a dollar for each of the A's?" If asked about the C, he or she would say something like: "That teacher wouldn't give her own child an A. In her class, a C is equal to an A."

The potential victim, on the other hand, would immediately react to the C with apologies and promises to improve, in a guilt-ridden, pleading manner, and would never emphasize the A's. When a predatory teacher (or some other predatory authority figure) observes this reaction, he or she immediately focuses on this child or adolescent as a potential victim.

When this pattern of perfectionism is consistently repeated, the child, at some point, usually around emerging adolescence, adopts this value as his or her own, and it remains so for life unless changed through therapy.

Fulfilling Early Developmental Needs

A positive self-image begins at home from the earliest years through parents emphasizing the positives and not the negatives in a child's or adolescent's behavior. Children who are appreciated, liked, and loved from an early age learn to like and love themselves.

Communication also begins from the earliest age and also at home. If children or adolescents constantly fear anger, belittlement, insults, threats, and punishment whenever they admit to a failing or misbehavior, communication will never exist between those individuals and their parents. They will also project this fear onto other adults and authority figures and see them in the same way that they see their parents. Predators are experts at dealing with these type of potential victims and actually prefer victims in this situation since it tends to guarantee them the safety and secrecy they need.

As soon as a child enters school, he or she is now under the new influences of teachers and peers for at least fifty hours per week, plus the additional hours that he or she plays and socializes with peers. Most parents today, especially when both are working, spend as little as an hour or two with their children daily, though possibly more on weekends. This time is usually spent at meals or in watching television. Children and adolescents who come home with an important question have little chance under these circumstances of being heard and either come up with answers themselves or go to peers for answers, which is the worst possible choice.

I have personally never met a survivor, child or adolescent, whose family put aside an hour per day strictly for communication. Many of the survivors that I have treated complained that there was never time for personal communication at home. Either the parents were too tired, too busy, or watching the news or their favorite program, or they were out of the home attending meetings or other social activities. If one of the children or adolescents of this type of parent really wanted to talk about a serious problem, he or she would be unable to. Survivors need a great deal of courage to discuss an incident of attempted or actual sexual molestation with anyone, and normally they make only a single attempt to do so. If rejected or not given the opportunity for an intimate discussion with their parents, they most likely will never try again.

Where daily communication is available with positive parents, a child or adolescent who is touched in a way that makes him or her feel uncomfortable or who is approached openly for sex will communicate this immediately to these parents or other authority figures. Unfortunately, most of the survivors I have treated over the last thirty-three years were unable to do this. None of the eight children molested by **PETER** in chapter 5 were ever able to talk to their mother or to teachers, priests, or other authority figures in their lives. The damage is still compounding.

Finally, sex education is critical in preventing sexual abuse. The lack of sex education in the home remains, in my mind, a major contributor to the increasing number of children and adolescents who are being sexually molested. Predators look for sexually naive children and adolescents to abuse because these children and adolescents are gullible and also fascinated with the "forbidden." Sex education is one of the most frequent ploys that predators use to get children and adolescents interested, then undressed, and then actively engaged in sex. **MR. DON**, in chapters 1 and 4, **KEIF**, in chapter 2, **HANS**, in chapters 3 and 11, **JIMMY, OLIVER**, and **PETER**, in chapter 5, **VINNY,** in chapter 8, and many others referred to in this work all used this "sex-education technique" to molest their victims.

A CAVEAT REGARDING MALE SURVIVORS

Male victims who do not report have an extremely high probability rate of becoming adult sexual predators themselves to "undo" what happened to them. This is usually acted out in a ritualistic way. My final example will clarify most of these issues.

BUDDY was sexually molested from age nine to ten. Buddy's father was an "incurable" alcoholic who was never home except late at night, when he would arrive in a drunken stupor. He and Buddy never got along, and Buddy remembers their mutual animosity beginning around the time he was five. Buddy's mother was a weak, dependent, nonassertive, self-centered person who was always whining about her plight in life and never had time for her son. If he attempted to talk to her, the conversation would instantly be focused on herself and her problems. She was also antisocial in that she would not attend school functions, scouting events, and so on, but never gave Buddy a reason.

Buddy preferred to be out of his home as much as possible since it was so depressing and negative in all ways. One day, while walking alone in a neighborhood park, one of his favorite places, he stopped in the men's room. Standing at the urinal and believing he was alone, he began playing with his penis in preparation for masturbating (his "only pleasure in life"). He didn't hear the man enter. Suddenly, while lost in his own pleasures, a hand reached around him and grasped his penis. The man said: "Don't waste any of it!" He then turned Buddy around, pulled down his shorts, knelt, and fellated him. Buddy thoroughly enjoyed this act that resulted in the most pleasurable orgasm he had ever experienced.

When he finally took note of the man, he noticed that he was fairly young, well dressed, and obviously well-to-do. When the man finished, he smiled, thanked Buddy, and pressed a ten-dollar bill in his hand. He then asked Buddy to meet him again next week, at the same time, and left. His new "friend" never asked Buddy to reciprocate in any way, nor did he even expose himself to him.

Lying in bed that evening and "replaying the tape" of his adventure in the park, Buddy was excited, got an erection, and masturbated to thoughts of the man fellating him. He decided he would meet the man again and did on many successive Wednesday afternoons. This pleasurable and profitable adventure continued for approximately six months, and then the man disappeared. Buddy faithfully showed up in the park for the next several weeks, but the man never reappeared.

Buddy missed his weekly adventure and began looking for other boys in the park to have sex with. Within a week, he followed another boy, his age, into the men's room and almost ritualistically repeated the incidents with his "friend" but added reciprocation (he had the boy fellate him). These adventures continued until Buddy reached adolescence. His masturbation fantasies, however, remained focused on his adult male friend in the park.

In the gym, in the locker room, and on the way home from school, Buddy now began hearing about the sexual adventures of his peers. All of his peers bragged about their heterosexual conquests, and Buddy began to realize that he was different. He had no interest in what he was hearing about girls or the wonders of his peers' newfound heterosexuality and continued to masturbate to fantasies of being fellated by his adult friend in the park.

When Buddy became sixteen, his sexual behavior abruptly changed. He was no longer interested in trying to find age-peers to have sex with in the park but began looking for nine-year-old boys (the age of his first molestation). He followed one nine-year-old boy into the men's room, waited for the boy to stand at the urinal, walked over quietly, reached around the boy, and grasped his penis saying: "Don't waste any of it!" The boy pushed his hand away and ran out of the men's room. Buddy stood there in shock. A few minutes later the boy returned with a policeman, and Buddy was arrested for sexual molestation. An enlightened judge listened to his story and gave him probation with the mandate of therapy, and I met him in my practice.

Could this sexual molestation and its subsequent traumatic event have been avoided? Who did Buddy have to talk to? What did he really know about sex? Who could he ask for help from? How did Buddy perceive his own molestation? The following excerpt is from my treatment notes and is used with Buddy's permission.

The man in the men's room was the only person in my life who made me feel good. He worried only about my pleasure and not his own, and then gave me a reward for just being "Buddy." Then he thanked me. I just wanted to be like the man in the men's room and make other boys feel the same way he made me feel.

Without being apprehended and referred for therapy, Buddy would have continued his pedophilic molestations and eventually would have ended up in prison.

KEY REPORTING ISSUES

Where can children like Buddy go when they feel their parents are unwilling or too negative to communicate with about their problems?

While there are many, many agencies that deal with these problems, child and adolescent survivors of sexual abuse are not made aware of these agencies and the ways to contact them. When they are informed of where to go to report sexual abuse, most survivors have expressed to me their fears of

1. the police, who might arrest them or make their cases public;

2. child-protective agencies like DYFS, which might remove them from their homes against their wishes; or

3. courts, where the predators appear to have more rights than the survivors and where survivors often fear that their cooperation or return to the molestation situation (in long-term molestation) will be seen as prostitution or equal guilt with the predator. (Buddy feared that if anyone knew that he accepted the ten dollars, he would be seen as a male prostitute, and he knew that that was illegal.)

Those fears notwithstanding, parents and other legal guardians must encourage children and adolescents to report any situations that involve either attempts at sexual contact or actual sexual contact. Parents also need to arrange therapy for children or adolescents who either are behaving sexually abnormally or have been sexually abused. Too often, parents fear the "stigma" of having a member of their family see a "shrink." What would the neighbors and relatives say? I say: Who cares what they say? The well-being of the child or adolescent should come first.

Parents also need to be constantly alert to children or adolescents suddenly having money coming from unknown sources or suddenly purchasing expensive goods such as a Walkman, Nintendo games, expensive game cartridges, new clothing or sneakers, gifts for family members and siblings, and so on. (Buddy did all of these things, and his parents never questioned him about the source of his newfound wealth.)

Sex therapists and other professionals dealing with sexual assault and abuse need to find a way to let children and adolescents know that they are available and will help. Unfortunately, due to parents' rights and fears of law suits, I do not anticipate this will happen.

Sexual predators have serious psychological problems, and while this explains their behavior, it most certainly does not justify it. Therapists need to feel comfortable in treating potential sexual molesters who are fantasizing future child or adolescent sexual molestation without fears of legal reprisal or law suits should their patient/client, while in therapy, actually act out on his or her fantasies. This is the main reason that so many good therapists will not accept potential sexual predators in their practices.

OTHER SUGGESTIONS FOR PREVENTION

Stressing Adults' Responsibilities for Children and Adolescents

All adults (relatives, friends, teachers, ministers, child-activity leaders, and so on) should become involved in the problems of our children and adolescents. Rapport is an individual and unique phenomenon that does not accompany a graduate degree, and many professionals that I know are incapable of the necessary rapport with children and adolescents that is required for trust in cases of sexual molestation or assault.

Discriminating Reporting

Laws need to be changed so that mandatory reporting is changed to discriminating reporting with the survivor's consent. Each case should be handled individually, and this decision should be made by a qualified therapist in the field, not by a blanket, so-called child-protection legal system that often does more harm than good.

Voluntary Treatment for Nonexposed and Nonapprehended Sexual Molesters

I also strongly feel that a first-time sexual predator who wants help should be treated without fear of imprisonment unless he or she poses an imminent threat to society. We need alternate settings where these individuals can go and be treated professionally with other individuals like themselves. Sex offender treatment does work if effectively given and if given by specially trained individuals.

My last word is that we all seriously need to collectively care for our children and adolescents. They are our future. While the majority can be saved from sexual abuse, we also need to be sure that the victims receive professional treatment with supportive love and care from everyone with whom they are associated. Only then will we begin to have a more normal, less abusive, and less sick society.

I wish to end this work with three poems written by one of **PETER'S** daughters who never reported and whose adult life was traumatically affected by her long-term molestation. She and so many other survivors like her deserve our love, our care, our concern, and our help.

PAIN

The poetry of **Katherine** bears eloquent testimony to the deep scars that resulted from her untreated incest.

Unnatural Disaster

Devastation along the Jersey shore / And major inland waterways / Hurricane George hit /

Twenty-five years ago / Or yesterday / Leaving in his wake / The following injuries: At least / one abortion / venereal disease / severed thumb / fractured ankle / concussion /

crushed car / head injury / speech impediment / drug addiction / alcohol addiction /

divorce / aborted career / thwarted ambition / slaughtered dream / sex addiction /

night terror / proliferation / breathing cessation / emotional amputation / social

humiliation / psychotic hallucination / suicidal ideation / delayed maturation /

epileptic annihilation / asthma / food addiction / hunger addiction / nausea /

cervical cancer / tipped uterus / ulcerated colon / duodenal ulcer / thyroid malfunction /

spiritual alienation / migraine affliction / relationship dysfunction / sexual compulsion /

clinical depression / memory suppression / imagination suffocation /

Jesus Christ fixation / penis obsession / self-revulsion / joy repression.

The damage reported thus far has been validated / verified / cross-referenced /

witnessed / testified / notarized.

All estimates of destruction / Must be considered Preliminary, and / Authorities warn

that More may yet be revealed.

In the interim, God has declared a State of emergency, / And
    is Standing by
In Case

Me

My mind screams / I'm not enough / Not enough
Not enough for normalcy / For real jobs / Real friends / Real
    family
Not enough / For God and country / And Recovery
Not enough / For fun and love / And sexuality
Not enough / For healing and warmth / And serenity
A massive mistake / Of a life / Stunted, shrunken, And
    deformed, / Is my kismet, /
My piece of the pie, / My portion of fate.
Failures feel like friends, / Familiar;
And faults, / As comfortable as home!
Because they're so / Well-worn / They're so / Everyday
They're so / Fitting /
To my massive Mistakeness / My shroud of shame /
Where "I'm not enough" / Is all there is.

Why I Am the Way I Am

Because / Before I could talk / Or walk,
I could trust, / And feel.
That was enough / To be damaged
Maybe (and maybe not) / Beyond repair
By someone who could / Rip the darkness / And bite it into two,
And hand my trust / And feelings / Back to me
Bloody, / And torn, / And bitten, / And blue.[1]

---

1. The poems are copyrighted by the author; reprinted by permission.

SUGGESTED READING

Interested readers will find listed below many of the books and workbooks that I use with the survivors of sexual abuse. I have also included a reading list on cults and satanic abuse for those readers or counselors interested in that topic.

SELF-HELP BOOKS FOR NONPROFESSIONALS

Alberti, Robert E., and Michael L. Emmons. *Stand Up, Speak Out, Talk Back!* New York: Pocket Books, 1975.

Bode, Janet. *The Voices of Rape.* New York: Franklin Watts, 1990.

Borcherdt, Bill. *You Can Control Your Feelings: 24 Guides to Emotional Well-Being.* Sarasota, Fla.: Professional Resource Press, 1993.

Brady, Katherine. *Father's Days.* New York: Dell, 1979.

Corneau, Guy. *Absent Fathers, Lost Sons.* Boston: Shambhala, 1991.

Deaton, Wendy, and Kendall Johnson. *No More Hurt.* Alameda, Calif.: Hunter House, 1991.

Engel, Lewis, and Tom Ferguson. *Imaginary Crimes: Why We Punish Ourselves and How to Stop.* Boston: Houghton Mifflin, 1990.

Freeman, Lucy, and Herbert S. Strean. *Guilt: Letting Go.* New York: John Wiley, 1986.

Harary, Keith, and Eileen Donahue. *Who Do You Think You Are?* San Francisco: Harper San Francisco, 1994.

Harris, Michael. *Unholy Orders: Tragedy at Mount Cashel.* New York: Viking Penguin, 1990.

Hawkes, Daniel. *Violation! A New Look at Sexual Violence.* London: Luxor Press, 1970.

Horton, Martha. *The Seashell People: Growing Up in Adulthood.* New York: M. Evans, 1990.

Lew, Mike. *Victims No Longer: Men Recovering from Incest and Other Sexual Child Abuse.* New York: Nevraumont, 1988.

Madow, Leo. *Guilt: How to Recognize and Cope with It.* Northvale, N.J.: Jason Aronson, 1988.

Madaras, Lynda. *The What's Happening to My Body? Book for Boys.* New York: Newmarket Press, 1988.

Madaras, Lynda, with Area Madaras. *The What's Happening to My Body? Book for Girls.* New York: Newmarket Press, 1988.

Manshel, Lisa. *Nap Time: The True Story of Sexual Abuse at a Suburban Day-Care Center.* New York: William Morrow, 1990.

Napier, Nancy J. *Recreating Your Self: Help for Adult Children of Dysfunctional Families.* New York: W. W. Norton, 1990.

Nichols, Michael P. *No Place to Hide: Facing Shame So We Can Find Self-Respect.* New York: Simon and Schuster, 1991.

Oksana, Chrystine. *Safe Passage to Healing.* New York: Harper Perennial, 1994.

Parks, Penny. *Rescuing the "Inner Child."* London: Souvenir Press, 1990.

Phillips, Gerald M. *Help for Shy People.* New York: Dorset Press, 1981.

Ross, Victor J., and John Marlowe. *The Forbidden Apple: Sex in the Schools.* Palm Springs, Calif.: ETC Publications, 1985.

Saward, Jill, with Wendy Green. *Rape: My Story.* London: Bloomsbury, 1990.

Seagrave, Ann, and Faison Covington. *Free from Fears.* New York: Poseidon Press, 1987.

Thomas, Gordon. *Enslaved.* New York: Pharos Books, 1991.

Viscott, David. *Emotionally Free: Letting Go of the Past to Live in the Moment.* Chicago: Contemporary Books, 1992.

PLAYS AND SKITS

Red Flag, Green Flag People. Red Flag, Green Flag Resources; c/o Rape and Assault Crisis Center; PO Box 2984; Fargo, ND 58108–2984. Tel.: 1–800–627–3675.

Touch! Illusion Theater; 528 Hennepin Ave.; Suite 704; Minneapolis, MN 55403. Tel.: 612–339–4944.

FURTHER READING FOR COUNSELORS AND THERAPISTS

Finkelhor, David. *Child Sexual Abuse: New Theory and Research.* New York: Free Press, 1984.

Giardino, Angelo P., et al. *A Practical Guide to the Evaluation of Sexual Abuse in the Prepubertal Child.* Newbury Park, Calif.: Sage, 1992.

Hedges, Lawrence E. *Remembering, Repeating, and Working through Childhood Trauma.* Northvale, N.J.: Jason Aronson, 1994.

Helfer, Ray E., and Ruth S. Kempe. *The Battered Child.* 4th ed. Chicago: University of Chicago Press, 1987.

Lifton, Robert Jay. *Cults in Our Midst.* San Francisco: Josey-Bass, 1995.

Meyers, John E. B. *Legal Issues in Child Abuse and Neglect.* Newbury Park, Calif.: Sage, 1992.

Pallone, Nathaniel J. *Rehabilitating Criminal Psychopaths: Legislative Mandates, Clinical Quandaries.* New Brunswick, N.J.: Transaction Books, 1990.

———, ed. *Young Victims, Young Offenders.* Vol. 21, nos. 1 and 2, of the *Journal of Offender Rehabilitation* (1994).

Russell, Diana E. H. *The Secret Trauma: Incest in the Lives of Girls and Women.* New York: Basic Books, 1986.

Sipe, A. W. Richard. *Sex, Priests, and Power: Anatomy of a Crisis.* New York: Brunner/Mazel Publishers, 1995.

Terr, Lenore. *Unchained Memories: True Stories of Traumatic Memories, Lost and Found.* New York: Basic Books, 1994.

Yapko, Michael. *Suggestions of Abuse.* New York: Simon and Schuster, 1994.

TEXTS ON CULTS AND SATANIC ABUSE

Bach, Marcus. *Strange Sects and Curious Cults.* New York: Dorset Press, 1992.

Davies, Maureen. *Helping Individuals and Agencies Deal with Problems of Ritual Abuse.* Rhyl-Clywd, Wales: Beacon Foundation, 1991.

Diamond, Vera. "Satanic Ritual Abuse Syndrome." Unpublished paper, London, the Cornelian Trust, 1992.

Kahaner, Larry. *Cults That Kill.* New York: Warner Books, 1988.

Lavey, Anton Szandor. *The Satanic Bible.* New York: Avon Books, 1969.

———. *The Satanic Witch.* Los Angeles: Feral House, 1989.

Oke, Isaiah. *Blood Secrets: The True Story of Demon Worship and Ceremonial Murder.* New York: Prometheus Books, 1989.

Otter, G'Zell, ed. *Witchcraft, Satanism and Occult Crime: Who's Who and What's What.* Los Ippilotos, Calif.: Green Egg, 1989.

Pazder, Lawrence, et al. "Michelle Remembers." Paper presented at the American Psychiatric Association Annual Meeting, New Orleans, 1980.

GLOSSARY OF TERMS

AHD   *American Heritage Dictionary,* 1989.

DBS   Benjamin B. Wolman, *Dictionary of Behavioral Science,* 2d ed. (San Diego: Academic Press, 1989).

PD   Robert J. Campbell, *Psychiatric Dictionary* (New York: Oxford University Press, 1989).

WEP   William E. Prendergast.

Adonis complex: The need to be like Adonis, a young man of great physical beauty. [AHD]

AIDS phobia: The abnormal fear of catching AIDS to the extent that it affects sexual performance, often leading to sexual dysfunctions or choosing celibacy. [WEP]

Ambivalence: The coexistence of opposing emotions, attitudes, or traits in the same individual. [DBS] Most commonly: love and hate, attraction and repulsion, wanting and not wanting, at the same time.

Anorexia or anorexia nervosa: A pathological loss of appetite and self-inflicted starvation. [DBS]

Assertiveness training: (1) A behavior-therapy technique by which anxiety habits of response to interpersonal situations are overcome by encouraging the patient to express other spontaneously felt emotions in the actual situation. [DBS] (2) A group-therapy process wherein situations are acted out that usually are frightening to an individual and he or she is taught to deal with them on a direct basis. For example, telling an individual how one feels or what emotional reactions his or her behavior generates. [WEP]

Barbie Doll complex: The need to be the most physically beautiful, attractive, and sexually stimulating young girl or woman in a group. [WEP]

Bisexuality: Being equally attracted to both sexes. [WEP]

Blow job: Slang term for fellatio, oral sex performed on a male. [WEP]

Bulimia: Insatiable hunger related to both appetite as well as increased intake of food. [DBS]

Chemical castration: A sex-inhibiting technique used by some psychiatrists with rapists and pedophiles or hebophiles. The technique consists of using hormone therapy, usually estrogens in the male, to diminish sexual thoughts, obsessions, and arousal. It is less effective after puberty than before and can easily be made ineffective with injections of testosterone. Monitoring is essential if it is to work. [WEP]

Compulsion: The state in which a person feels forced to behave against his or her own conscious wishes and judgment. [DBS]

Defense mechanism: A term introduced by Freud in 1894 and still used today. (1) Defense mechanisms are methods used by the ego (self) in fighting off the instinctual outbursts of the id and the attacks of the superego. [DBS] (2) When an inner conflict arises in an individual due to wants, desires, or fantasies that go against the individual's moral or religious beliefs and values, anxiety results. The individual then uses a defense mechanism (denial, repression, rationalization, and so on) to ward off the anxiety. [WEP]

Delusion: A perception contrary to reality despite evidence and common sense. [DBS]

Denial: Withdrawal of the ego (self) from reality, breaking away from the truth and refusing to acknowledge the existence of painful facts. It occurs when life becomes too painful to accept. [DBS]

Dependency: Almost total reliance of a weak and inadequate person on the nurturing, helping, caretaking, and affectionate behavior of another person. [WEP]

Desensitization: The weakening of an unwanted and negative response to a stimulus by repeated confrontation with that stimulus. [WEP]

Desire-phase dysfunction: A sexual dysfunction involving the loss of interest in any or all sexual activity, due to a negative and traumatic experience. For some, masturbation is practice whereas in others no sexual behavior at all is tolerated. [WEP]

Deviant: An individual who differs markedly from the social standard usually in terms of attitude, moral standards, and overt behavior. [DBS]

DYFS: In New Jersey, the Division of Youth and Family Services.

Ego-strength: A trait consisting of good emotional stability and the capacity to cope with problems on all levels in a mature manner. [WEP]

Equalizing. *See* **Undoing/Equalizing.**

Etiology: The study of origins and causes of a problem, symptom, disease, dysfunction, and so on. [WEP]

Externalization: The projection of one's own personal feelings or perceptions onto someone else. [WEP]

Fellatio: Oral stimulation of the penis. [WEP]

Flashback: A sudden recurrence of a memory, feeling, or other perceptual experience from the past even though no adequate stimulus for its recurrence is readily identifiable. [PD]

Frigidity: The inability of a woman to achieve orgasm through intercourse; a psychosexual dysfunction with inhibited sexual excitement; the analogous condition in the male is termed impotence. [PD]

Hebophile: Adult sexual preoccupation with, interest in, and/or obsession with postpubertal boys or girls. In sex offenders, this includes the desire to find a younger, orgasmic partner for sexual activities. [WEP]

Homophobia: Negative attitudes to homosexuals and homosexuality, reflecting both conscious and unconscious fears and reactions. Homophobia includes not only irrational and persistent fear of homosexuality (often manifested in extreme rage reactions) but also the self-hatred experienced by gay men and women because of their homosexuality. [PD] Homophobia is often used unconsciously to deny one's homosexual impulses.

Homosexual panic: An acute, severe episode of anxiety related to fear (or the delusional conviction) that the subject is about to be attacked sexually by another person of the same sex, or that he or she is thought to be homosexual by others. [PD]

Impotence: Sexual dysfunction consisting of the male's inability to perform sexual intercourse due to erectile failure. [PD]

Imprinting: A learning process occurring early in the life of a social animal in which a behavioral pattern is established through association with a parent or other role model. [AHD] *See also* **Sexual imprinting.**

Inadequate personality: (1) Inadaptability, ineptness, poor judgment, lack of physical and emotional stamina, social incompatibility, and so on. [PD] (2) An individual who perceives himself or herself as always being below or inferior to his or her peers, even in the face of concrete evidence. [WEP]

Incorporation: (1) Assimilation of external objects into the body and making them part of oneself. [DBS] (2) Taking the attributes of another person into oneself with the hope and desire of becoming equal to that person. [WEP]

Internalization: Taking things from the external world and making them part of the personality. [PD]

Judgmentalism: Critically evaluating a person, object, or situation. [WEP]

Minimization: Decreasing the seriousness, severity, or damage that results from an act, statement, or behavior to decrease guilt. [WEP]

Obsession: An idea, emotion, or impulse that repetitively and insistently forces itself into consciousness even though it is unwelcome. [PD]

Orgasm: (1) The peak of excitation in the genital zone; the sexual climax. [PD] (2) The physical sensations at the climax of a sexual act (to be distinguished, in males, from ejaculation).

Overcompensation: Doing much more than is necessary to make up for a feeling of inadequacy, weakness, or deficiency. [WEP]

Pedophile: An adult interest in or obsession with prepubertal children, both boys and girls; in opposition to hebophiles, who only want and need postpubertal children. [WEP]

Perception: (1) A process of obtaining information about the world through the senses. [DBS] (2) A process of subjectively viewing an event, a person, a behavior, or a situation and forcing it to fit into the individual's system of beliefs or needs. [WEP]

Perfectionism: Setting extremely high standards for oneself and accepting nothing else. [WEP]

Predator: One who uses and/or abuses others for his or her own needs or profit without concern for the effects on them. [WEP]

Premature ejaculation: Inability to control the ejaculation process; usually refers to ejaculation shortly after penetration or upon penetration, followed by feelings of guilt, frustration, and unmanliness. [WEP]

Projection: Placing blame or fault onto others for an individual's behavior or faults. [WEP]

Puberty: That stage of growth in boys and girls that extends from the end of childhood into the beginning of adolescence. Usually it is noted from the emergence of the secondary sex characteristics and continues for two to three years after. [WEP]

Rationalization: Attempting to justify or make something appear reasonable when otherwise it would be perceived as irrational. [WEP]

Readiness: A subjective time when an individual is willing and able to share experiences, memories, or details of a trauma. [WEP]

Regression: Returning to some former stage of development or behavior. [WEP]

Repression: An unconscious exclusion from the consciousness of objectionable impulses, memories, and ideas. The ego, as it were, pushes the objectionable material down into the unconscious and acts as if the objectionable material were nonexistent. [DBS]

Retarded ejaculation: Like premature ejaculation, an inability to control the ejaculation process. This term usually refers to individuals either who cannot ejaculate while having sex with another person or whose ejaculation takes such a long time that both parties are frustrated and complain of pain later. [WEP]

Ritual: A formal way of conducting a religious ceremony. [WEP]

Ruler: A measurement used by all human beings to compare or evaluate themselves on a single trait or on many norms.

Sadomasochism: A simultaneous existence of both submissive and aggressive attitudes in social and sexual situations with others, usually with a considerable degree of destructiveness. [DBS]

Satyr: A male with an excessive sex drive. [WEP]

Seductive molestation: Sexual molestation accomplished with bribes, proffered friendship, offered affection and loyalty, and so on, as opposed to force. [WEP]

Self-confrontation: Therapeutic technique wherein individuals face themselves and their problems, faults, deficiencies, and so on, without placing the blame on others or making excuses. [WEP]

Self-esteem: Self-worth; a positive attitude toward oneself. [WEP]

Self-image: The way one sees oneself; it is affected by early taught values and the reactions of adults toward a child or adolescent. [WEP]

Sexual assault: Any sexual behavior imposed on another person by means of threat, intimidation, a weapon, or physical strength. The act must be against the victim's will. [WEP]

Sexual dysfunction: An inability to perform a desired sex act: that is, impotence, frigidity, premature or retarded ejaculation, vaginismus, and so on; or sexual urges and sexually arousing fantasies that are unacceptable in society: that is, sex with animals, sex with children, sexual assault, and so on. [WEP]

Sexual imprinting: Phenomenon that occurs when an individual experiences his or her first orgasm with another human being. If the result is pleasant and if the act is performed with a person who is liked or loved, the imprinting will be positive; if the result is painful and frightening and if the act involves a person who uses force, threat, or intimidation, even though an orgasm may occur, the imprinting will be negative. [WEP]

Sexual preference: In general, the ability of any person to choose his or her type of sexual behavior and his or her sexual partner. Sexual preference is changeable, as opposed to sexual identity, which experts say is not. [WEP]

Sexual trauma: Psychological damage resulting from a sexual encounter with another human being, either due to force and physical damage or due to damage resulting from the unacceptability of that act by society, that is, pedophilia and hebophilia, sexual assault, public exhibitionism, and so on. [WEP]

Sodomy: Anal penetration. The term's legal usage often includes oral sex acts as well. [WEP]

Trait: An inherited or acquired characteristic that is consistent, persistent, and stable. [DBS]

Trigger: A word, action, memory, or behavior that initiates or produces an emotional or behavioral reaction that is unplanned and often unwanted. [WEP]

Unconscious, the: That part of the human mind that one is unaware of, as opposed to the conscious (consciousness), which encompasses that part of the mind that one is aware of. [WEP]

Undoing/Equalizing: A sexual predator's exact repetition of a behavior that was used on him or her as a child or adolescent. The purpose, conscious or unconscious, is to avoid being the only one against whom the act was committed or to justify submitting to the seduction of an authority figure. [WEP]

Vaginismus: A symptom of frigidity; a painful contraction of the vaginal muscles that prevents sexual intercourse or, at times, even digital penetration. [WEP]

INDEX